WITHDRAWN

Ethnic Leadership in America

THE JOHNS HOPKINS SYMPOSIA
IN COMPARATIVE HISTORY

THE JOHNS HOPKINS SYMPOSIA IN COMPARATIVE HISTORY are
occasional volumes sponsored by the Department of History at The Johns
Hopkins University and The Johns Hopkins University Press, comprising
original essays by leading scholars in the United States and other countries. Each volume considers, from a comparative perspective, an important topic of current historical interest. The present volume is the ninth.
Its preparation has been assisted by the James S. Schouler Lecture Fund.

Ethnic Leadership in America

Edited by JOHN HIGHAM

THE JOHNS HOPKINS UNIVERSITY PRESS
Baltimore and London

The Johns Hopkins Symposia in Comparative History, no. 9
Copyright © 1978 by The Johns Hopkins University Press

Manufactured in the United States of America

The Johns Hopkins University Press, Baltimore, Maryland 21218
The Johns Hopkins Press Ltd., London

Library of Congress Catalog Number 77–17257
ISBN 0-8018-2036-7

Library of Congress Cataloging in Publication data
will be found on the last printed page of this book.

Contents

78-2948

Preface

To a reader seeking instruction on the day-to-day tasks of ethnic leadership—how to run an organization or edit a newspaper or represent constituents—this book offers precious little. The authors are not men of affairs. We are scholars with a special interest in ethnicity, and our undertaking had its origin in broadly historical and theoretical questions. We set out to study leadership in order to gain a fresh perspective on the nature of ethnic groups in American society.

My own attention was drawn to the neglected subject of ethnic leadership in the course of reflecting on the significance of boundaries. In America ethnic groups have in some instances been rigidly circumscribed; but more often their boundaries are highly permeable. When boundaries weaken, I speculated, the survival or at least the vitality of an ethnic group would seem to depend increasingly on what is happening at the foci of group activity.[1] In other words, within the leadership. If that is true, ethnic groups in an open society are, in some degree yet to be specified, the creation of their leaders.

The James S. Schouler Lecture Fund provided a means for making a preliminary reconnaissance of the topic and discovering how others might approach it. The papers presented here are, therefore, the products of a symposium held at The Johns Hopkins University on February 5–6, 1976, under the auspices of the Schouler Fund. Instead of concentrating on one moment in time or one type of ethnic community, I sought participants who could speak with authority about widely divergent groups that have been prominent in the nineteenth and twentieth centuries.

It was not possible to examine more than a handful of the myriad peoples who have constituted the heterogeneous society of the United States; so I had to reconcile myself to woeful lapses from the hallowed American principle of equal time. For example, the opportunity (presented by Josef Barton's unusual researches) to include a comparative study of several immigrant nationalities was too tempting to resist, even though no one of the southern or eastern European peoples could then

ix

receive the full-bodied treatment accorded to single groups in other chapters. I can only hope that my selectivity, though partly fortuitous, will seem a challenge rather than an affront to the many ethnic groups whose unique leadership experience has not been assessed in these pages.

Another problem a book of this kind must face is the difference in point of view between insiders and outsiders. In ethnic studies the insider is likely to have a special empathy with the people he writes about. On the other hand the outsider may bring to bear a more critical attitude, a more demanding standard of judgment. It is tempting but I believe stultifying to see these tendencies as dichotomous—to think that only insiders can understand "us" or that only outsiders can be objective. We need both perspectives, overlapping and enriching one another. In recruiting coauthors I sought a mix of insiders and outsiders and came up in the end with a nearly equal balance.

For assistance in this enterprise I am greatly indebted to the authors of the papers, and they share my further debt to the other participants in the symposium—Hopkins colleagues and visitors from other institutions —whose remarks enlivened and extended the occasion. I appreciate especially the willingness of my colleague in anthropology, Sidney Mintz, to join fully in this mostly historical enterprise and to expand his own comment into the Afterword of this book.

The symposium also benefited from the sympathy of Dean George E. Owen, who saved my precarious budget from disaster, and from the services of Janet Tighe and Joanne Bracken, who managed local arrangements with energy and aplomb. In offering, as part of the Introduction, an account of modern Hawaiian leadership I have drawn in good measure on personal interviews with informants who may not in all cases agree with my conclusions and who may prefer therefore to remain anonymous. I am grateful to them and to Professor Donald D. Johnson of the University of Hawaii, who put his own rich knowledge of Hawaiian affairs fully at my disposal. In writing the Introduction I enjoyed the stimulus and support of the Woodrow Wilson International Center for Scholars.

NOTE

1. John Higham, *Send These to Me: Jews and Other Immigrants in Urban America* (New York, 1975), pp. 12–13, 242–46.

Introduction: The Forms of Ethnic Leadership

John Higham

WHAT ROLES HAVE LEADERS PLAYED in the history of America's ethnic groups? What objectives have ethnic leaders sought? What methods have they employed, what styles exhibited, what problems faced, what results achieved? How important have such leaders been in making modern American ethnic groups and putting an imprint on our society and culture? To bring these questions forward, the essays in this book were written. Although they provide few answers, they supply for the first time an informed basis for cross-cultural comparisons.

To ask about the special character and impact of ethnic leaders is at once to reflect and to challenge the current "revival" of ethnicity. Our inquiry reflects the revival by taking ethnic initiatives seriously: by expecting the ethnic impulse to come to focused and intentional fruition. Yet raising the question of leadership also challenges current assumptions. The reassertion of ethnic identities in recent years is connected with a general distrust of elites and (on the part of scholars) a desire to look at history from the bottom up. Leaders must in some sense stand above the rank and file and move in a larger world. That is why the problems and tasks of leadership are easily neglected in ethnic studies today. This book is designed therefore to offer a corrective as well as a supplement to studies of ethnic voting, of mobility, patterns of work, education, and the like.

We also have a practical reason for giving more attention to ethnic leaders than historians and social scientists have customarily done. The American ethnic group, as Nathan Glazer points out in Chapter 2, is an amorphous entity, difficult to define and in the great majority of cases

1

very incompletely separable from other elements in the population. Except for unusual instances of great internal discipline or external resistance, ethnic boundaries are vague, fluid, and indeterminate. An ethnic group fades out—like a magnetic field—as the distance from its center increases. Its history is one of the energy it generates and the direction in which it moves. Accordingly we may find in configurations of leadership a distinctness and clarity that disappear when we look at the group as a whole. Leaders focus the consciousness of an ethnic group and make its identity visible.

One of the very few contributions yet made to a sociology of ethnic leadership came from the outstanding social psychologist Kurt Lewin more than thirty years ago. Lewin brought to attention the tendency for ethnic leaders in America to be "marginal" to their own groups and therefore (he believed) unreliable as strategists and spokesmen.[1] A group that is underprivileged, Lewin pointed out, is likely to choose leaders whose economic success or professional attainments make them relatively acceptable outside the group. Such persons "may, under a thin cover of loyalty, be fundamentally eager to leave the group." Against the weak or divided allegiance of these "leaders from the periphery" Lewin set a more positive and dynamic leadership oriented toward the center of the group.

Lewin's distinctions between center and periphery sprang from a special concern about Jewish self-hatred at a time when pressures for assimilation and threats to the self-esteem of minority peoples were far more intense than now. In other circumstances the periphery might be viewed differently: not as a dangerously exposed location but as an expanding frontier or a zone of reciprocal influence and mutual accommodation. Under suitable historical conditions, the periphery can be just the place for a leader to be.

Although we should beware of Lewin's bias, his distinction between center and periphery remains a fruitful insight, which needs further elaboration. At one end Lewin's polarity suggests a question that no one has clearly addressed: where, in fact, is the "center" of an ethnic group to be found? In its traditional, unreconstructed elements, or in its advanced or innovative strata? In Spanish-speaking villages where old crafts and rituals survive, or in Cesar Chavez's United Farm Workers? We will return to this question later.

At the opposite end, one may observe that the periphery of a group does not always set the outer limit of its leadership. Under some conditions ethnic groups may be led by persons located beyond the periphery, outside of the group altogether. Thus slavery imposed a white leadership on the mass of southern blacks before the Civil War; that heritage of dependence on (and resentment toward) white leaders left a long-enduring impact on the subsequent development of Afro-American leadership. In subtler but still effectual ways, immigrants too have sometimes fallen under outside leaders. In Chapter 3 Roger Daniels shows how the Japanese government before World War I kept the first generation of Japanese Americans under its thumb through the Japanese Associations. The government of Hungary endeavored during the same period to maintain a comparable hegemony over Magyar immigrants. Through secret financial subsidies it gained control of immigrant churches, schools, and newspapers, all with the object of persuading Hungarians to return to their homeland. American corporations and political parties have also practiced a covert manipulation of ethnic associations. The corruption of foreign-language newspapers in the late nineteenth and early twentieth centuries has never been adequately investigated. The record of those years is studded with glimpses of editors begging for subventions and of big corporations distributing their advertising to politically "reliable" newspapers. There was, for example, Louis Hammerling, a Galician Jew who eventually returned to Poland, married a countess, and was elected to the Polish Senate. Beginning as a protégé of the Republican boss Boies Penrose, Hammerling induced hundreds of newspapers and magazines, published in twenty-nine languages, to join his American Association of Foreign Language Newspapers. Though essentially an advertising agency, the Association was regarded as a powerful force counteracting labor unrest and supporting Republican candidates.[2] Hammerling operated outside the periphery of the groups he influenced.

Along such lines Lewin's topological approach might be extended and revised, but the authors of the present volume have moved in other directions. Their mandate was broad and open. I asked each scholar simply to examine the history of leadership in a single ethnic sector, in more or less recent times, with a view to understanding the extent to which such groups had reconstituted themselves in coping with American life. Considering the variety of approaches the subject permitted and the diversity of peoples under discussion, it is striking how many of the essays pivot on a common axis. Five out of seven chapters deal primarily with the conflict between a leadership of accommodation and a leadership of protest.

The distinction between accommodation and protest, as alternative strategies for dealing with the host society, was given classic formulation in Gunnar Myrdal's great work, *An American Dilemma* (1944). Myrdal described his fascinating chapters on Negro leadership as a "sketch . . . frankly impressionistic and partly speculative."[3] The probing subtlety of his analysis remains, nonetheless, an unrivaled challenge to students of American culture and society. That his categories still seem useful should not surprise us. To apply those categories to a variety of ethnic groups will first require, however, some consideration of their diverse objectives or, as I would prefer to say, their "concerns."

Among the basic concerns of American ethnic groups, four stand out. One has to do with relations between the United States and the homeland of the group. For American Indians the problem of the homeland that was torn from them is chronic. For ethnic groups that left their homeland voluntarily, this concern may not ordinarily be troublesome; but an international crisis can give it a searing intensity.

A second great concern of ethnic groups is their own status in American society. The conservation or enhancement of group status takes various forms: the display of cultural attainments, combatting prejudice and discrimination, raising the socioeconomic level of the group. Beyond these outward-looking endeavors, a third concern must be the internal integrity and cohesion of the group, which is rarely secure. Finally, an ethnic group must sometimes confront the elemental issue of survival. Nearly all of these basic concerns pose for ethnic leaders alternatives of accommodation or protest; the outcome in some major cases may be studied in Chapters 2 through 6 below.

In the first three of these chapters the key problem is that of the homeland as it has affected different immigrant groups. In each case a people's attachment to its ancestral home is (or may be) suddenly violated by a dramatic shift in American foreign policy and public opinion. This, in turn, gravely endangers the status of the group. For Nathan Glazer, who writes about American Jews with an eye to the future as much as the past, the homeland question is only potentially disruptive, the Jewish community having for the present attained (in a favorable climate of opinion) extraordinary unanimity in its support of Israel. Nevertheless, Glazer argues, Israel's survival is the only great problem still hanging over American Jews. His discussion of earlier issues, which agitated the Jewish community from the 1880s to the 1950s, seeks to account for their resolution or subsidence. Two factors stand out. For one, the underlying social cleavage between "uptown" and "downtown" Jews has largely disappeared. For another, the bitter conflict over Zionism has given way to consensus on Israel. "Downtown" protest and "uptown" accommodation have flowed together, mingling in a single effort of assistance and pressure. Going a step beyond Glazer's own conclusions, we may note that the major Jewish organizations seem to have effected a highly successful blend of protest and accommodation.

Among Japanese Americans and German Americans no such convergence took place. Instead, events compelled a drastic choice that Jews and most other minorities have never had to face: a choice between the United States and the homeland. That meant, in respect to American policy, an attitude either of total acquiescence or of embittered resistance.

In the Japanese American case, Roger Daniels makes clear, the triumph of an accommodationist leadership was absolute. Pledged to unswerving support of United States authorities, the Japanese American Citizen's League (JACL) rejected the homeland, and it prevailed over every variety of protest. It overcame the Japanese nationalists on the one side and, on the other, those who chose America but insisted on vindicating their constitutional rights before accepting military service.

The virtually unassailable preeminence which the JACL won in the Japanese American community during the 1940s obviously owed much to its expedient response to the war crisis. But Daniels suggests that the roots of the JACL approach lay further back, in a conflict of generations. The Japanese in the United States never developed the fruitful dialectic between protest and accommodation, which in American Jewry was given a broad, objective base by the social cleavage between two distinct immigrations. The product of a single immigration accomplished under tremendous external pressures, the Japanese community was dominated by a more physically painful rift between alien fathers and native sons. When authority inevitably passed to the sons, no rallying point for protest survived. Now that the objectives of the accommodationist leaders have been largely fulfilled, and the sons are giving way to a third generation, one must ask whether Japanese Americans will in the future have any central leadership at all.

In Frederick Luebke's careful study of German American leadership after World War I, we observe still another consequence of the homeland issue. Neither a stimulus, as it has been to Jews, nor a constraint, as it became for Japanese Americans, the problem of the homeland proved insoluble for German Americans. It resulted, quite simply, in the destruction of a national leadership. During the prewar years (as Luebke and others have shown in previous works[4]) that leadership turned toward a kind of protest that was compensatory and defensive. Many German American spokesmen grew belligerent and chauvinistic. They championed the fatherland with increasing shrillness as the ravages of assimilation eroded the ethnic base on which they stood. The defensive arrogance of this unrepresentative leadership intensified the tragic persecution of German Americans in 1917–18. After that massive humiliation, a new generation of accommodationist leaders emerged in the 1920s, preaching the recovery of cultural respect and opposing the politics of revenge. But the issues had hardly been joined when the American Nazis captured attention and brought about the final discrediting of efforts to organize the German American community as a whole or to speak for it. The German case underlines the high risks of ethnic protest in a situation that tests national loyalties.

In one way or another the choice between protest and accommodation has ceased to be a live option for Jews, Germans, and Japanese. All three groups have attained a relatively favorable status in America, and that has greatly lightened the tasks of leadership. It is among underprivileged groups, such as blacks and Indians—groups which must continue to try to overcome historic injustices—that the tension between protest and accommodation remains urgent.

Writing about black leadership, Nathan Huggins points up the special features of both styles in the classic period of the emergence of a modern black consciousness, the period from the 1890s to the 1930s. To highlight those features, Huggins has adopted a slightly different terminology. Leaders who have customarily been described as accommodationist, like Booker T. Washington, Huggins calls "emblematic" in order to emphasize their dependence on the whites who recognized them as emblems. The leaders we associate with open protest, most notably W. E. B. DuBois, Huggins identifies as reformers. Apostles of an interracial reform movement, they counted on ideals to reach and to move the conscience of America. The overpowering constrictions of the American caste system, Huggins argues, diverted both types of leadership from any effort to mobilize the black masses along racial lines.

In this perspective what stands out are the frustrations, the dilemmas, and above all the powerlessness afflicting protesters and accommodationists alike. Some of these afflictions persist to our own day. But Huggins also sees, as early as the 1930s, the beginnings of a transition from the "soft protest" of the DuBois era to a new level of demand and a tougher pursuit of power. Tactics of confrontation and direct action have prepared the way for a leadership of office-holders, legitimized and sustained by black votes.

What the respective roles of protest and accommodation may be in the present era Huggins does not say. We may guess that they are becoming more interdependent as black politics gains stability and maturity. Protest of some sort is a long established, institutionalized feature of the urban black community. Varying in intensity but always expressing a passionate moral appeal tinged with threat, it has been a staple of black journalism and a major instrumentality of black leadership since antebellum times.[5] In the main, however, harsh necessity made protest ineffectual and abstract, or drove it inward at a heavy cost of pride and integrity.[6] With the rise of black mayors and congressmen, both principle and expediency can become less absolute. In this context accommodation is no longer the obligatory posture of leaders who depend on white patrons; protest is no longer a strangled cry in a dream. Both strategies become dimensions of the political process for black leaders whose constituencies grow more diverse as their power increases.

Robert Berkhofer's somber analysis of American Indian leadership gives us no obvious grounds for expecting a similar fusion of clashing tendencies in the oldest of America's peoples. His story of Indian politics is one of unceasing turmoil. Every effort to stabilize power and to reconstitute authority seems to foster antagonisms and to multiply factions. Several reasons are suggested. First, a propensity to distrust all leaders springs from the high value placed on equality and consensus in traditional North American Indian cultures. Second, among Indians tribalism and village loyalties have fragmented authority geographically to a degree unequaled in other segments of the population. Third, the legal recognition of tribal entities by the United States has compelled Indians—unlike any other ethnic group—to struggle among themselves over the distribution of their own resources. Finally, the special legal status Indians cherish, and all attendant economic benefits, depend ultimately on the will of the dominant white society; that immoveable reality arouses continual frustration and distrust among Indians over the efforts of their own leaders to strengthen and advance the group.

Nonetheless the lines of cleavage among Indians conform broadly to the pattern we have observed in other groups. Accommodation, which may be understood here as a posture of negotiation or partial acceptance of white initiatives, has collided over and over again with attitudes of defiance and resistance. Among Indians "protest" has meant defending the "old ways," or what passed as such, against the "progressives" who have more often been beneficiaries of the status quo.

Berkhofer raises for us a difficult question. In the Indian context can protest and accommodation fertilize one another, as in Jewish and perhaps in black leadership? Or must one approach thwart the other, as Berkhofer's account might seem to imply? It is possible that a close examination of the interplay between protest and accommodation in Indian leadership might reveal successful instances in sufficient number to permit a ray of optimism. One thinks, for example, of the remarkable Seneca prophet Handsome Lake, who revitalized his people through a unique amalgam of western values and traditionalist beliefs.[7] In recent times the capacity of the National Congress of American Indians to contain both tendencies and to adapt to powerful cross-currents of opinion gives additional evidence that accommodation need not betray and that protest need not dissolve in futility. It is reasonable to suppose that the gradual development of pan-Indian organizations and urban spokesmen is in some measure checking the fragmentation of authority in American Indian life, which should, in turn, permit a more effective convergence of accommodation and protest.

From the experience of the five ethnic groups reviewed thus far, it is possible to conclude that neither accommodation nor protest can sustain a viable leadership on the national level over the long run. That does not, however, tell us very much. The circumstances of these groups have dif-

fered so strikingly—the options of their leaders have been so disparate—
that a consistent strategy effective for all groups is hardly conceivable.
Rather than broad efforts to generalize, one might hope henceforth for
critical assessments of a much more specific kind. Only one of the authors
of this book, Frederick Luebke, has ventured to criticize the principal
leaders of his assigned group; in that instance both oblivion and collective
repentance have facilitated his candor. In comparative ethnic studies,
unfortunately, criticism is less welcome than in any other area of American life.

An examination of issues and strategies might profitably extend to
many other American ethnic groups. Our understanding of what protest
and accommodation have meant would surely benefit, for example, from
a look at the Norwegians, whose vigorous political leadership in the upper
Middle West swung sharply from left to right after World War I; or the
Spanish-speaking people of the southwest, whose leaders used to be so
conservative and are now in many cases so militant.[8] Still, a review of
issues and strategies gives only a limited sense of what ethnic leadership
is all about. The alternatives of protest or accommodation arise when a
group faces a choice in its relations with the surrounding society. But a
very large part—perhaps the greater part—of ethnic leadership has to
do primarily with internal processes. Leaders create the structures of the
ethnic community; they produce (or confirm) its symbolic expressions;
they exemplify the style that enables the group fully to experience itself.
We are fortunate that the last two essays in this book deal centrally with
the constitutive functions of ethnic leaders.

In the making of an ethnic group, two levels of identification and interaction may be distinguished. At the local level of face-to-face association
exists the small community. Its institutions are the parish, the saloon,
the *landsmanshaft*, the singing society, the Indian band, the neighborhood gang. Above this infrastructure is the large community which binds
together the entire ethnic group through federations, newspapers, political
leaders, and other highly visible figures. The connections between the
small community and the large community, and the characteristics of
leadership at both levels, are not very well understood. But it is clear that
the large community ordinarily handles the external relations of the
group, so its leaders stand out in the areas discussed in the first five chapters. The small community, on the other hand, creates and sustains the
web of daily life. To leadership on that level Josef Barton's paper is
addressed.

Discussing six of the nationality groups from southern and eastern
Europe, Barton has not attempted to survey the entire range of small-
community builders who emerged in the decades from 1870 to 1920. He
tells us nothing about the *padroni*—the labor bosses, who met arriving

immigrants, found jobs for them, collected their wages, and even arbi-trated their disputes. He does not touch on the immigrant bankers, who received their fellow countrymen's paltry savings, sent remittances to relatives overseas, and usually sold steamship tickets as well. Barton also passes over the wardheelers, who introduced the immigrants to American politics, and the priests, whose authority varied from group to group but was always imposing. In order to have a single institutional setting for comparative analysis, while focusing on a kind of leadership that arises outside of already established structures, Barton has concentrated on the founders of voluntary associations: chiefly mutual aid societies but also labor unions, theatrical companies, and other cultural groups.

What is most striking in this close scrutiny of the grass-roots of ethnic affiliation is, first, the sheer abundance—the almost prodigal richness—of its exfoliation within every nationality Barton has studied, and, second, the direct transfer of these institutions from the old world. Voluntary associations sprang up in the villages of southern and eastern Europe in the late nineteenth century to arrest the disintegration of community life. Very ordinary people—peasants, laborers, artisans—assumed leadership in these societies and acquired thereby the capacity to recreate a dense social matrix in the cities of America.[9]

Barton's research enables us to ask, as he does in conclusion, how asso-ciational patterns in the small community have shaped the larger struc-ture of ethnic groups. American cities have teemed with voluntary societies since the 1840s.[10] Not every ethnic group, however, has matched the organizational vitality southern and eastern Europeans displayed around the turn of the century. In studying English and Scottish immi-grants who settled in industrial towns in the United States in the nine-teenth century, Charlotte Erickson was struck by their lack of interest in any ethnic societies. In Hawaii in the twentieth century Japanese immi-grants have generated a veritable honeycomb of particularistic societies; the native Hawaiians, on the other hand, have very few.[11] Does this dif-ference in the organization of the small community help to explain a cor-responding contrast in the solidarity of the whole ethnic group? At present one can only guess.

Whatever the answer may be, the small community as Barton describes it was a deeply conservative force, dedicated essentially to preserving what could be salvaged from the breakup of peasant society. In America, as in Europe, the new network of affiliations provided a modicum of sta-bility for people who had to cope with great mobility and change. In time, however, the small community weakened. Its myriad forms eroded, and larger centralized institutions took over what they could of its work. Big insurance companies absorbed the little mutual aid societies; big unions took the place of workingmen's circles. Voluntary associations have survived best in affluent and highly educated sectors of the population. Today the Catholic working class ranks low in organizational participation.[12] Its ethnic loyalties are therefore more fully invested in the large community, insofar as they survive at all.

We come back, then, to the men and women who have managed the big ethnic organizations and provided the popular symbols of ethnic power and prestige; we have on that level a concluding chapter about the ethnic group that has surpassed all others in dramatically visible leaders. Robert Cross's panoramic essay on the Irish brings home a major dimension of leadership touched on only indirectly in the preceding chapters. The analysis of issues and strategies in the early chapters, and the examination of community-building in Chapter 7, tell us little about the psychological attributes of ethnic leaders: the emotional needs they address, the personal qualities they embody, the subjective meanings their words and gestures convey. The Irish, undoubtedly the most theatrical of American ethnic groups, offer a particularly vivid example of the psychic functions of ethnic leaders.

Cross ranges widely over the many sorts of leaders the Irish produced: the politicians, the priests and the bishops, the journalists and the writers who "helped the Irish see themselves as they wanted to be seen," the labor leaders and the policemen. All these roles the Irish performed with a special style in which discordant qualities were often marvelously blended. It was a style of exuberance mixed with pessimism, or belligerence combined with bonhomie. On the one hand, Irish leaders showed a fierce loyalty to their own kind and a combative hostility toward all enemies, real and suspected. On the other hand, they acquired a cheerful talent for working with people of different backgrounds in the pragmatic operation of big organizations. So men of Irish descent pushed to the top of general or multi-ethnic institutions, like the Roman Catholic Church and the Democratic party, without ceasing to be distinctively Irish.

We are very much in need of sensitive portraits of the style of leadership in other American ethnic groups. The importance of philanthropy in the attainment of leadership in the American Jewish community, the distrust of leaders of all kinds in Italian American culture, the German image of the good citizen who acts independently and the consequent undoing of ethnic solidarity—tendencies such as these have been noted but never carefully studied in comparative perspective.[13] If it is true that leaders must give to the culture they represent a dramatic rendition of the values it honors, the comparison of leaders should offer a promising means of illuminating ethnic subcultures.

Issues and strategies, community building, ethnic style: such are the themes these essays explicitly address. It remains to ask what more they tell us, what overall lesson they may have for the history of American ethnic groups when read together.

One impression these pages leave is of a certain decline. Here Luebke and Daniels are most explicit. The German American ethnic group has outlived any recognized national leadership. Japanese Americans seem well on the way to the same condition. Huggins, in contrast, acclaims the rise of an elective leadership among blacks; but none of the black mayors or congressmen to date has commanded the same devotion and trust inspired by Martin Luther King and Malcolm X during their lifetime, not to mention W. E. B. DuBois, Booker T. Washington, and Frederick Douglass. One might say as much of the Jews. There are, of course, eminent American Jews, but no Jewish organization today has a leader as widely known and respected as Louis Marshall, Louis Brandeis, or Stephen S. Wise. In a comparable way the Irish, while continuing to provide leaders for America, have themselves seemed less and less led. The Indians, in this respect as in others, may form a partial exception: they have produced in recent years a self-conscious intelligentsia (Vine DeLoria, N. Scott Momaday) to take the place of the great chiefs of the past. This difference may follow from the fact that the Indians are only in our time becoming a self-conscious ethnic group.

For the rest, the fading of a visible national leadership may be understood as a consequence of modernization.[14] For American ethnic groups modernization has meant either one of two things, and sometimes both. It has greatly weakened the group as a locus of individuals' associations and interests; or it has given rise to an increasingly differentiated, professional, and bureaucratic type of leadership, which works to contain modernization within the ethnic structure. In an early stage, the modern leader is a centralizer, building the big organizations that take over some of the functions of the small community Josef Barton has described. At that point the modernizer can dominate his organization and make himself felt throughout the ethnic group. Later, the organization loses its centrality or becomes more impersonal. Modernization calls for increasingly technical knowledge. Leaders become submerged in their organizations.

Since modernization tends to lessen the distinctiveness and visibility of ethnic leaders, the process is not easy to document or to describe; only tentative suggestions can be offered here. Among Indians the relatively anonymous bureaucratic leaders probably originated within the Bureau of Indian Affairs, as it opened executive positions to former tribesmen. Indian influence in the Bureau goes back to the late nineteenth century, but only in recent years through the encouragement of Indian preference acts has it become predominant. Indians have filled the office of Commissioner of Indian Affairs since 1966, and by 1974 62 percent of the

Bureau's employees had Indian ancestry.[15] Among blacks the National Urban League played a pioneering role in bringing forward a professional elite. Founded in 1910 by a trained social worker, the League insisted that its local affiliates be led by paid professionals. Only later, in the 1930s, did the rising distinction of the black bar enable the National Association for the Advancement of Colored People to rely heavily on Negro lawyers for its crucial legal talent.[16]

It is among Jews that professionalization has been carried farthest. Traditionally, Jews turned for leadership to wealthy men who validated their title to authority in the ethnic community by philanthropic generosity. In the twentieth century power has shifted more and more from the volunteers who provide the money to the professional administrators who know how to spend it. This shift has been especially evident in the growing complexity and importance of the local Jewish federations during the last two decades.[17] A recent memo from the Council of Jewish Federations on "The Role of the Professional" stipulated that the executive of a Federation must "exert effective professional leadership and supervision" over a specialized staff and, in doing so, coordinate "volunteer fund-raising, budgeting and financing, community planning, policy formulation, administration and management, program design and development, research and evaluation [and] community relations."

The transition to a modernized leadership is likely to create for ethnic groups a major dilemma, which appears with unusual sharpness in the case of one of the less well known of American peoples, the Hawaiians. For most American ethnic groups, a distinction between "modern" and earlier kinds of leaders is blurred by the recency of the group's formation and by our uncertainty over what may be called "traditional" in an American context. The Hawaiians illuminate vividly a traditional-modern dichotomy because their leadership until recent decades was so unambiguously anchored in ancient prescriptions. Hawaiian leadership consisted of the high chiefs and chiefesses, their rank and lineage elaborately defined, their sacred authority over the common people beyond all question. In the early nineteenth century these *ali'i* were drawn together in a royal court and topped by a reigning dynasty. All honor and initiative in Hawaiian society flowed from a single source, and the commoners' deference toward these superiors was unqualified.[18]

The overthrow of the Hawaiian monarchy in 1893 by an American clique was profoundly humiliating to the *ali'i*. Most of them withdrew completely from public life. In order not to recognize American sovereignty, some have never voted.[19] The *ali'i* remained, however, the unchallenged emblems of Hawaiian tradition. A new leader who embodied the old order arose among them in the early twentieth century in the person of Prince Jonah Kuhio Kalanianaole, a favorite of the fallen Queen and an intended heir to her throne. Educated and trained for high office, an orator, wit, and athlete, Prince Kuhio accepted the new American government. In return the white organizers of the Republican party designated him as its standard bearer and spokesman among the Hawaiians. For twenty years (1902–22) he was the elected delegate from the Territory of Hawaii to the U.S. Congress. Courtly, genial, thoroughly accommodative in approach, he corralled the Hawaiian vote for the Republican party while extracting from the federal government whatever benefits could be secured for his people and urging them to greater efforts in their own behalf.[20]

Wanting to freshen the memory of Hawaiian greatness, in 1903 Kuhio founded the elite Order of Kamehameha. It fostered the observance of Kamehameha Day as a major public holiday and set a pattern for other upper class societies, such as the Daughters and Sons of Hawaiian Warriors, which joined in the work of collecting genealogies and staging public festivals. Yet Kuhio also had in mind the needs of the poor and the requirements of pressure politics. In 1918 he organized the Hawaiian Civic Club to gain support for a "rehabilitation" program that would enable landless Hawaiians to return to the soil. Resembling Booker T. Washington in many ways, Kuhio was the traditional leader operating in a modern setting.

The rehabilitation law was passed, but it did not work very well. When Kuhio died, no one took his place. More and more, the old chiefly class became integrated into white society and indifferent to the plight of the ordinary Hawaiian. The Hawaiian Civic Club grew, but its interests shifted from social issues to pageants and fancy balls. Abandoned by their traditional leaders, the rank and file of Hawaiians fell into an intensified dependence on whites.[21]

Beginning in the 1950s, a new type of leadership has slowly materialized. It consists of politicians, social workers, and labor organizers who are primarily concerned to throw off the old psychology of dependence and to enable Hawaiians, through knowledge and power, to take fuller charge of their own destinies. Their initial opportunities came through the rejuvenation of the moribund Democratic party under John A. Burns. Demanding that every group should have a fair share in governing Hawaii, Burns (a white man) forged an interethnic coalition which transformed Hawaiian politics. Elected governor in 1962 with an ethnic Hawaiian as running mate, he created a cabinet that included five whites, four Japanese, four Hawaiians, two Chinese, and one Filipino.[22] Prominent among his Hawaiian aides were William Shaw Richardson, a lawyer who has been Chief Justice of the State Supreme Court since 1966, and Myron B. Thompson, a social worker who has been in the forefront of many efforts to improve social services.

Yet the new leadership, for all of its appeal to ethnic pride and all of its commitment to programs for social and economic advancement, was not very successful in mobilizing the Hawaiian people. Apathy remained high, and of the Hawaiians who voted many stuck with the Republican party. This was partly because the major beneficiaries of the Burns coalition were the already more energetic and numerous Japanese. The latter surged ahead in every field so spectacularly as to intensify among many Hawaiians a sense of failure and victimization. But the tepid response these modern leaders elicited also had another cause, which brings out a crucial dilemma of modernization.

Intrinsically, the ethnic group is a link with the past and a bulwark of stability. It depends on instinctive sympathies and ancestral loyalties of a wholly nonrational kind. Modernization, on the other hand, demands rationality, calculation, progress, and material incentives. It brings deracinating forces into the ethnic group and sets up an inner tension between "modern" techniques and goals and ethnic loyalty. The modernizing leader, to revert to Kurt Lewin's terminology, necessarily stands somewhere near the periphery of the group. His approach may actually weaken ethnic identity unless he can also evoke the symbols and focus the passions of a distinctive tradition. However colorless and bureaucratic modern Jewish leaders may have become, they are champions of Israel, and the defense of the homeland gives them a strong hold on Jewish hearts. The Hawaiians had lost their homeland and still grieved over it; but its recovery in any substantial degree seemed unrealistic to the established leaders of the Burns coalition. They worked for better education, for counseling services, for welfare reforms, but they had no cause that could rouse and inspire the Hawaiian people.

In the 1960s a wave of discontent and assertiveness spread through underprivileged ethnic groups in America and other modernized societies. Rational, bureaucratic leaders were thrown on the defensive. Hawaii was no exception. By the end of the decade the new militancy had reached the Islands; and in 1971 it touched a Hawaiian taxi driver, the mother of twelve children, with the force of a divine revelation.

The occasion was a fire, which destroyed Louisa K. Rice's taxi without harming a book she had left in it but had not read. Sensing a providential purpose at work, she read the book with intense excitement. It was the autobiography of Queen Liliuokalani, *Hawaii's Story*, originally published in 1898 as an appeal to Americans to return Hawaii to her people. On top of this summons, Mrs. Rice was visited with a dream, in which a symbolic orange was placed in her outstretched hand. Clearly she had work to do. She started a society for the recovery of Hawaiian lands and named it ALOHA (Aboriginal Lands of Hawaiian Ancestry). Somehow the homeland could be restored.[23]

For more than a year hardly anyone joined the ALOHA Association. Then the founder, still driving her cab, learned that Congress had awarded to the Eskimos, Indians, and Aleuts of Alaska a huge settlement of money as well as land to extinguish their ancient claims to the rest of the state and make way for an oil pipeline. With borrowed funds Mrs. Rice induced an Alaskan lawyer to come to Hawaii and explain how a similar claim might be pressed there. Through these friendly auspices, ALOHA secured a crack lobbyist in Washington. A specific proposal was formulated for reparations for the public lands the Hawaiian Kingdom lost when it was overthrown in 1893 with the connivance of U.S. representatives. According to the ALOHA scheme, Congress would charter and fund a Hawaiian Native Corporation, to be owned jointly by all persons of Hawaiian or part-Hawaiian descent, and to engage in business activities and welfare programs for their benefit. ALOHA did not challenge existing land titles. The land itself might be irrecoverable, but cash could take its place.[24]

In 1973–74 the ALOHA Association came to life. It swept through the Islands like a religious revival. It raised more than $100,000 from a state-wide telethon, secured endorsements from leading newspapers and politicians, and signed up thousands of members. No Hawaiian movement had awakened such enthusiasm since the days of Prince Kuhio. But trouble soon followed. The Association was wracked with quarrels over the practical details of the project and ways of implementing it. Kekoa Kaapu, a Harvard-trained urban renewal coordinator in Honolulu, rose to the helm of the Association and tried to put its operations on a professional management basis. Nevertheless, over-spending brought ALOHA to the verge of bankruptcy in 1975. Kaapu was relieved of the presidency. His successor lasted only a few months. Mrs. Rice denounced everyone and threatened to create a schism.[25]

Whatever its failings, the ALOHA Association aroused countless Hawaiians from apathy and defeatism. It showed how essential to ethnic mobilization the vision of a violated homeland can be. Yet the confusion and wrangling into which the Association fell demonstrated the inadequacy of a romantic and traditionalist vision in the absence of modern management.

The ferment of the early 1970s produced many other Hawaiian organizations, some more conservative than ALOHA, some more radical. What is striking is that virtually all of them focus on the land question. Most of the new organizations also push a vigorous cultural revival—a rediscovery of Hawaiian language, chants, navigational skills, and religious traditions. The two themes—land and culture—intertwine. Militant young Hawaiians think of the land as sacred. They regard the U.S. Navy's use of the small island of Kahoolawe for bombing practice as a desecration of their heritage. First in 1976 and again a year later, small groups of angry activists invaded Kahoolawe. The bombing continued. George Helm, a nightclub singer who became the charismatic leader of the agitation to reclaim the island, appeared before the Hawaii state legislature and held its members transfixed with an anguished appeal: "God can hear us. Why can't the politicians?" A month later Helm and a companion vanished in the surf off the bleak, deserted coast of Kahoolawe.[26]

The outcome of these and other demands on the part of the young traditionalists is still unclear. None of the new organizations has gained ascendancy in the Hawaiian community; nor have the modern leaders been displaced. Recognizing the need for new initiatives, they have profited from the challenge. Who else can relate so effectively to non-Hawaiian authorities? Prompted by modern leaders, a broadly based Coalition of Hawaiian Organizations came into being in 1975, providing for the first time a forum where all shades of opinion could find expression. To the Coalition Myron Thompson brought a proposal for obtaining a planning grant from the U.S. Department of Health, Education and Welfare under provisions of a law to assist "Native Americans." The object of the grant, which was duly approved and received, is to learn with some precision how many people can be counted as Hawaiian and how their needs and desires can best be met.[27] Meanwhile, in 1976, an appealing middle-of-the-road Hawaiian who got his start in the Burns administration was elected to Congress. Daniel Akaka is the first person of Hawaiian descent to sit in either house of Congress since the attainment of statehood.

Can Thompson and Akaka, through patient social research and all-around good will, frame a program capable of healing the rift between tradition and modernity? Such a program will have to attack the Hawaiian's heritage of dependency without destroying their distinctive culture and identity. It will have to respond to their longing for a lost homeland while strengthening and expanding their participation in modern society. That is a tall order. But the evidence presented in this book suggests that it is necessary and in some measure realizable.

Severe though the tensions between tradition and modernity can be, the opposition between them is far from absolute. In societies as tradition-bound as India, ancient prescriptions can facilitate new departures.[28] By the same token, in societies as emancipated as the United States new methods do not always (or only) endanger old loyalties, but may also serve them. Although modernization has attenuated ethnic leadership, it has proved essential to ethnic organization. That is the lesson of Hawaiian experience. It is a lesson that gives continuing relevance to the memory of Prince Kuhio and continuing significance to the rise and decline of the ALOHA Association. To invigorate tradition while embracing modernity is the crucial challenge and opportunity of ethnic leadership in our time.

NOTES

1. Kurt Lewin, *Resolving Social Conflicts: Selected Papers on Group Dynamics* (New York, 1948), pp. 190–97. This essay was first published in 1941. Alvin W. Gouldner reprinted part of it, together with supporting essays on leadership among Jews, Negroes, and Italian Americans, in his valuable reader, *Studies in Leadership: Leadership and Democratic Action* (New York, 1950).

2. Paula Kaye Benkart, "Religion, Family, and Community among Hungarians Migrating to American Cities, 1880–1930" (Ph.D. diss., The Johns Hopkins University, 1975), pp. 60–132; John Higham, *Strangers in the Land: Patterns of American Nativism, 1860–1925* (New Brunswick, N.J., 1955), pp. 126, 190, 258. On Hammerling see also his official organ, ironically entitled *The American Leader* (1912–?), and New York *World*, March 19, 1924, p. 3. On subsidies to German-American and Irish-American newspapers in 1872, see Leon Burr Richardson, *William E. Chandler Republican* (New York, 1940), pp. 148–49.

3. Gunnar Myrdal, *An American Dilemma: The Negro Problem and Modern Democracy* (New York, 1944), p. 779. My formulation in the next two paragraphs is much indebted to remarks by Professor Nathan Glazer at the Schouler Symposium.

4. Guido A. Dobbert, "German-Americans between New and Old Fatherland," *American Quarterly* 19 (1967): 663–80; Klaus Wust, *The Virginia Germans* (Charlottesville, 1969); Frederick Luebke, *Bonds of Loyalty: German-Americans and World War I* (De Kalb, 1974), pp. 44–46, 86–100.

5. Peter K. Eisinger, "Racial Differences in Protest Participation," *American Political Science Review* 68 (1974): 592–606, is an illuminating study of the importance of protest in black culture today. For a fuller historical dimension see Robert C. Dick, *Black Protest: Issues and Tactics* (Westport, Conn., 1974).

6. Myrdal, *American Dilemma*, pp. 768–78.

7. Anthony F. S. C. Wallace, *The Death and Rebirth of the Seneca* (New York, 1970).

8. Jon Wefald, *A Voice of Protest: Norwegians in American Politics, 1890–1917* (Northfield, Minn., 1971); Rodman W. Paul, "The Spanish-Americans in the Southwest, 1848–1900," in *The Frontier Challenge: Responses to the Trans-Mississippi West*, ed. John G. Clark (Lawrence, Kans., 1971).

9. Kathleen Neils Conzen has recently made a parallel discovery of a direct transfer of the associational impulse from the homeland by German immigrants. See her *Immigrant Milwaukee, 1836–60: Accommodation and Community in a Frontier City* (Cambridge, Mass., 1976), pp. 154–91.

10. Robert Ernst, *Immigrant Life in New York City, 1825–1863* (New York, 1949), pp. 124–34.

11. Charlotte Erickson, *Invisible Immigrants: The Adaptation of English and Scottish Immigrants in Nineteenth-Century America* (Coral Gables, Fla., 1972), p. 261. On Hawaii see Dennis Ogawa, *Jan Ken Po: The World of Hawaii's Japanese Americans* (Honolulu, 1973), pp. 6–12, and Honolulu *Advertiser*, April 16, 1943, p. 7.

12. David L. Sills, "Voluntary Associations," in *International Encyclopedia of the Social Sciences* (1968), 16: 365–66.

13. Norman Miller, "The Jewish Leadership of Lakeport," in *Studies in Leadership: Leadership and Democratic Action*, ed. Alvin W. Gouldner (New York, 1950), pp. 195–227; Herbert Gans, *The Urban Villagers: Group and Class in the Life of Italian Americans* (New York, 1962), pp. 108–15.

14. I have tried to make reasonably clear in the text what I mean by a term that allows us to describe, by a kind of conceptual shorthand, several interlinking concomitants of technological growth during the last century. For criticism of the concept see Dean C. Tipps, "Modernization Theory and the Comparative Study of Societies: A Critical Perspective," *Comparative Studies in Society and History* 15 (March, 1973): 199–226.

15. S. Lyman Tyler, *A History of Indian Policy* (Washington, D.C., 1973), pp. 221–26; United States Department of the Interior Bureau of Indian Affairs, *The American Indians: Answers to 101 Questions* (Washington, D.C., 1974), p. 11.

18   JOHN HIGHAM

16. Nancy J. Weiss, *The National Urban League, 1910–1940* (New York, 1974), pp. 73–79, 112; Allan Spear, *Black Chicago, 1900–1920: The Making of a Negro Ghetto, 1890–1920* (Chicago, 1967), p. 173; August Meier and Elliott Rudwick, "Attorneys Black and White: A Case Study of Race Relations within the NAACP," *Journal of American History* 62 (March, 1976): 913–46.

17. Daniel J. Elazar, *Community and Polity: The Organizational Dynamics of American Jewry* (Philadelphia, 1976), pp. 90, 181–89, 203, 264–67.

18. Irving Goldman, *Ancient Polynesian Society* (Chicago, 1970), pp. 199–242. On the habit of dependence see, for example, "The Future of the Hawaiians," *Pacific Commercial Advertiser* (Honolulu), January 21, 1889.

19. Honolulu *Advertiser*, August 6, 1974, p. A6.

20. William H. Beers, *Prince Jonah Kuhio Kalanianaole* ([Honolulu] 1974).

21. Ernest Beaglehole, *Some Modern Hawaiians*, University of Hawaii Research Publications, no. 19 (Honolulu, n.d.), pp. 98–101; Tony Todaro, "The Hawaiian Civic Club," *Paradise of the Pacific* 67 (1955), pp. 94–96; Honolulu *Advertiser*, November 26, 1975, p. 4.

22. Samuel Crowningburg-Amalu, *Jack Burns: A Portrait in Transition* (Honolulu, 1974), p. 98.

23. Honolulu *Star-Bulletin and Advertiser*, August 4, 1974, pp. 1, 4. The early stirrings of Hawaiian nationalism at the beginning of the present decade are described in Francine du Plessix Gray, *Hawaii: The Sugar-Coated Fortress* (New York, 1972), pp. 117–33.

24. Honolulu *Star-Bulletin and Advertiser*, August 4, 1974, pp. 1, 4; *The Alohagram* 1 (August, 1974). On the Alaska Native Claims Settlement Act of 1971 see *New York Times*, August 16, 1975, pp. 1, 20. The legal basis of the Hawaiian claims is analyzed in Neil M. Levy, "Native Hawaiian Land Rights," *California Law Review* 63 (July, 1975): 848–85. See also William E. Tagupa, "Native Hawaiian Reparations: An Ethnic Appeal to Law, Conscience, and the Social Sciences," *Journal of Ethnic Studies* 5 (Spring, 1977): 45–50.

25. Honolulu *Advertiser*, August 7, 1974, p. A3; February 11, 1975, p. A8; May 2, 1975, p. A9; November 17, 1975, p. A3; November 25, 1975, p.1; Honolulu *Star-Bulletin and Advertiser*, July 20, 1975, p. A3.

26. *New York Times*, January 11, 1976, p. 51; Pam Smith, "The Ohana: Birth of a Nation or Band-aid Brigade?" *Hawaii Observer*, no. 104 (May 19, 1977), pp. 19–25.

27. Honolulu *Advertiser*, October 17, 1975, p. A15, and November 26, 1975, p. 1; Alu Like, Inc., *Quarterly Report No. 1 to Region IX of the Office of Human Development (DHEW)*, October 1, 1975–December 31, 1975.

28. Lloyd I. Rudolph and Susanne Hoeber Rudolph, *The Modernity of Tradition: Political Development in India* (Chicago, 1967).

The Jews

Nathan Glazer

THE ETHNIC GROUP in American society is an amorphous entity. It is not defined in law, except for the special case of the American Indian. And of course its "leadership" is not defined formally or publicly for any ethnic group, as it might be in other nations with other polities. Thus we are given no easy handles in approaching the question of leadership in ethnic groups. For the society in general, we can take up initially, in considering leadership, the firm structure of political organization. Presidents, governors and mayors, congressmen and legislators, secretaries and judges, are clearly arranged in hierarchies. This as least permits us to select a group of leaders who hold unambiguously defined positions to begin an analysis of leadership, even though, as we know, our analysis must soon extend to consider variously defined "power elites" whose position is not signified by formal office.

In other areas, we are given other aids. If one studies business leaders, one has no great difficulty in selecting the most distinguished business leaders in the country. All one needs is a list of the five hundred leading corporations and their top officers. Admittedly, just as in the case of political leaders selected by the offices they hold, it can be argued that there are powers behind the throne who do not hold major or visible office but who nevertheless are more important than the leaders who do. The selection of a group of cultural or intellectual leaders is admittedly more difficult, but one can—with peril—resort to lists of Nobel prize-winners, or members of the National Academy of Sciences. Real influence in the intellectual sphere is more difficult to assess; Charles Kadushin's ingenious effort is only one, and it has not been without critics.[1]

What do we do with ethnic group leadership? How do we sort out the dignitaries from the powers, the mellifluent orators from the doers? How do we distinguish—an important issue for ethnic groups—the men who

19

are leaders because they have gained distinction in the large world for their talents or wealth or political office from those who are known only to the internal world of the ethnic group? Is it important to distinguish them? In groups without formal definition and formal structures of leadership, we lose the initial assistance given to us by the armature of a given structure in studying leadership in the large society. All the problems of distinguishing position from influence are made more complex[2] when we consider the ethnic group. Nevertheless, it is clear there are leaders within ethnic groups; even more surprising, in view of the enormous variation among American ethnic groups—in size, wealth, power, geographic distribution, cultural character, internal differentiation, etc. —rather similar questions can be raised about leadership in ethnic groups. Clearly, even if we have no theory, and may not have, we may have some common questions. Thus, for example, Gunnar Myrdal's fruitful distinction between "accommodationist" and "protest" leaders, developed in discussing black leadership, is one that may be applied with profit to at least the American Jewish group and, one suspects, to all. The two styles are more or less implied by the position of any ethnic group in American society: they are *in* it, but not wholly *of* it. They are shaped by the realities of the American polity, a society in which any interest group might alternate between protest and accommodation in trying to further its interests, or divide between protest and accommodationist styles and segments at any given time in advancing its interests.

I would like to raise a few broad questions about ethnic leadership and consider how they have been—at least at this point in time—resolved within the American Jewish community. The questions are:

1. Who is entitled to exercise leadership, and by what charter? This is the issue of "democracy" vs. the "self-appointed" leader.

2. What should be the *style* of leadership—in particular, how is the conflict between "accommodationist" and "protest" styles resolved?

3. Finally, how does ethnic group leadership deal with conflicts between "ethnic group" interests and "the public interest," taken in its largest dimension?[3]

The first large question—who should exercise leadership, and by what charter—is closest, to my mind, to resolution within the Jewish community. A number of variants of this question have agitated the Jewish community for at least seventy years. For example:

a. Should it be the wealthy and the prominent who exercise leadership? In this case, what of the interests of the poor and unknown?

b. Should it be the "Jewish" Jews who exercise leadership, those closest to the masses and the folk, and drawing their authority from them? Or should it be the prominent people, those known to the outside world, for whatever reason, who exercise authority?

c. Finally, should there be an internal democratic process for the choice of leaders? Or should one reconcile oneself to multiple leaderships, self-appointed, appointed by organizations, risen to prominence for one or another reason, and not chartered by a formal democratic process of the entire community?

In dealing with these questions in a brief paper, one must characterize large swatches of American Jewish history in rather summary form and undoubtedly many will be able to object to one or another nuance, fact, or generalization, but I think the picture I draw is generally accepted.

Between the 1840s and the 1880s the American Jewish community was a remarkably homogeneous one. Before the 1840s there were also Jews in this country—indeed, the first Jewish community is dated from 1654, in New York—and one can distinguish considerable heterogeneity among them: Sephardic Jews, with backgrounds that included, distantly, Portugal and Spain, more recently, Holland and Brazil and the West Indies; Jews who had sojourned for longer or shorter times in England; Jews from Germany, Poland, Hungary. Jews were generally grouped in small communities or settled as individuals, subject to disappearance as Jews as they married non-Jews or converted. But with the "German" immigration—a term which covers Jews from all the German-speaking lands, or lands in which Jews spoke German, and thus includes Bohemia and to some extent Hungary—a rather homogenous community was created. To begin with, German was the common language; all these immigrants had given up Yiddish. There were common occupations, basically trade, rising in the case of the most successful families to banking. In any case, agriculture, common labor, and even artisanship were scarcely found among the Jews of the German-speaking lands. There was the common religion, Judaism, and the common variant of it, the Ashkenazic, undergoing Westernization, that is, "Reform." There was the common experience in the lands of origin of being treated as a special and outcast group, somewhat relieved by the ragged progress of emancipation during the middle part of the nineteenth century in most of these countries.

All these circumstances, we may point out, distinguished the German Jews clearly from the East European Jews who began to come in a huge flood after 1880. These did not speak German; included many common laborers and artisans among them, "proletarians"; practiced a more intense and less Westernized form of Judaism; and far from experiencing emancipation, they were experiencing a diminution of their rights; for in Russia and Rumania the political and civil position of the Jews steadily became worse.

The relative homogeneity of the German Jewish community of the nineteenth century did not mean there were no issues of leadership within it: it did mean, however, that—at least in retrospect—these conflicts seemed more modest and reconcilable, as indeed we may see from the career of Isaac Mayer Wise, the organizer of Reform Judaism. He wrote its prayer book, created its seminary, founded its congregational and rabbinical organizations, was the dominant figure in what was expected to be a national organization of American Jews. By the 1880s, the transformation of the American Jewish community into a homogeneous community with a common religion, culture, occupations, and institutions of leadership was complete. There was even a certain uniformity of political outlook: the German Jews of the 1880s were Republicans.

The coming of the great masses of the East European Jews broke all these uniform patterns. Jews became socially, religiously, economically, and politically more diverse. There were now poor Jews, working-class Jews, intensely Orthodox Jews, Socialist and Anarchist Jews, in large numbers, creating new organizations, with very different interests and outlooks. A period of conflict over *who* were the proper leaders of American Jews began. Was it to be wealthy and prominent and well-connected Jews who spoke for the new Jewish masses in the United States? Was it to be Jews who had become separated from the intense folkish culture of their fathers and forefathers and who had taken up the dignified, high Protestant style of well-to-do Americans? Was it to be leaders who held their positions by some form of popular election, or was it to be leaders who appointed themselves to defend Jewish interests as they understood them? All of these issues can be summed up crudely as the conflict between "uptown" and "downtown." The reference is to New York City, where, until the expansion into the suburbs after World War II, half or more of all American Jews lived. The remarkable thing to my mind was that even while this conflict was most intense—between, let us say, the early 1900s and the 1940s, or between the Kishinev pogrom and the World War II holocaust—a sense of common interests seemed again and again to draw together the opposing elites. Thus, Moses Rischin has described the close involvement of the uptown leaders in the life of the Lower East Side—in education, reform, religion, the stabilization of the ghetto economy—indeed, one may say, in all things but politics. In politics the downtown Jews were either staunch Socialists or drawn into the Tammany machine, while the uptown Jews remained Republicans, even if progressive Republicans.[4] Arthur Goren has described how, when the Lower East Side stormed and seethed in response to Police Commissioner Bingham's assertion in 1908 that half the criminals of New York were Jews, and demanded that the uptown leaders speak up, the downtowners were simultaneously—while denouncing the uptowners—seeking their leadership and their intervention. One is reminded of children who, while violently attacking their parents, nevertheless try to induce them to take authoritative responsibility.[5] After remaining silent for two weeks, Louis Marshall, the very image of the self-appointed, self-confident, uptown German Jewish leader, arranged for Bingham to retract his statement and for the spontaneous Lower East Side Committee—which included many who undoubtedly denounced Marshall on other occasions as an imperious, uptown, undemocratic magnate—to accept it, thus closing the incident. (Marshall wrote the apology *and* the acceptance—he took no chances.) Despite the fact that the American Jewish Committee, created by the German Jewish leaders in 1906 to defend Jewish interests, was entirely self-appointed, its leadership—Louis Marshall was the dominant figure in it—was generally accepted by downtown.

The poor and downtrodden *wanted* the wealthy and well connected to assume leadership, in same areas; in others, they counted on their indigenous leaders—Socialist, Zionists, labor leaders. They voted for these in elections, they gave them loyalty as trade union members, and it was the indigenous leaders who symbolized for them, whether in Socialism or Zionism, the better world they sought. They listened to and joined in denunciations of the uptown leaders, the "shtadlanim," the "court" Jews who mediated with the princes and powers; but they nevertheless looked upon them with awe and rejoiced when they emerged from the corridors of power in which they made their arrangements to provide settlements on specific issues.

I wonder whether this is not a regular pattern of ethnic group leadership. From the point of view of ordinary people, there is more that ties together the fierce ideological opponents within an ethnic group than would appear to be the case if one takes statements and writings at face value. Thus, to the Jewish masses both Meyer London, the Russian Jewish Socialist, and Louis Marshall, the Republican corporation lawyer, were great leaders. Both reflected honor on the group; both were defenders of group interests, in their own way. One wonders whether the same pattern may not be found in other groups—so that it was the intellectuals and ideologues who trumpeted the differences between say, a Booker T. Washington and a W. E. B. Dubois, but to the people they were both heroes.

This is not to say there were no real issues, real points of conflict between uptown and downtown. But these differences, I believe, were rooted less in interests, despite the differences in wealth and economic power, than in style, culture, and approach. Both uptown and downtown were equally concerned to secure the civil position of Jews in the United States. Both uptown and downtown were equally concerned with overcoming the savage discrimination and persecution of Jews in Czarist Russia and Rumania. It would be hard to find in the accounts of the long struggle to secure the civil rights of Jews in Eastern Europe—against Czarist Russia, at the peace conference after World War I, in the newly independent successor states of Eastern Europe, and during World War II—any real divergence in interest and concern between uptown and downtown. All Israel, it seemed, was one. One could have imagined possible divergences of interest. For example, there is a good deal of evidence that the mass migration of East European and Russian Jews after the 1880s hurt the social position of the well-to-do established German Jewish community, and there were many expressions of dismay, annoyance, and antagonism. And yet the overwhelmingly dominant response was one of compassion and concern. From the beginning, the wealthy and influential Jewish leaders were ready to expend their wealth and influence to assist Jews of a very different level of culture and wealth.[6]

What, then, were the points at issue between uptown and downtown? They were not the religious practices, the Orthodoxy of the East European Jews. After all, Marshall, Schiff, and other leading German Jews reestablished and endowed the Jewish Theological Seminary of America as a basically Orthodox institution to serve them. There was no argument over the desire of the East European Jews to advance educationally and economically: the uptown Jews established institutions like the Educational Alliance on the Lower East Side to assist them in this desire. There were two substantive issues on which they parted and one procedural one. The substantive issues were Socialism and Zionism, and the procedural issue was whether Jewish leadership in the United States should be established through popular elections or through organizational representation and self-appointment.

On the first issue, Socialism: To my mind, this was the less important one, even though Socialism was repugnant to the conservative Jewish leaders. Socialist rhetoric might be turned against Schiff, Marshall, and the others, but the fact remained there was no major direct conflict between the substantive economic interests of the German Jewish aristocracy and the economic interests of the Jewish masses. The wealth of the German Jewish aristocracy came from banking, the practice of law, the ownership of department stores. The greatest Jewish banker, Schiff, was known for his compassion and philanthropies; the wealthiest Jewish department store owners, such as the Strauses of Macy's, had a similar reputation. If Schiff exploited anyone with his major railroad reorganizations, it was not the Jewish garment workers; if Marshall exploited anyone with his legal fees, it was not they either; nor was it easy to cast department store owners in the role of leading exploiters of the Jewish workers, who were neither employed by nor shopped in such stores. The leading "exploiters" of the needles-trades workers of the Lower East Side were men just like themselves: East European Jews recently risen to the point where they could employ a few sewing machine operators or rent a loft for a very minor manufacturing enterprise. (The line between worker and employer was a very easy one to pass: there was hardly an employer who had not been or was not still a worker, or would not be a worker again, hardly a worker who did not have hopes of becoming an employer.) Indeed, it was the uptown leaders who intervened and tried to settle the fierce strikes waged by Jewish needles-trades workers against Jewish employers. Thus Louis Marshall and Jacob Schiff intervened to end the devastating cloakmakers strike of 1910; and it was this strike that brought the wealthy Boston Jewish lawyer, Louis D. Brandeis, into Jewish affairs for the first time. The uptown intervention into classic labor conflicts had nothing or little to do with their economic interests. Uptown intervened to overcome internecine warfare in the Jewish community and to assist the impoverished needles-trades workers.[7]

The whole question of how socialist Jewish Socialism (as well as American Socialism) was is, of course, a complicated one. In any case, the fact that uptown was Republican and downtown was Socialist did not prevent close relations between them in the common interest of improving the condition of the Jewish workingman. Whatever the rhetoric, the workers' leaders welcomed the intervention of the powerful uptown leaders, who could generally tip the scales in favor of a settlement with slightly better terms than the labor leaders could get on their own.

Zionism was perhaps a rather more serious source of conflict. The Zionist movement had deep roots in Eastern Europe, but it began to take something like a modern secular form only in the 1880s. Theodor Herzl transformed it into a fully secular political movement in the last few years of the nineteenth century. The Zionist movement had a very modest impact in the United States, though there were some Zionists here, until World War I. The Jewish workers were socialist for the most part; they were not interested in a Jewish homeland in Palestine; the Jewish wealthy and the Reform movement opposed the Zionist movement because it questioned their image of themselves as members of a religion, not a nation or a people. Thus before 1914 the Zionist movement had little support, whether among the East European workers or the German Jewish upper middle class. It did have adherents who were drawn to it for various reasons.

The war required immediate relief for the Jewish colonies of Palestine, cut off from their accustomed funds, and for the Jews of Eastern Europe, whose areas of settlement now became the battlefields of the Eastern war. And during the war the Zionist movement mushroomed and became briefly the dominant power in American Jewish life, a position it lost rapidly after the war. It is not easy to explain this explosive growth. One hesitates to attribute this transformation to one man, but it is hard to think of an alternative explanation. Louis D. Brandeis was converted to Zionism—a surprising conversion in view of his background, which contained almost no connection with Jewish life—in 1912, emerged to become its dominant leader in 1914, and placed his enormous energies and influence into building the Zionist movement in America, both before and after he went to the Supreme Court in 1916, and helped it gain national and international recognition and support. In 1914 there were 12,000 members of the Federation of American Zionists, in 1919 176,000.[8]

Zionism became a power that drew support from all the levels of Jewish life, with converts (few but important) among the old established German Jews, among the Jewish middle classes, and among Jewish workers. Despite the fact that Brandeis was able to bring many Americanized German Jews into the Zionist movement, most remained outside, either actively hostile or else willing to cooperate only for the philanthropic ends of Zionism, such as salvaging the Jewish colonies in Palestine, helping build up Palestine as a place of refuge for Jews who would not or could not go to the United States and other countries (during the war the immigration restriction movement waxed ever stronger, and Jewish leaders could foresee the possibility of the closing of the gates that came in the early 1920s), and developing Palestine as a cultural and religious center for Jews. The conflict over the political aims of Zionism did not really come to an end in American Jewry until the establishment of a Jewish state after World War II, when the issue became moot.

But during World War I and afterwards the conflict over Zionism was intense, and it became one of the major issues dividing East European Jews from German Jews. It then became closely linked to the question of the *means* by which American Jews should try to influence the postwar settlement for the benefit of Jewish minorities in Eastern Europe and the Middle East: whether through the intervention of the established Jewish dignitaries with their political and economic influence, or through elected representatives of the Jewish people. The East Europeans for the most part wanted popularly elected representatives and urged an American Jewish Congress; the German Jews for the most part resisted this approach. The line was not simply drawn between the plutocrats and the leaders of mass organizations, between the German Jews and the East European Jews. Stephen S. Wise, a progressive Reform Rabbi, led the fight for the Congress; the Zionists, now led primarily by German Jews—Brandeis, Wise, Judge Julian Mack—supported it. The American Jewish Committee opposed it, as it generally opposed mass intervention in what it conceived of as the necessarily delicate issue of the management of Jewish affairs. The Jewish labor leaders joined them in opposition. The Jewish labor leaders were not Zionists, but socialists, and as such their hope for the Jews of Eastern Europe was the establishment of states under Social Democratic government, providing minority rights to Jews for culture, education, and religion. They did not favor the Zionist solution, but in view of the temper of Jewish public opinion during World War I as the Zionist movement exploded, they could see that an elected body would be under Zionist domination. The American Jewish Committee and the trade union leaders managed to wring a compromise: there would be an American Jewish Congress, but it would be a purely temporary organization. Meanwhile, the Jewish delegation to the Paris peace conference would consist of non-Zionists and Zionists, under the chairmanship of the ubiquitous Louis Marshall.[9]

The Congress movement did not create a permanent organization based on popular election to represent all of American Jewry. The deal held, and only one general election for an American Jewish Congress was held at the end of World War I. But it did create a second and more popular national Jewish organization, alongside of and competing with the American Jewish Committee, which continued the name of the American Jewish Congress, and was dominated for many years by the impressive figure of Rabbi Stephen S. Wise. It was chiefly differentiated from the American Jewish Committee by its strong commitment to Zionism and to a more public approach to pressing for Jewish interests. What it could not do—what no organization could do—was to replace or speak for the multifarious organizations that reflected the various tendencies in American Jewish life.

The creation of a central leadership for American Jewry was basically made impossible, I believe, because of the American political framework, in which private organizational efforts were unregulated by government. They could flourish, or die, as they wished. They received neither official public recognition, which might have permitted them to become dominant within their group, nor any public discouragement (indeed, tax exemption may be considered a form of encouragement). As a result, in each area of Jewish life parallel organizational structures came into existence. In the area of "defense," as it was called—Jewish rights in the United States and abroad—there were the American Jewish Committee, the American Jewish Congress, and the Anti-Defamation League of B'nai B'rith. In the area of religion, there were the three major "denominations" of Reform, Conservatism, and Orthodoxy, each with its Seminary, its Congregational organizations, its Rabbinical organizations, and other attendant organizations. The Jewish trade unions—which at first were Jewish both in membership and in leadership, later were Jewish primarily in leadership—had their own organizations for Jewish interests. And so on.

Yet if the patterns of American life encouraged the flowering of hundreds and thousands of organizations, the crises of Jewish life raised again and again the need for unified action. The rise of Hitler, the stripping of the Jews of Germany and then of the lands conquered by Germany of rights, property, and life, the withdrawal by the British Government during the 1930s of support for the creation of a Jewish homeland in Palestine and the restriction of Jewish rights to immigration to Israel, the rise of anti-Semitism in the United States, spurred by Nazism, the holocaust, the tragic problem of the surviving Jews of Europe, the Palestinian crisis, and then, with the creation of the State of Israel, the permanent need to assist in its upbuilding and defense—all these seemed to require a central organization, a central voice.

In World War II the story of the American Jewish Congress movement of World War I was largely repeated. If the conditions of the Jews in Europe and Palestine in World War I called for a single voice for American Jewry, the call was a thousand times stronger in World War II. The Jews of Europe were being hunted down and killed in the incredible death factories while the gates of Palestine remained closed, while indeed the gates of the United States remained closed. The immigration laws were enforced with an unbelievable severity, and no mechanism for providing even a temporary refuge for those who could escape was put into effect until near the end of the war. Once again, the Zionist movement grew rapidly, and once again, it failed to get universal support. The American Jewish Committee was still suspicious of a mass democratic organization and the political line to which it would be committed if it became subject to it. A central organization was formed temporarily (first called the American Jewish Assembly, then the American Jewish Conference). It was not terribly effective.

Could the Jews of the United States have done more to help the Jews of Europe if they had been united in a central democratic organization? One analyst of the scandalous failure of the United States to do more to help the doomed Jews of Europe believes so. But a full case has not been made out, and conceivably the varied organizations, with their varied techniques of agitation and influence and their varied means of access to power, did as much as a central organization might.[10]

Popular election of a single central body thus has never been established in American Jewry—clearly, it never will be. But neither is it true that American Jews therefore continue to be represented by the self-appointed and self-selected, the wealthy delegates to the Gentiles, so to speak. Rather, a rich and complex organizational life has come into being, which nevertheless represents a community that has become remarkably homogeneous economically, socially, and politically. Today, the distinctions between Eastern and German Jews is of minor significance, and few organizations can be found that represent one or the other. The Jewish working class has almost disappeared. Yiddish-speaking Jews are few and declining. And, with the creation of the state of Israel, the issue of Zionism, which had so long agitated and divided American Jews, in effect disappeared. Zionism was an issue as long as it could be debated *whether* Palestine should become a Jewish state or something less than that, a Jewish homeland, a cultural and religious center, or a refuge. It stopped being an issue *when* part of Palestine became Israel, because all Jewish organizations and tendencies agreed on the prime necessity of defending Israel, and it became a matter of indifference that some who defended it had once been interested only in saving Jews, and others who defended it had once been interested in creating a Jewish state. On this central issue, there is no longer any difference—or any discernible to the naked eye—between the position of the American Jewish Committee and the American Jewish Congress, between wealthy and poorer Jews, German and East European Jews, Yiddish-speaking and English-speaking Jews. The "roof" organization of the American Jews, when it comes to key political matters, is the Conference of Presidents of Major Jewish Organizations, but it is not popularly elected, has no control over any of its members, does not coordinate their actions; it is a consultative body, which, on issues of overwhelming unanimity, such as the right to emigration of Russian Jews or the defense of Israel, may take some common action.

To my mind, when one considers the long conflict over democracy in Jewish leadership, one must conclude that it has lost much of its urgency. One reason is because a new homogeneity has been created in the American Jewish community to replace the homogeneity broken by the mass immigration of the 1880s and after. Another is to be found in the fact that a single overwhelming issue dominates American Jewry, the protection of the State of Israel from destruction, and on that issue divisions are relatively minor, though one may see, as the danger increases, the possibility of substantial splits within the American Jewish Community over what policies Israel should pursue, whether American Jews should intervene in affecting those policies, and how, and what attitude they should take regarding their own government's policies toward Israel.

The issue of democracy in American Jewish life, while it has become less urgent, has not disappeared. In the late 1960s, a movement developed among some Jewish youths that was critical of Jewish leadership for ignoring what we may call the new spiritual needs that arose out of the youth ferment of the 1960s. The concrete issue that arose dealt with the distribution of communal funds. These go overwhelmingly to Israel on the one hand, and to established community institutions in this country —hospitals, old-age homes, social service organizations—on the other. Jewish leaders were attacked because they achieve their position through wealth, because they are ignorant of Jewish culture and religion, because they ignore youth, because they are not representative of the people. One can see a continuity between this kind of criticism and the criticism of the leadership of the *shtadlanim* in the first few decades of the century. And yet in my judgment it does not have great weight today. There has actually been a decline in the role of great wealth in Jewish leadership, first of all because more Jews are wealthy enough to take on communal responsibilities; second, because the unpaid lay leaders—the Presidents of organizations—have generally become less important than the paid officials. Leaders, it is true, do not generally have a deep Jewish education, but then neither do most Jews. And they are, I would guess, more representative of rank-and-file Jews than are the new youth activists who want more commitment to what they feel is relevant Jewish education.

Just as the question of who should represent American Jews was a major issue of the first half of this century, so, too, was the question of the style of leadership, the means whereby Jewish issues should be brought to public attention—or, indeed, whether they should be brought to public attention at all. Here the American Jewish Committee generally insisted that Jewish needs could best be met by influentials talking to influentials. Not that it always opposed popular agitation. On the question of the abrogation of the trade treaty with Czarist Russia to protest its treatment of Jews, the Committee was perfectly happy to, and itself initiated, public protest, though basically it operated through all the means of bringing influence and pressure on decision makers, rather than through mass meetings.[11] Its point of view was perhaps best expressed by Louis Marshall when he argued against an American Jewish Congress in 1915: "One of the gentlemen says, 'We will not beg a gift, we will ask for nothing, we will demand!' Now that is the very thing which I fear with respect to any Congress of Jews. There will be those who will accompany their demands with the most extraordinary arguments and with the most ineffectual assertions. And demand from whom, and demand what, and demand how? People who demand must have some sanction for that demand. . . . We have no armies, we have no country of our own, we have no power. . . . What can we accomplish by the passage of resolutions? Who will listen to them, who will present them to the leaders of the armed bands who are perpetuating [the pogroms]?"[12]

Perhaps World War I and its aftermath justified this approach to Jewish problems. There were, after all, considerable successes: the abrogation of the Russian Treaty, the Balfour Declaration, the Minorities Treaties with the successor states that protected Jewish rights, all owed much to Jewish men of influence. With the rise of Hitler, "accommodationism" became ineffective and helpless—not that "protest" could necessarily do more. But sometimes the soul must cry out, and perhaps protest *could* have done more. Stephen S. Wise, who had long expressed the spirit of protest par excellence, insisted that the atrocities of the Nazis must be exposed from the beginning and denounced in as loud a voice, and with as strong actions, as Jews were capable of. The American Jewish Committee opposed mass meetings and provocative acts such as the boycott of German goods. It was true that every act of Jewish resistance was treated as a provocation by the Nazis and resulted in further restrictions, confiscations, violence, visited on German Jews. But in view of what we now know of Hitler and his government, we can conclude that even if protest did no good, accommodation would have been even worse.[13]

Stephen S. Wise was vindicated in his insistence on the broadest and strongest possible protest against Nazi Germany. But the most painful dilemma for Jewish leadership was what kind of pressure to bring, on their *own* government, in wartime, to help save the Jews of Europe? Because six million Jews were killed, American Jews will always ask themselves whether enough was done, whether more could have been done, but whatever answer they give will be unsatisfying simply because of the scale of this numbing event.

"Accommodation" and "protest" are still issues in Jewish life, now wrapped up with the question of Israel. Just as the United States was the only nation that American Jews could influence when it came to the Jews of Europe, so, too, it is the only nation they can influence when it comes to the defense of Israel. The borders of protest have since been expanded. The extreme of protest is now, in our terror-ridden world, no longer a Madison Square Garden meeting—that is pretty tame today— but it may be placing a bomb at the United Nations. All the issues are raised for American Jews with which we have become familiar from the analysis of black protest in recent years: Is protest more effective than lobbying and working through "the system," what kind of protest, doesn't even extreme protest, and terrorism, help the moderate leaders who would never resort to such methods, and the like? But terrorism and extreme protest are not today major issues in the Jewish community. Almost all denounce the American Jewish Defense League, and almost all agree that quiet negotiation must be accompanied by public demonstration. The issue of protest versus accommodation has been reduced in significance, though it is always present in some degree. Thus, Jewish opinion is not uniform on the question of what kind of pressure should be exerted on the Soviet Union. The issue continues to surface on the question of what kind of pressure to exert on the American government or American elected officials when it comes to policy toward Israel.

It is the permanent danger to Israel that raises most sharply the third and last question I have proposed. How does ethnic group leadership deal with conflicts between "ethnic group interests" and "the public interest"? Israel has become the dominating issue in American Jewish life. The issues of the past have been reduced to relative insignificance. Thus, the issue of the rights of the Jews of Eastern Europe and the Arab lands, which was the dominant concern of the American Jewish Committee until after World War II, is no longer of great importance. These Jews have been killed or have emigrated to Israel, and the remaining communities are numbered in the hundreds or thousands, rather than the hundreds of thousands and millions, except for Soviet Russia, where a large Jewish population of two or three million survives. This is not to say that Jewish organizations are not concerned about the fate of the remnants of Polish or Iraqi Jewry, but the numbers involved are tiny. The issue of organized anti-Semitism in the United States is now not a major one. There is no *Dearborn Independent*, supported by a Henry Ford, regularly publishing anti-Semitic propaganda, as there was in the twen-

ties. The organizations of the thirties and forties have disappeared or
have been greatly reduced. The issue of limitations on admission of
Jews to colleges and medical schools is no longer a major one, though
there is some concern over the rise of ethnic goals and quotas. But this
is not a specifically Jewish issue. The question now is not, should quotas
limit Jewish attendance in colleges or medical schools? but, should quotas
be used so that a minimum of other minority groups—blacks, Spanish-
surnamed—gain admission? There is no public disrespect for the Jewish
religion, though there are local community arguments over such matters
as the public celebration of Christmas. The point is not that anti-Semitism
does not exist; but public or organized anti-Semitism hardly exists. Thus
only one major issue is left, and it is an issue of overwhelming urgency and
great complexity—the safety and survival of the state of Israel. It has almost totally dominated American Jewish life for thirty years, and its power
to obliterate other issues has risen over time. It inevitably has the capacity
to raise the question of "dual loyalty," of the problem of the attachment of
American citizens to a foreign state.

There is one respect in which perhaps this problem is not as serious
as similar ones which have faced other ethnic groups attached to their
homelands: there is no danger that the United States and Israel will be
on opposite sides in a war, which was the fate of German Americans and
Japanese Americans. But in every other respect the problem of Israel
raises the question of dual loyalty more sharply. Thus, Israel evokes a
much deeper and more emotional commitment by American Jews than I
think any homeland issue has for other American immigrant groups.
Israel is unique in many respects, among them the fact that Israel is not
actually the country from which most American Jews come. But it has
become a substitute for the destroyed homelands of Eastern and Central
Europe and the Arab world because Jews from all these countries have
gone there. Thus, a very substantial proportion of American Jews have
relatives in Israel or have visited Israel; hundreds of thousands have
lived in Israel. Further, Israel is unique in that its international position
has never been regularized, it has never received the recognition or acceptance of its neighbors. It has fought four wars with them, and during
these wars American Jews have believed, with reason, that Israel was
threatened not merely by defeat and the loss of territories, but also by
the annihilation of the state and the massacre of its inhabitants. Not only
did the antagonism that Israel aroused among the Arab states, one un-
paralleled by other cases of international relations, raise this possibility,
but also the fact that history provided a recent example of large-scale
extermination of Jews, and what has happened once may happen again.
Perhaps only the issue of Ireland, when it was ruled by England, aroused
the same intensity for an American ethnic group, and the Irish, as we
know, were quite ready to go very far in support of Irish freedom. But

there is no equivalent of Ireland for any ethnic group today, and thus Jews are alone in the intensity of their commitment, and the kinds of actions they will engage in to ensure American support (we have to add the additional point that support is not possible from other quarters, owing to Arab power and Communist hostility). Jews would like to point to other ethnic groups that act as they do, and in measure they can, but the difference in degree of involvement with homeland that marks Jews, owing to the special position of Israel, reaches to a difference in quality. Thus, we know that there was Greek pressure on Congress in connection with arms to Turkey, but all that was involved, serious as that was to Greeks, was the division of the island of Cyprus. Greece itself was hardly threatened.

The oddities of history further make the Israeli-Arab issue not one in a distant corner of the world. It now involves all the great powers intimately and the world's most important source of energy, and it is seen as the one issue that may well lead to world war. Thus it is not only the intensity of Jewish feeling which attracts notice, it is also the centrality of the Middle East in world affairs.

If Jews were a small and uninfluential group, it would perhaps not matter much that they were deeply committed to the fate of Israel. Jews make up less than 3 percent of the American population, and that proportion is declining. But despite these relatively small numbers as a proportion of the population, there are enough of them—perhaps six million— and they are prominent enough, owing to how they are distributed through business, the professions, the academy, that they matter politically; yet there are not enough of them to matter decisively. It is an odd position to be in, and if the needs of American foreign policy dictate, as they have for our leading allies, the lessening of support for Israel, what will American Jews do—and what will other Americans think of them?

Now there are various answers to the dual loyalty problem. Some argue that it does not exist—that every American has the right to support his homeland. We generally act as if that is so, and yet we know that dilemmas do arise. Ethnic groups, their leaders, their publications, their organizations, must often choose between what is seen as a homeland interest and what is seen as an American interest. I have already referred to the most drastic circumstance when they must choose—that is, when the United States goes to war against the homeland. I have suggested Jews do not face such a drastic possibility. But the possibilities they may be faced with are bad enough. The United States is deeply engaged in the conflict in the Middle East, for reasons we need not enter into, and it will not revert to being a by-stander, or one power among many, in the conflict. The United States tries to preserve a neutral stance. But being such an important factor, American policy is analyzed carefully by Jewish organizations, and, even without the involvement of Jewish organizations, it provokes strong responses from great numbers of American Jews. Because the policy of the United States has been seen by the Arab countries up to now as being unbalancedly pro-Israel and because United States relations with the Arab countries are so important, it is inevitable that American policy will be seen by American Jews as increasingly pro-Arab. As I write these lines, a striking change has occurred in the Middle East, and for the first time in thirty years direct face-to-face negotiations for peace are taking place between Israel and the largest Arab nation. The immediate threat of another war has been lifted. But the radically changed perspective created by the unexpected actions of the president of Egypt does not wipe out the fears and possibilities of thirty years. In any case, peace will be a long time coming, and these fears—of war and of what may happen if Israel loses a war—will not disappear.

The overwhelming importance of Israel's safety to American Jews, in addition to the crucial role the United States plays in the Middle East, raises every day the question, What kind of influence or pressure should American Jews exert in affecting American policy?

Israel's present military strength, and the turn in Egyptian policy, seem to have temporarily eliminated the fear of Israel losing a war. But these fears reached agonizing levels in 1967 and 1973; only a short-sighted view would argue that they can never again play a role in American Jewish thinking and in American Jews' relationship to the American polity. When the possibility of Israel losing a war was vivid to American Jews, they could not help comparing their situation to that of World War II when Jews were being killed in vast numbers and opportunities existed—or so many Jews believed—to save some by giving money to individual Nazi leaders. It was a tragic dilemma indeed. What pressure, after all, could one, should one, place on one's nation at war?[14] Or—as in 1973—what pressure does one place on one's nation and one's leaders when each day's action or inaction may mean the destruction of the homeland and its people?

One may now hope that such a dilemma will never again confront American Jews. And yet there are many issues that have arisen, that will arise, even if, and as, the Middle East moves toward peace, that will raise the "dual loyalty" question. How much aid to Israel? How strong the pressure against aid to Israel's antagonists? Should American soldiers be used to guarantee peace in the Middle East? Should there be a clear military guarantee by the United States of Israel? And regardless of what American Jews do to push for one position or another, what would be the reaction of their fellow Americans to this urgent intervention by one group to affect American foreign policy?

Thus, at a time when Jewish leadership is more unified than ever before, when fewer issues of interest, culture, style, and orientation divide it, when it is more united in spirit—if not organization—than ever before, one central problem of ethnic group leadership rises up more intensely for Jews than for any other group: How does one defend group interests without affecting—or being seen to affect—adversely the public interest? It is not a comfortable position.

NOTES

1. Charles Kadushin, *The American Intellectual Elite* (Boston: Little, Brown & Co., 1974).
2. I refer here to the long debate among sociologists and political scientists over community power. Floyd Hunter, Robert A. Dahl, Nelson Polsby, and many others have contributed to it. For a convenient summary, see Nelson Polsby, "The Study of Community Power," in *International Encyclopedia of the Social Sciences* (New York: Macmillan Co. and The Free Press, 1968), 3: 157–63.
3. In this paper, I limit myself to the leadership of a group that deals with the large political issues which face the group. Thus, I do not discuss—as one might—religious leadership; or the leadership of the complex structure of fund-raising institutions which form so prominent a role in Jewish life; or "social" leadership. Many studies deal with leadership in one or another of these manifestations. But there is as yet not much research on political leadership, in the sense in which I use it here.
4. Moses Rischin, *The Promised City* (Cambridge, Mass.: Harvard University Press, 1962), pp. 95–115.
5. Arthur A. Goren, *New York Jews and the Quest for Community* (New York: Columbia University Press, 1970), pp. 25–37.
6. The best picture of this response is given in Charles Reznikoff, ed., *Louis Marshall: Champion of Liberty, Selected Papers and Addresses* (Philadelphia: The Jewish Publication Society of America, 1957), passim; and Cyrus Adler, ed., *Jacob Schiff* (Garden City, N.Y.: Doubleday Doraan, 1929); as well as the two excellent histories of Jews in New York of Arthur Goren and Moses Rischin.
7. On the relations between uptown and downtown in dealing with labor strife, see Rischin, *The Promised City*, pp. 236–57; Goren, *New York Jews*, pp. 196–213.
8. Melvin I. Urofsky, *American Zionism from Herzl to the Holocaust* (New York: Doubleday & Co., Anchor, 1976), p. 134. For Brandeis's path to Zionism, see pp. 11–126; for his role in American Zionism, pp. 109–229.
9. For accounts of the Congress movement, see Goren, *New York Jews*, pp. 218–77 (for the position of the Socialists, see p. 227), and Urofsky, *American Zionism*, pp. 151–81.
10. Henry Feingold, *The Politics of Rescue: The Roosevelt Administration and the Holocaust, 1938–45* (New Brunswick, N.J.: Rutgers University Press, 1970).
11. Reznikoff, ed., *Louis Marshall*, pp. 49–108.
12. Goren, *New York Jews*, p. 224.
13. Stephen S. Wise, *Challenging Years* (New York: G. P. Putnam's Sons, 1949), pp. 233–66; and Urofsky, *American Zionism*, pp. 365–69.
14. See Wise, *Challenging Years*; Arthur D. Morse, *While Six Million Died* (New York: Random House, 1967); Henry L. Feingold, *The Politics of Rescue* (New Brunswick, N. J.: Rutgers University Press, 1970).

The Japanese

Roger Daniels

IT HAS BEEN TRADITIONAL for historians and other students of ethnic groups in the United States to treat immigrants from Asia as if their experiences were entirely divorced from those of peoples who came from other parts of the world.[1] This view has, I am convinced, not only blurred the image of Asian Americans but has also contributed to an increasingly significant distortion of the composite picture of American ethnic groups, since the Asian American element is almost always either completely ignored or vastly underrepresented.[2] Although Asian Americans represent less than one per cent of the total population, the Asian-American element of recent immigrants has grown spectacularly since the modifications in our once blatantly racist immigration laws that began with the McCarran-Walter Act of 1952 and culminated in the Immigration Act of 1965. By the early seventies immigrants from Asia were accounting for nearly one fifth of all immigrants to the United States, the highest such percentage in our history. By contrast, if one takes the entire century and a half of enumerated immigration from 1820 to 1971, immigrants from East Asia[3] amount to about 2.5 percent of the total.[4] The hostility and discrimination which immigrants from Asia have faced since the 1850s is too well known to require narration here. Although it is true that both popular prejudice and statutory bias have either abated or largely disappeared since the end of World War II, the instant revival of many anti-Asian notions that accompanied the bungled Vietnamese refugee program cannot be ignored by any student of the subject.

If it is legitimate in one sense to speak of East Asians as if they were a coherent group—because they were so perceived by Americans—in another and more important sense such a classification imposes a largely arbitrary and artificial unity on peoples whose experience and cultures were and are radically different. Very little except the perceptions of Occidentals can unite such diverse peoples as Chinese, Japanese, Koreans, Filipinos, and Vietnamese, not to speak of several of the varied peoples of the Indian subcontinent, all of whom are subsumed under the rubric "Asian American." That such a catchall can still be appropriate—and I speak as a contributor to a recent volume entitled *The Asian American*[5]—clearly indicates the retarded state of scholarship in this field. A part of the problem has been that scholars—on both sides of the Pacific—have treated immigrants as part of the international tensions existing between the developed and less developed parts of the globe, leading to an examination of conflict resolution rather than the lives of human beings, an emphasis on the excluders rather than the excluded.

Any serious look at the experience of immigrants from Asia shows that most of the generalizations made about immigrants generally apply as well to Asian groups as they do to any others. Most of the million and a half East Asians who came here arrived during the great agricultural and industrial expansion which occurred between the 1850s and the outbreak of World War I. Most of them did not have the capital necessary to set up their own enterprises; few of them had the education to practice a learned profession or to enter one of the skilled trades (and even those who possessed these attributes were largely stopped by either statute or custom). Most immigrants from Asia were thus proletarians: they had only their labor to sell. From this point of view then, Asians, like most immigrants of the period whatever their origin, entered the labor force at the very bottom. Unlike most immigrants, the Asians came almost exclusively to the western United States, so that their labor was largely employed in agriculture. Their ability to labor was contested by none. Woodrow Wilson, writing in 1902, insisted that the Chinese

were more to be desired, as workmen if not as citizens, than most of the coarse crew that came crowding in every year at the eastern ports. They had, no doubt, many an unsavory habit, bred unwholesome squalor in the crowded quarters in which they most abounded in the western seaports, and seemed separated by their very nature from the people among whom they had come to live; but it was their skill, their knack at succeeding and driving duller rivals out, rather than their alien habits, that made them feared and hated. . . .[6]

Similar statements could and would be made about later Asian migrants, especially those from Japan and the Philippines.

Although it would be possible to pile on quotations to demonstrate the similarity of both experience and perception, this essay is devoted to a discrete analysis of one aspect of the history of one group: the kinds of leadership that were developed by the Japanese who resided in the continental United States. The geographical limitation is important. The experience of Japanese immigrants to Hawaii and their descendants there is so strikingly different that it must be treated separately. Persons of Japanese descent or birth constitute the largest single ethnic group in our fiftieth state, the only state in which white persons are a minority. The Japanese ethnic group—which comprises about 28 per cent of the population—has a virtual stranglehold on elective and appointive political power in the islands. At this writing the governor, one of two United States senators, both federal representatives, the majority of both houses of the state legislature, and the president of the state university are Japanese Americans, a degree of political clout not demonstrated, I think, by any other immigrant group in modern American history.

The special Hawaiian case apart, Japanese have been and remain a tiny minority in the rest of the United States. Even in California, where they have been most numerous and had the highest incidence, Japanese have never amounted to more than 2.1 percent of the population. (The 1970 census figure is a hair over 1 percent.) Apart from their small numbers and geographical concentration there are several special characteristics which have given immigrants from Japan and their descendants a history in the United States somewhat different from that experienced by other contemporary immigrant groups; perhaps the two most important of these differences are race and their special continuing relationship to the government of Japan.

Without in any way attempting to resolve here the complex question of whether or not traditional racial divisions are viable entities, this paper will accept the racial distinctions recognized by American immigration and naturalization law. Those statutes stipulated the existence of four racial groups: whites (later Caucasians); persons of African descent; American Indians; and Asians, sometimes described as Mongolians. These categories were never described with any serious attempt at ethnological exactitude; by administrative decision, to cite merely one example, all Mexicans were classified as "white." What was eventually crucial for immigrants from Asia was that the naturalization statutes, rewritten after the passage of the Fourteenth Amendment, limited naturalization to "white persons and persons of African descent." These statutes, as interpreted by both the executive and judicial branches of the government, meant that all Asian immigrants, regardless of their place of birth, were in a separate and unequal category: they were "aliens ineligible to citizenship." No matter how long they resided here, they remained, in law, perpetually alien. Their native-born children, of course, by virtue of the Constitution, were citizens. It should be noted that West Coast anti-Oriental groups were quite aware of this anomaly, and endeavoured for a number of years to eliminate it. What they proposed was a constitutional amendment which would have proscribed even native-born Asians from citizenship, thus creating a perpetual caste of persons ineligible for citizenship by reason of race.

Although several East Asian governments were aware of and resented this discrimination, only one government, that of Japan, was able to do very much about it in a positive way. The seemingly inordinate interest which the government of Japan displayed in its subjects who migrated to the United States should not be interpreted as stemming from a humanitarian concern for their welfare. By the 1880s, as Hilary Conroy has observed, Japan's "ever jealous watch against discriminatory treatment abroad" to emigrants from Japan was chiefly motivated by the desire to protect "her own prestige as a nation."[7] Even before significant numbers of Japanese had emigrated anywhere, the Imperial government, observing the ways in which Chinese, natives of the Indian subcontinent, and other East Asians had been shipped to and exploited in all parts of the world in what Hugh Tinker has rightly called "a new system of slavery,"[8] concluded that allowing Japanese emigrants to suffer such degradation would be incompatible with Japan's aspirations to great power status.

As early as 1891, when there were only about 3,000 Japanese immigrants in the entire United States, representatives of the Japanese government in the United States were already evincing their concern. In that year Consul Sutemi Chinda argued that the presence of Japanese prostitutes in San Francisco was impairing "Japan's national honor." The "ignominious conduct" of some Japanese in America, he warned Tokyo, would "be used, sooner or later, as a pretext for attacking the Japanese residents by those who openly advocate the exclusion of the Oriental race from the country." Telling the Foreign Ministry what it already knew, he argued that Chinese in the United States "are now detested and discriminated against simply because they failed to grasp the seriousness of the situation at the outset. Their failure must be a lesson to us Japanese."

As is so often the case when political figures try to read the lessons of history, Consul Chinda read them incorrectly. After an investigation of the nascent Japanese American community along the West Coast, Chinda concluded that it was the presence of "undesirable Japanese"—prostitutes and procurers—that was likely to cause trouble and he urged his government to prevent the emigration of such persons to the United States. It is instructive to note that Japanese officials in the United States tried to apply a higher standard of morality to emigrants from Japan than that which prevailed in either Japan or the western United States at the time. This is in sharp contrast to the emigration policies of other nations, many of which consciously exported their less desirable population and tried to keep what they regarded as the "better sort" at home.[9] This attitude of the Japanese government, manifested in the early 1890s, helps explain both the willingness of that government to collaborate later with the

United States in such policies as the Gentlemen's Agreement and the high degree of supervision which the Japanese government later tried to exercise over the lives and fortunes of Japanese emigrants to the United States.

The policy both succeeded and failed. The Japanese government was able, largely by a system of passport control, to limit immigration to what it regarded as the "better sort." Most of the Issei immigrants before the Gentlemen's Agreement seem to have been upwardly mobile male members of the lower middle class, with a not inconsiderable admixture of students, and a sprinkling of merchants and political radicals. Yet, as is well known, the tiny Japanese-American community on the West Coast was, from 1905 on, under heavy attack in large part because of its very success and partly because of the success of Japan in gaining a measure of international prestige as a result of her victory in the Russo-Japanese War. Observing the hostility which her emigrants were engendering, the Imperial government bowed to the wishes of the United States government in 1907–8 and virtually stopped the migration of male Japanese to this country. Under the terms of that agreement, Japan undertook not to issue passports good for the continental United States to laborers, skilled or unskilled, but would continue; at its discretion, to issue passports to "laborers who have already been in America and to the parents, wives and children of laborers already resident there." All the evidence indicates that the Japanese government scrupulously kept the agreement. It has been hailed by most historians as a great achievement of honest and patient negotiation. Designed by both sides to improve relations, it actually helped to exacerbate them because neither government fully understood the nature and the dynamics of the problem which confronted them.[10]

At the time of the Gentlemen's Agreement there were perhaps 60,000 Japanese in the entire United States, with about two-thirds of them in California. Some 90 percent of these immigrants were males. For the next fifteen years a net immigration of perhaps 25,000 women ensued, creating a more balanced but still heavily male population. These women, some of whom were "picture brides" married by proxy to immigrant men they had never seen before they left Japan, began having children at what seemed to many Caucasian observers to be an intensive rate. By the end of the 1920s the children of these immigrant marriages—the Nisei generation—outnumbered their parents. The majority of these Japanese American families found their way into agriculture or horticulture and achieved a degree of economic success that placed most of them at least in the lower middle class as small-scale proprietors. According to the preconceptions of Japanese officials like Consul Chinda, the successes of these "better sort" Japanese should have accorded them an entirely different kind of treatment than that received by their Chinese predecessors. That, of course, was not the case.

In the nineteenth century attacks against the Chinese had been justified partly on the ground that they brought no women and had no families. In the twentieth century Japanese were attacked because they brought women with them and had families. As late as 1905 the California legislature complained in an official resolution passed unanimously by both houses that Japanese immigrants were "mere transients [who] do not buy land [or] build or buy houses. . . . They contribute nothing to the growth of the State. They add nothing to its wealth, and they are a blight on the prosperity of it, and a great and impending danger to its welfare."[11] Eight years later the same body—and many of the same individuals—exacerbated relations between the United States and Japan by passing an alien land act designed solely to prevent Japanese from purchasing agricultural land, and later tried to extend the ban even to its lease or rental.

Under such circumstances a nation less concerned with its prestige might have written off the Japanese immigrants in America, but the Imperial government remained convinced that such an action was not appropriate. From the 1890s until the outbreak of World War II the Japanese government tried to exercise, with varying degrees of success, a degree of control over its subjects in the United States that is unprecedented in the history of immigrants to this country.

This control was exercised in a number of ways, but in all of them the role of Japanese consular personnel was crucial. Starting with Consul Chinda in San Francisco in 1891, Japanese officials organized a succession of ephemeral associations intended to embrace all Japanese in an area. These associations seem largely to have been responses to anti-Japanese activity in various localities. When, for example, sporadic violence erupted against Japanese in and around San Francisco in the chaotic conditions following the earthquake and fire of 1905, it was the Japanese consulate that marshalled most of the evidence which was later used by Secretary of Commerce and Labor Victor H. Metcalf in his famous report to President Theodore Roosevelt on the condition of the Japanese population in San Francisco. In the wake of the Gentlemen's Agreement, which followed shortly thereafter, special responsibilities were placed on the Japanese government. Since it was responsible for determining the status of Japanese resident in the United States, it needed some method of comprehensive registration and control of Japanese resident here. In February, 1909, the Japanese Consulate General in San Francisco caused the founding of the Japanese Association of America. In theory, all Japanese resident in the United States would belong to this organization through local chapters which were to be established in every part of the country in which there were significant numbers of resident Japanese.

In practice, of course, not all resident Japanese belonged to the Association. Some undoubtedly stayed out as a matter of principle; others, particularly those residing outside of major centers of Japanese American population, stayed out because of indifference or convenience; while a third group, perhaps the most numerous, stayed out because it cost money to join. In the beginning annual membership ranged from $1 to $3 a year. Both for its own bureaucratic convenience and to apply pressure on individual Japanese to join the appropriate local association, the Japanese government gave the various Japanese Associations an official role and made them the intermediaries through which individual Japanese residents had to pass if they wished to retain official connection with the Japanese government. Both Japanese law and the Gentlemen's Agreement required the Japanese Consular service to issue certain documents to resident Japanese. The responsibility for these certificates was delegated to various Japanese Associations, which, in turn, were empowered to collect fees for their issuance.

Certificates required by the Gentlemen's Agreement related largely to travel outside the country with the right to return and the ability to bring into the country wives, parents, and other relatives. Thus, any Japanese who wished to keep or establish family ties across the Pacific was forced to do so through the appropriate Japanese Association. In addition, Japanese law required that men of military age who had not fulfilled their service obligations register every year that they resided abroad. Other certificates were required to register marriages, divorces, births, inheritances, and other vital statistics.[12]

The true role of the Japanese Associations has been much misunderstood. Exclusionists, like V. J. McClatchy of the Sacramento *Bee* McClatchys, insisted long ago that the Associations were a sinister "invisible government," part of the Japanese plan to take over America. This was a charge that kept reechoing in anti-Japanese propaganda in this country, having been repeated as late as the early 1940s by the Dies Committee. Apologists for the Japanese, on the other hand, insisted that the Associations were merely self-help and protection groups analogous to similar organizations existing in other immigrant communities.[13]

As we have seen, neither was true. The Associations were, in fact, semiofficial organs of the Imperial government. Their function was essentially bureaucratic, not sinister. Many of these functions were dictated, not by Imperial ambition but rather by Japanese governmental attempts to comply with an executive agreement entered into with the United States government, and contemporary documents indicate that the United States government at times pressed the Japanese to exercise an even greater control over the immigrant Issei than the Imperial government either desired or was able to accomplish.

The special relationship between the Associations and the Japanese government meant that leadership in the Japanese community devolved upon individuals who were far from independent. At the apex of the Japanese Associations stood Japanese consular officials; much of the income of the Associations depended upon their ability to charge fees for certificates and other official documents which most immigrants would need at one time or another. This "right" could be, and in fact was, withdrawn from a local association at any time. The leaders of official Associations thus had to be persons who were acceptable to the Japanese consular officials. These leaders were almost always economically well-established individuals. Businessmen, editors of Japanese language newspapers, and successful agricultural entrepreneurs were typical "establishment types" who headed local associations.

Of all the certificates which the Associations came to control, the most crucial was the one which gave the right to bring one's wife, proxy or otherwise, to the United States. From the point of view of the Japanese government, which tried to abide by the terms of the Gentlemen's Agreement, the problem was how to determine the socioeconomic status of each Issei male who wished a passport for his wife. Eventually a rule of thumb was established so that anyone who could show an established bank account or other liquid assets of $800 or more would be eligible to have his wife join him. Once a local association certified that such was the case, the consulate would arrange for the issuance of the necessary passport and other travel documents. The amount of potential power that this placed in the hands of petty association officials is obvious. Interviews with surviving Issei and others knowledgeable about the community make it clear that these regulations were not hard to circumvent. Even for hard-working and frugal Issei $800 was a sizeable nest egg to accumulate. What happened in a great number of cases was that groups of men pooled their assets in what they called "show money," so that over a period of time the self-same $800 could provide travel documents for a number of wives, picture brides, and other relatives.

Often there were, not surprisingly, conflicts between local associations and the central body in San Francisco which was subject to direct pressure and control by the various consuls general. A number of local associations, for example, had protested, futilely, that $800 was too high a figure and that perhaps half that would be more reasonable. The most bitter controversy came in 1919 when the Japanese government, hoping to blunt the growing postwar anti-Japanese movement led by United States Senator James D. Phelan (D-Cal.) and others, decided to stop issuing passports to "picture brides" and got the national Japanese Association to endorse this position. Some leaders, like W. K. Abiko, publisher of the San Francisco *Nichibei Shimbun,* one of the largest and most influential of the Japanese language newspapers in the country, and several local associations protested loudly but in vain what they rightly thought was an abandonment of their rights and privileges by the Imperial government and its agent, the Japanese Association, for reasons of state.

Apart from their role as agents of the Japanese consular service, the various associations and the central association performed two other major functions: they acted as conscious agents of acculturation and provided various defense functions when the rights of individual Japanese were attacked. Through the Associations and other channels such as the immigrant press and Japanese language schools, the Issei and their children were exhorted to dress in the western fashion, to attend schools and excel in them, not to carouse in public, and, in general, to make as low a social profile as possible.[14] Since this advice came from the Associations, which had real powers of control, the implication was clear that anyone who brought disgrace upon the Japanese image might well have difficulty obtaining certain certificates. That the Japanese government itself had protested when the San Francisco School Board tried to segregate Japanese pupils into long-established schools for Chinese, and had involved even the president of the United States in the successful struggle to avoid this loss of face, was clear evidence that all Issei parents could understand of the value that their home government placed upon education. At a time when most immigrant groups were, at best, indifferent to anything more than a rudimentary education for most of their children, the commitment of the leadership of the Japanese American community to a maximization of schooling for as many young Nisei and Issei as possible is remarkable. It would lead, within a generation, to native-born Japanese Americans having considerably more education than the average American.

The Japanese Associations also organized, and, to a significant degree financed, the legal defense of the rights of the Issei and their children. Much of the litigation involving Japanese Americans stemmed from the California Alien Land Acts of 1913 and 1920 and from similar statutes in other western states which sought, largely without success, to inhibit first the ownership and then the leasing of agricultural land by "aliens ineligible to citizenship." The Japanese Associations kept on retainer firms of lawyers in both northern and southern California. When individual Japanese litigants could afford to pay their own fees, they did so; in the more numerous instances when they could pay only a portion, the Association made up the rest. The amount of litigation involved was considerable, relative to the size of the population, and often involved appeals within the state court system and subsequent appeals to the federal judiciary. In the final analysis, the courts held that while a state could properly place limits on alien landholding, it could not inhibit American citizens, even when they were minor children of aliens ineligible to citizenship, from exercising any of their fourteenth amendment rights. Thus, much, if not most, of the considerable acreage in prime agricultural land controlled by members of the Japanese American community was, in law, placed in the name of minor children. Had the community been atomized, it is doubtful that it would have been able to uphold its property rights so successfully.[15]

The development and maintenance of this sense of community solidarity was surely the most significant accomplishment of the first generation of leadership among Japanese Americans. Virtually all of the leaders came to the United States as adults. Even those who strove hardest for Americanization, such as George Shima (born Kinji Ushijima), a spectacularly successful agricultural entrepreneur who was probably the first Issei millionaire and became the first president of the Japanese Association of America in 1909, were essentially Japanese in culture and political orientation. Many of the leaders were officials of banks and other corporations headquartered in Japan, while still others were heavily involved in trans-Pacific commerce. In the larger urban Japanese American communities visits from Japanese officials, naval officers, and touring celebrities from the old country held the highest place on the social calendar, along with patriotic Japanese holidays like the emperor's birthday or the anniversary of Admiral Togo's victory over the Russian fleet. The natural attachment of most Issei to their homeland can only have been strengthened by their legal status as permanent aliens, by the social ostracism which they encountered, and by the continuing and effective guardianship that the Imperial government exercised, both directly and through its creatures, the Japanese Associations.

By the end of the 1920s, however, the situation began to change. The unilateral abrogation of the Gentlemen's Agreement by the United States Congress in 1924 ended the responsibilities of the Imperial government for a continuing supervision of immigration. Although it never abandoned its subjects in America—births and deaths continued to be registered, for example—its direct involvement with the Japanese Associations markedly lessened after 1924. In addition, the first generation of Japanese born in the United States, the citizen Nisei, was beginning to come of age. Generational conflict is, of course, a natural phenomenon in all human communities. It is probably more dramatic and polarized in immigrant communities than in others. The legal and social situation in the Japanese American community from the late 1920s until the outbreak of the Great Pacific War in December, 1941, was such that the clash of generations was perhaps more acute than in any other American immigrant community. I believe that this is the case because, in addition to the "normal" generational antagonisms, the special legal status of the Issei as aliens ineligible to citizenship—and in the states where most of them lived ineligible to own agricultural land—meant that the second generation often had legal title to the property of the first. While other Asian immigrants, notably the Chinese, suffered the same legal disabilities, they were not sufficiently concentrated in agriculture to feel serious disadvantage from the alien land laws. In addition, the demographic situation of the two major Asian-American communities was strikingly different.

By 1930 native-born Japanese Americans were almost as numerous in the United States as their alien parents, and in the years that followed the older generation was increasingly outnumbered. Using the extraordinarily complete data gathered during the wartime incarceration of the West Coast Japanese, we can reconstruct a typical Issei family.[16] Children were born in the years 1918–22 to a thirty-five-year-old father and a twenty-five-year-old mother. This meant, ironically, that the numerically most significant group of Nisei was coming of legal age between the years 1939 and 1943, the time of the greatest crisis in the relations between the United States and Japan. While the Japanese American community was growing dynamically—waxing more than fivefold between 1900 and 1930—the Chinese American community, its growth by immigration stopped in 1882, shrank by about half between the 1880s and 1920. Since few Chinese women emigrated—females comprised under 5 percent of the Chinese-American community throughout the nineteenth century—the Chinese-American population was an aging one in which the old always outnumbered the young, thus delaying significant generational conflict for decades. The picture bride immigration of the years after the Gentlemen's Agreement plus a predominantly male return flow to Japan after 1920, gave the Issei generation a sex distribution that more closely resembled the norm for the immigrant communities.

Thus, by the 1930s, the Japanese-American community was no longer unitary, but was becoming two communities: an Issei community, alien and largely Japan-centered, and a Nisei community, native-born and distinctly American-oriented. The Issei generation, aging and shrinking, both absolutely and relatively, saw its influence wane; even without the external crisis that foreign affairs produced in 1941–42, an overt generational leadership struggle was apparent in the 1930s. While this conflict had many causes, its essence was lifestyle and national orientation.

The Issei, like many immigrant groups before and since, tried to re-create a Japanese society in America, but the image of Japan that most of them held was static. They remembered, as immigrants usually do, the Japan of their youth, not the emerging, industrializing Japan of the twenties and thirties. Since the United States, by both statute and custom, deliberately tried to keep them separate, the Issei were probably better insulated against Americanization than were most contemporary immigrant groups. All the institutions of the first generation—the Japanese Associations, the press, the churches, the associational groups based on place of birth in Japan, the business associations of the Little Tokyos and Little Osakas—were Japan- and Japanese-language centered. At the same time, membership in a broad spectrum of Americanizing institutions was denied to them. Denied the right of naturalization, they could not become voters. Most trade unions barred them from membership. If they went to a Buddhist temple, the priest was subsidized by the Japanese government; if they adopted a western religion, as a sizable minority did, it was likely to be in a segregated congregation with a pastor who was either a former missionary or a convert from Japan.

On the other hand, despite their own almost total cultural isolation, the Issei insisted—partly at least because of the urgings of the Japanese government through the Associations—that their children not only accept an American education but excel in it. The Nisei thus went to school and were subjected to the most powerful of Americanizing influences; fortunately for them, their number in any school was generally so small that the classrooms they attended were truly integrated. Therefore, they participated from early childhood in at least a part of the larger society. Even in California, where anti-Orientalism was most rampant, the educational establishment seems to have been exceedingly fair to the Nisei children, who, from the very first, charmed their American teachers and exceeded the norms in academic achievement.[17]

Outside of school, however, the Nisei found a society that rejected them regardless of their accomplishments. Fully credentialed Nisei education majors, to cite merely one example, were virtually unemployable as teachers in the very schools in which they had excelled. John Modell has described the prewar Nisei dilemma well: "[The Nisei] had inherited from his parents a remarkable desire to succeed in the face of hardship, but had also learned the American definition of success, by which standard the accommodation made by his parents could not be considered satisfactory."[18] Despite what Modell calls their "American definition of success," all but a few of the maturing Nisei generation found that their real economic opportunities were circumscribed by the ethnic economic community. One Young Nisei described his situation in 1937: "I am a fruitstand worker. It is not a very attractive nor distinguished occupation. . . . I would much rather it were a doctor or lawyer . . . but my aspiration of developing into such [was] frustrated long ago. . . . I am only what I am, a professional carrot washer."[19] The young Nisei went on to argue that the realistic zenith of his aspirations was to save some money and get a business of his own, which would probably be a fruit or vegetable market. An exceptional number of both generations became petty proprietors. Sociological observers of this phenomenon have tended to misinterpret it. Thirty years ago Gunnar Myrdal noted that Chinese and Japanese in the United States "owned one-and-a-half times as many stores, restaurants, and eating places per 1,000 population as other residents of the United States" and contrasted this to Negro operation of only one-sixth as many. More recently Ivan Light has made similar comparisons. Each argues that the poor showing of blacks vis-à-vis Asians is somehow related to a lack of enterprise on the part of the former, but neither comparison is well taken.[20] The Japanese American business community was a trifurcated one. The largest segment was based on far western agriculture and horticulture and was vertical in that it included both wholesale and retail marketing. A second segment, not unrelated to the first, was in small shops that catered primarily to the ethnic community and, secondarily, in terms of curio shops and restaurants, to the larger public. The third and smallest segment, in terms of persons involved, was in trans-Pacific oriented enterprises, largely the export-import trade. Prior to the 1950s, few Japanese corporations had branches or offices in the United States, but those that existed—chiefly a few banks and steamship lines—employed significant numbers of Japanese Americans. Only the first segment did most of its business with the larger society. The largest number of Japanese American retail establishments were family-owned and operated, had small capital investment, and essentially served the immigrant community. Wages were lower, hours longer, and prices higher than in comparable establishments in the larger society. One patronized Mr. Watanabe's grocery store, despite its higher prices, because it was closer, and, even more important, one could speak one's own language there. In addition, of course, if you wanted Aji-no-moto sauce, only he had it. The basic function of these establishments was to fill needs that could not be filled by the larger society. However satisfactory this economic ghetto was to the immigrant generation, it did not fit within what Modell has called the "American definition of success" accepted by most Nisei. Throughout the 1930s, however, all but a few of the second generation adults were confined within the ethnic economic structure, even those who consciously tried to break out. The first Japanese American to graduate from the University of Oregon Law School, for example, could find professional employment only with a consulate general of Japan.

The dissatisfaction of Nisei with the ethnic economic structure was merely one aspect of the growing generational conflict. There was cultural and political conflict as well. Despite the establishment and maintenance of a relatively large network of Japanese language schools, which were subsidized by the Japanese government and which functioned after school hours and on weekends, few Nisei acquired any significant facility in the Japanese language, as the United States Army later learned when it recruited thousands of them to do military intelligence work during World War II. The Issei resented this manifest loss of Japanese culture and young Nisei resented the hours in what were, in essence, after-school parochial schools.

What little participation Issei had in politics was almost exclusively Japan-oriented. Their organizations—for example, the Japanese Chamber of Commerce of Los Angeles—tended to support or at least to find a rationale for imperial Japanese aggression. In a 1931 publication, the Chamber complained of "China's oppressive policy toward the Japanese" and insisted that the purpose of Japanese troops in Manchuria was "purely to protect the life and property of our countrymen," and similar treatment was later given to what the Japanese liked to call the "China incident" of the later 1930s.[21] The Los Angeles Chamber and similar organizations elsewhere raised funds for the support of Japanese War Relief.

Most Nisei were either indifferent to or opposed such efforts. Their political activities, such as they were, were essentially America-oriented. Some energy went into the formation of such groups as Japanese American Young Republicans and Young Democrats, but the key organization of the emerging citizen generation was what became, in 1930, the Japanese American Citizens League (JACL) which arose out of preexisting local and regional organizational groupings. Even before the Great Pacific War broke out, the JACL was on a collision course with the organizations of the older generation. Since it was an organization for citizens, Issei were effectively barred from membership. Since it stressed Americanization and the exercise of civil rights and minimized even cultural ties with Japan, its goals were somewhat repugnant to most of the Issei, especially the community leaders. The JACL creed, written in 1940, best expresses the Americanized ideology of the more articulate Nisei leaders. It stressed accommodation rather than conflict, it swallowed, in one patriotic gulp, the American dream.

I am proud that I am an American citizen of Japanese ancestry, for my very background makes me appreciate more fully the wonderful advantages of this nation. I believe in her institutions, ideals and traditions; I glory in her heritage; I boast of her history; I trust in her future. She has granted me liberties and opportunities such as no individual enjoys in the world today. She has given me an education befitting kings. She has entrusted me with the responsibilities of the franchise. She has permitted me to build a home, to earn a livelihood, to worship, think, speak and act as I please—as a free man equal to every other man.

Although some individuals may discriminate against me, I shall never become bitter or lose faith, for I know that such persons are not representative of the majority of the American people. True, I shall do all in my power to discourage such practices, but I shall do it in the American way—above board, in the open, through courts of law, by education, by proving myself to be worthy of equal treatment and consideration. I am firm in my belief that American sportsmanship and attitude of fair play will judge citizenship and patriotism on the basis of action and achievement, and not on the basis of physical characteristics. Because I believe in America, and I trust she believes in me, and because I have received innumerable benefits from her, I pledge myself to do honor to her at all times and places; to support her constitution; to obey her laws; to respect her flag; to defend her against all enemies, foreign and domestic; to actively assume my duties and obligations as a citizen, cheerfully and without any reservations whatsoever, in the hope that I may become a better American in a greater America.

Clearly this hypernationalism did not spring from the Nisei experience or accurately reflect the status of the second generation. It was, rather, a declaration of faith, a hopeful vision of what the future would become. Although many Nisei were so Americanized that they actually believed the creed as written, it is also clear that the creed was, in part at least, an overreaction, a conscious rejection of the ethnic heritage that was seen as retarding the aspirations of the second generation. The creed not only failed to reflect reality, but it surely failed to convince many Nisei. Certainly the professional carrot washer quoted earlier could not have subscribed to it.

In addition, the JACL deliberately avoided in the later 1930s and early 1940s what had become topic "A" among Japanese-American leaders of both generations: the growing likelihood of a war between America and Japan. As early as 1937 a young Nisei intellectual writing in a student publication at the University of California voiced the fears of many of his generation: ". . . what are we going to do if war does break out between the United States and Japan? . . . In common language we can say "we're sunk." Even if the Nisei wanted to fight for America, what chances? Not a chance! . . . Our properties would be confiscated and most likely [we would be] herded into prison camps—perhaps we would be slaughtered on the spot."[22]

If, for most Americans, the attack on Pearl Harbor came as a bolt from the blue, for many Japanese Americans, particularly the older Nisei, it was the fulfillment of their most dreaded nightmare. For most, the attitude was resignation, often using a common Japanese expression—*shi-ga-ta ga-nai* (it can't be helped)—to express their feeling of utter helplessness in the face of impersonal forces over which they had no control. For the Issei, particularly the community leaders, the situation was impossible. Every immigrant still in America became an enemy alien. By the opening of business Monday morning, December 8, every Issei bank account in America was frozen.[23] During the night the Federal Bureau of Investigation, using selective but not particularly intelligent criteria, had taken into custody about 1,500 male Issei and started the process of interning them. Although the relevant internal FBI documents are not yet public, it is easy to reconstruct the process by which the government compiled its roundup lists. Working, as security agencies often do, on the principle of guilt by association, the Justice Department, which seems not to have had anyone who could even read Japanese on its staff, simply grabbed any alien who was prominent in any Japanese community organization. This meant officers of the Japanese Associations, leaders of business groups like the Japanese American Chambers of Commerce, teachers in language schools, Buddhist priests, and officials of Japanese-American agricultural and horticultural groups. Although the total number was small—between one and two per cent of the Japanese-American population—it, in effect, wiped out the entire leadership group of the Issei generation. At the time of its greatest crisis, the Japanese-American community had to depend on new and untried leaders of the citizen generation.

Most of the Nisei were stunned, and only a very few were capable, especially in the hectic weeks just after Pearl Harbor, of any organized activity. Farmers continued to farm, but many enterprises, cut off from their bank accounts, found it impossible to do any business. But most of the leaders of the JACL, some of whom had been covertly cooperating with United States government intelligence agencies, were not paralyzed. They were but a tiny minority of a minority. One source estimates that, in Los Angeles, the JACL had but 650 members in a population of 20,000,[24] but, given the leadership vacuum created by the roundup of the prominent Issei, it was the only visible group with any kind of a program at all. Its leaders quickly wired President Roosevelt affirming their loyalty. (The White House sent the telegram to the State Department, the department of the government which dealt with foreigners, for reply!) In the larger communities, and particularly in Los Angeles, the metropolis of Japanese America, feverish activity took place.

Togo Tanaka, a Nisei editor, went on the radio to tell his fellow citizens that "as Americans we now function as counterespionage. Any act or word prejudicial to the United States committed by any Japanese must be warned and reported to the F.B.I., Naval Intelligence, Sheriff's Office and local police."[25] A JACL Anti-Axis Committee formally resolved, on December 9th, to allow no one who was not a citizen to contribute either time or money to its work, even though this meant, in most instances, deliberate disassociation from their own parents. Since one of the favorite American indictments of totalitarian regimes is that they destroy the family by turning children against their parents, it is instructive to note that this, too, happened here.

The young Nisei leaders were, of course, in an impossible situation. Most of them were quite Americanized, yet all of them had Japanese faces and were identified with a perfidious enemy. Most of them wished only to protect their people and themselves from the concentration camps that many expected. West Coast newspapers and radio stations daily called for their incarceration, or worse. To cite only one example, the Los Angeles *Times*, in the first issue after the attack, warned against "spies, saboteurs and fifth columnists." "We have thousands of Japanese here, [the paper warned]. Some, perhaps many, are . . . good Americans. What the rest may be we do not know, nor can we take a chance in the light of yesterday's demonstration that treachery and double-dealing are major Japanese weapons."[26]

In addition there was a flurry of violent but nonfatal incidents against individual Japanese. Most of them seem to have been perpetrated by Filipinos, who, as migrant agricultural laborers, had economic as well as patriotic grievances against the rural Japanese they assaulted. The constant verbal abuse against "Japs," "yellow vermin," the sale of "Jap hunting licenses," the insults and stares they encountered in public caused many responsible young Nisei leaders to fear mob violence, a not fantastic phobia in view of the western vigilante tradition. That this inexperienced, frightened, and largely demoralized leadership consciously chose accommodation to almost anything the government and Caucasian leadership proposed is not at all surprising. Even before the decision to evacuate the Japanese Americans was made by Washington in early February, 1942, Nisei leaders in California had proposed a voluntary evacuation to the governor of California. Under this plan, whose origin is unclear but which stemmed from fears by officials of the Department of Agriculture that vital California agricultural production would be hurt (as it was) by the removal of skilled Japanese agriculturalists from the fertile valleys of California, the Japanese would be removed from cities—or at least from areas considered strategic—and resettled in agricultural areas within California where there was already considerable Japanese settlement. This plan being rejected, most of the Nisei leadership cooperated with federal authorities and helped to organize the total relocation of the West Coast Japanese to concentration camps which began in mid-March, 1942. It should be noted, however, that most of the top JACL leadership removed to Salt Lake City before the federal government instituted the travel freeze which preceded the relocation.[27]

Given its deliberately accommodationist stance, it is not surprising that the JACL leadership encountered a great deal of resistance and hostility within the larger community. This can be best seen by examining two discrete events that occurred during the wartime incarceration: the

Manzanar riot of December, 1942, and the Heart Mountain draft resistance in early 1944.[28]

Manzanar, located in the desolate Owens Valley of southern California, close to both Mount Whitney and Death Valley, the highest and lowest points in the continental United States, was the first of the permanent relocation centers to be established. A "volunteer" group of Nisei, mostly JACLers, had gone in as an advance party. The active, accommodationist stance of this group, coupled with the fact that many JACLers received key positions in the internal governance of Manzanar, caused many to believe that they were taking advantage of a communal tragedy. One scholar has compiled some of the rumors that were rampant in Los Angeles and later at Manzanar during 1942.[29]

The J.A.C.L. was instructed by Naval Intelligence to send questionnaires to all members to report on their parents. The J.A.C.L. started their survey on Kibei in order to turn in information to the F.B.I. They are taking this as a protective move to whitewash themselves by blaming others.

The J.A.C.L. is trying to be patriotic and they are supporting the evacuation program. They do not have the welfare of the Japanese people at heart.

The J.A.C.L. is supporting the idea of cooperating with the government and evacuating voluntarily because they could go in and buy up all the goods in Japanese stores at robbery prices and make a substantial profit.

The J.A.C.L. big shots have their fingers in the graft. They are getting something out of the evacuation.

The J.A.C.L. is charging aliens for information that the aliens could get anywhere.

The J.A.C.L. is planning the evacuation with the officials. They are mixing with high government officials.

All J.A.C.L. leaders are *inu*. [A popular Japanese pejorative literally meaning "dogs" but in this situation "informers."]

At the same time members of the JACL minority and those who supported them had scapegoats of their own: the Kibei. Kibei were individuals, predominantly male, who, though born in the United States, had been sent back to Japan for a significant part of their education. Many, but not necessarily most, of them were strongly oriented toward Japan, and the opposition to the JACL was often, but not always, headed by Kibei. Kibei in the relocation centers often made symbolic demonstration of their attachment to Japanese culture by drilling publicly in the martial arts and by singing patriotic Japanese songs. This, of course, infuriated the America-oriented Nisei, whether or not they were involved directly in the JACL. Shibutani, in his contemporary study of Manzanar, described some of the Nisei reactions to Kibei as follows:[30]

Those Kibei are the guys we have to watch. They're so damned hotheaded they will do anything. Then all the rest of us have to suffer just because they happened to be technically American citizens. It'll get so the *hakujin* [the word normally used by Japanese to describe whites] won't trust any Nisei.

. . . If those son of a bitches like Japan so much why did they come over here in the first place? I never did like those guys anyway. They came over here with their Japanesy ideas and try to change all America to suit themselves. They don't seem to realize that 130,000,000 people might be right.

There was also sporadic violence, directed not at guards or administrators, but at fellow inmates. When, for example, a distinguished artist and University of California professor was brutally assaulted by an unknown assailant, the incident was characterized by JACL-oriented inmates as a "typical Kibei attack from the rear with a lead pipe."[31]

Exacerbating this polar situation among the incarcerated people at Manzanar—and it must be emphasized that only a tiny minority of the 10,000 people confined there took any significant part in its internal ideological warfare—was a spectacularly inept governmental administration split between a civilian War Relocation Authority (WRA) and a military component. To cite merely one example, on April 11, 1942, the camp administration caused the following to appear in the camp newspaper, which was nominally put out by Nisei inmates:

The citizens of Manzanar wish to express in public their sincere appreciation to General John L. DeWitt and his Chiefs of Staff, Tom C. Clark and Colonel Karl R. Bendetsen, for the expedient way in which they have handled the Manzanar situation.

The evacuees now located at Manzanar are greatly satisfied with the excellent comforts the general and his staff have provided for them. . . . Thank you, general![32]

Other stupidities included an attempt to forbid any meetings being conducted in the Japanese language—the only language in which most of the older persons could discuss anything intelligently—and a clumsy attempt to "fix" the camp elections by denying the right to hold elective office—but not appointive office—to noncitizens. The result was a truly polarized situation in which most of the camp's silent adult majority was aligned against the administration and its JACL collaborators. The result was the Manzanar riot, one of only three instances of mass violence and bloodshed in a program that lasted almost four years and involved over one hundred thousand inmates.

The evening before the riot, Fred Tayama, a restaurant owner who had been a leading JACL official and had a subordinate role in camp administration, was attacked by an unknown group and beaten seriously enough to require hospitalization. Although he could not identify his attackers, the administration arrested several Kibei malcontents for the assault. The most prominent of these was Harry Ueno, whose major demonstrable offense had been an attempt to organize a Kitchen Workers' Union. He not only agitated for better working conditions but also accused certain officials of appropriating sugar and meat intended for the evacuees, thus accentuating the food anxieties that are usually prevalent among imprisoned people.

Ueno's arrest sparked a mass demonstration led not by a Kibei but by Joe Kurihara, a Hawaiian Nisei who was the most effective anti–WRA-JACL agitator in the camp. A veteran of the United States Army who had been wounded in World War I, Kurihara was understandably embittered by his imprisonment, although another ex-doughboy inmate of Manzanar, Tokataru Slocum, was a staunch defender of the necessity of the evacuation. According to Bill Hosokawa, Kurihara swore, after he was put behind barbed wire, "to become a Jap a hundred per cent and never do another day's work to help this country fight this war."[33] After listening to Kurihara and others, the demonstrators made two demands: (1) the release of those arrested; and (2) an investigation of Manzanar by the Spanish consul (the Spanish government represented the Japanese government during the war). Some of the speakers also urged further violent action against the hospitalized Tayama and other "*inu*" who were suspected, correctly, of having urged the WRA to segregate the Kibei malcontents from the other evacuees, citizen and alien. In the course of this and other meetings, "death lists" and "black lists" of alleged informers were read over loudspeakers: almost all of those denounced were JACL leaders; many of them held relatively responsible positions under the WRA.

After some fruitless discussions with the Manzanar management, another and more heated mass meeting was held later in the day. More "death lists" were read, and the crowd was exhorted to kill Tayama immediately. One group from the mass meeting invaded the hospital to "get" him (he was successfully hidden under a hospital bed) while another group went to the jail, presumably to effect the release of the imprisoned Kibei. Some accounts say that these demonstrators hurled rocks at jail guards; others that the abuse was all verbal. In any event, no casualties were reported among the security forces. The WRA authorities then called in the military police, who pushed the crowd back from the jail but failed to disperse it. The troops then tear-gassed the crowd, estimated at several hundred, mostly teenagers and young men, which scattered in great confusion, but re-formed later. At this juncture the troops, apparently without orders, fired submachine guns, shotguns, and rifles into the unarmed crowd. Two young men were killed and ten other evacuees reported for treatment of gunshot wounds, as did one soldier, apparently hit by a misdirected shot.

Although an official WRA report insists that this crisis "cleared an air that had become heavy with distrust," the opposite is true. Sixteen malcontents were sent to isolation camps in Moab, Utah, and Leupp, Arizona, and sixty-five of the most prominent JACL leaders were taken into protective custody at an abandoned Civilian Conservation Corps camp in the Mohave desert, from whence most of them were eventually released as part of the WRA leave program. Within the camp a strike took place. Black armbands were distributed, and according to Togo Tanaka, one of the suspected "inu," two-thirds to three-quarters of the inhabitants wore them, some probably under coercion. This spectacular resistance to the JACL leadership can be characterized as "right" opposition, many of whose leaders, whatever the provocation, were essentially Japan-oriented.

There was also what I have called a "left" opposition as well, an opposition which opposed the centrist JACL position, but did so out of a stated dedication to the underlying principles of the American republic. If the late 1942 Manzanar riot can be used as an archtypical example of the right opposition, Heart Mountain, Wyoming, in 1943 and 1944 epitomizes the opposition from the left.[34] If the resistance at Manzanar exploded as the result of a trivial "accident," that at Heart Mountain was premeditated.

The Heart Mountain opposition was focused upon the reapplication of the draft to Nisei who had positively asserted their loyalty. Before Pearl Harbor, Japanese American citizens were fully liable to the draft. Shortly thereafter many who had entered the service were summarily discharged, and all those who otherwise would have been 1-A were classified 4-C and no longer subject to induction. The JACL leadership, in and out of camps, felt strongly—and I think correctly—that military service would be an excellent way for Japanese Americans to redeem their reputations. Their requests to Secretary of War Henry Stimson—and, more importantly, to his deputy, John J. McCloy—eventually led to the formation of volunteer Japanese American combat units, most of whose officers were white. In connection with this program—and with the WRA leave program by which many in the camps would be released and would relocate themselves in the interior of the United States—the government distributed to all inmates over eighteen years of age a loyalty questionnaire entitled "Application for Leave Clearance." We now know that the questionnaire had originally been devised by the Army for distribution to Nisei males of military age only, but the WRA issued it to citizens and noncitizens of both sexes.

The crucial questions were numbers 27 and 28, which read:

27. Are you willing to serve in the armed forces of the United States on combat duty wherever ordered?

28. Will you swear unqualified allegiance to the United States of America and faithfully defend the United States from any or all attack by foreign or domestic forces, and foreswear any form of allegiance or obedience to the Japanese emperor, to any other foreign government, power or organization?

To the JACLers and their followers, the loyalty questionnaires were an excellent chance to redemonstrate their patriotism, and they urged all to answer the questions "Yes-Yes." As one Nisei, who answered "Yes-Yes" and then volunteered for military service, put it in a letter, it was "a hard decision. . . . I know that this will be the only way that my family can resettle in Berkeley without prejudice and persecution."[35] The Kibei malcontents and others on the right had no problems either: they could answer "No-No" and not be subject to any immediate penalty. But for Issei, the questionnaire posed serious problems. Although most of them did not realize it, the mere issuance of such a questionnaire to Japanese nationals was a violation of the Geneva Convention. In addition, many of the older Issei were terrified of the outside world and did not want to leave the security of the camps. For uncommitted Nisei, both questions created problems. Many answered question 27 conditionally with answers like "Yes, if my rights are restored." Others argued that question 28 was a trap, and that to foreswear allegiance to the Emperor of Japan was to confess that such allegiance had once existed. Many of both generations originally refused to answer at all. After a long ideological campaign within the camps, and some modification of the governmental position, almost 75,000 of nearly 78,000 eligibles in the various relocation centers filled out their forms. Approximately 6,700 of the registrants answered "No" to question 28; nearly 2,000 qualified their answers in one way or another and thus were set down in the government's books as disloyal; and a few hundred simply left the question blank. The overwhelming majority—more than 65,000—answered "Yes-Yes" and became officially loyal.

The military recruiting that accompanied this questionnaire had less positive results. From those still in incarceration, some 1,200 volunteered for the proposed regimental combat team and about two thirds of those were accepted. This was not nearly enough for the Army's purposes, and, as a result, on January 20, 1944, regular selective service inductions were resumed for Japanese Americans of military age, whether in or out of camp. For those in camp, selective service procedures applied only to those who had answered "Yes-Yes," and persons who wished merely to avoid military service could do so simply by changing their answer to question 28.

Most Nisei still in camps who were subject to the draft complied with it for one reason or another. About 10 percent did not, and it is this 10 percent and their supporters whom I have dubbed the left opposition. Before telling their story it is important to understand how the selective service mechanism worked for camp inmates. Even the Director of Selective Service, Major General Lewis B. Hershey, not normally one of the nation's more sensitive citizens, refused to have any selective service facilities located behind barbed wire. Most draftees had a preinduction physical examination and, if they passed it, then received an order in the mail to report for induction. For Japanese American inmates the process was significantly shortened. The preinduction physical and induction were made one process. Anyone who wished effectively to resist the draft, therefore, had to do so before discovering whether he was physically fit; the general method for resisters was to refuse to board the bus which was to take them to the nearest selective service examination station. Throughout the camps about every tenth Nisei ordered to report for induction refused to do so; conversely, about 90 percent complied.

What is interesting here is to note the contrasting rhetoric of the left opposition and that of the JACL. I will concentrate, as indicated above, on what happened at Heart Mountain. Resistance to the WRA and the JACL started early in the camp's history, in October, 1942. Unlike the resistance at Manzanar, the historian of Heart Mountain has been unable to find "one expression of . . . pro-Japanese or anti-American sentiment." Among the loyal Nisei at Heart Mountain several leaders arose, all of whom were critical of the JACL. That organization, they insisted, "is not truly representative of the citizens . . . [and] should be willing to step aside if Niseidom cannot get together under its banner." Arguing against accommodation, the left opposition insisted that the Nisei should not enter the Army until the government admitted that the whole evacuation had been wrong. "We must demand [one of them insisted in February, 1943] that our name be cleared; and have it read to the world that there has never been a justification for our evacuation, and that we are fighting, not to redeem ourselves or to clear our names, but for what we have always believed in."

When the War Department announced the resumption of selective service for Japanese Americans, the Heart Mountain *Sentinel*, the camp newspaper which spoke for the WRA and the JACL, hailed it as "the most significant development in returning Japanese Americans to full civic status." When the left opposition, organized into a Fair Play Committee, questioned the constitutionality of drafting citizens who were still held in incarceration, the *Sentinel* commented that "during the last week, in the hidden recesses of boiler rooms and latrines, behind closed doors and under the protection of darkness, leaders of the Fair Play Committee have fired with fanatical zeal the weaker members and departed from their mimeographed statements which are purposely toned down for public consumption." It was of no avail, the *Sentinel* insisted, to fight "against issues that are beyond our control." As for the resisters' argument that those who advocated compliance were abandoning constitutional rights, the *Sentinel* replied that "the contention that a restriction of our rights means a loss of those rights [was fallacious]. We don't lose any rights unless the constitution itself is changed. . . . If the Supreme Court rules evacuation was constitutional, then we will not have been deprived of any rights."

All told, eighty-five young Heart Mountaineers refused to board the symbolic bus to the selective service center. All were eventually convicted in federal court and sentenced to three years in a federal penitentiary. The American Civil Liberties Union, apparently so urged by the JACL leadership in Salt Lake City, explicitly refused to have anything to do with the Japanese American draft resisters. Its director, Roger Baldwin, wrote to one of the resistance leaders: "men who counsel others to resist military service are not within their rights and must expect severe treatment."

By the time these trials began, in the summer of 1944, the once minority view of the JACL had probably come to prevail, at least among most of the Nisei. They seem to have come to believe, as the JACL leaders always had, that the only way that they could ever win a place for themselves in America was by being better Americans than most. In any event, in the immediate postwar years, the JACL, enlarged and expanded, became the voice of the Japanese American community. Its leaders, with influential friends in high places, were able to lobby successfully for the Japanese American Claims Act, which gave some victims of the relocation token fiscal compensation for property losses, and, even more importantly to the community, helped to get a provision allowing the naturalization of Issei and other Asians as well as a quota for Japan into the Immigration and Nationality Act of 1952. For at least twenty years after the relocation there was little if any challenge to the JACL within the larger community. Few questioned, at least in public, the correctness of the position of positive accommodation with the government and its demands which it had unhesitatingly taken in 1942 and continued to maintain. The Nisei were hailed as a "model minority," and some community spokesmen even gave public lectures to other minorities—particularly blacks—on how to get ahead in American society.[36]

By the middle of the 1960s, however, and in the decade since, there have been many evidences of change in both the Japanese American community and in its leadership. The very growth in the size of the population—within the continental United States there were about three times as many Japanese Americans in 1970 as there had been in 1940—the maturation of the third, or Sansei, generation, the change, relatively and absolutely, of the social position of Asians in the United States, and changes within American society itself have all contributed to a weakening of the once strong leadership tradition within the ethnic community.

Some outside observers still persist in seeing the Nisei and their children as the "model minority," clinging to the virtues of the Protestant Ethic even as it was being abandoned by the older stock, who supposedly brought it here. Older leaders within the community tend to have a different view. For them, Whirl seems to be king, or at least heir apparent, as they see the rising generations less and less differentiated by behavior and achievement from the general level of society.

Both views, it seems to me, are excessive. The current socioeconomic position of Japanese Americans is clearly middle to lower middle class.[37] As a group they have significantly higher educational achievement than the general population, but also receive less income than their educational accomplishments would suggest.[38] With this achievement of status has come increasing Americanization, including a growing tendency to marry outside of the Japanese ethnic group, once a rare phenomenon.[39]

In terms of leadership no single group or organization has displaced the JACL; at the same time, the third and fourth generations of Japanese Americans are no longer as responsive as they once were to an organization that remains essentially civil rights-oriented. A few young Japanese Americans have become identified with radicalism and with such "radical chic" concepts as the Third World Liberation Front, but I suspect that participation in radical organizations is distinctly lower for college student Japanese Americans than for all college students. In the mid-sixties, when the existence of numerically significant Japanese-American radicalism first emerged, the general reaction of community leaders was one of shock and repugnance, but there seems now to be a greater tolerance toward social deviance, real or imagined, than existed previously. Two recent *causes célèbres* provide tangible evidence of this new attitude: the ability of Wendy Yoshimura, an alleged member of the Symbionese Liberation Army, to raise a considerable bail bond through a community-wide solicitation and the way in which the entire spectrum of the Japanese American community rallied around the cause of Iva Toguri—the so-called Tokyo Rose of World War II—in the campaign for her rehabilitation, which ended successfully with a pardon by President Gerald R. Ford. These recent postures should be contrasted with earlier attitudes: when Toguri was originally tried in 1949, most of the Japanese-American establishment, still anxious about its "enemy" image, applauded her indictment and conviction.[40]

In short, one can no longer make viable generalizations about ethnic leadership because the most pressing issues and forces that once united most of the community have ceased to exist. This is not to say that discrimination against Japanese Americans has ceased or that Japanese Americans cannot unite when they perceive discrimination. Much more community energy has been spent in recent years in protesting and memorializing the wrongs of the past than in concerted action directed at present problems.[41] Japanese-American community leadership was most effective, as we have seen, when outside agencies—the Japanese government in one instance, the United States government in another—created situations in which community spokesmen were necessary. It is interesting to note that this leadership, whether of the Associations or of the JACL, was normally perceived as collective rather than individual. The influence of these external unifying forces having abated, with no pressing communitywide problems on the horizon, the prospects are that most Japanese Americans will function atomistically within the larger community rather than act cohesively as a tiny minority.

NOTES

1. For a more detailed statement see Roger Daniels, "Westerners from the East: Oriental Immigrants Reappraised," *Pacific Historical Review* 25 (1966): 373–83, and "Majority Images/Minority Realities: A Perspective on Anti-Orientalism in the United States," *Prospects* 2 (1976): 209–62.
2. Two recent examples of the failure properly to consider the Asian component of the American population are Joshua A. Fishman et al., *Language Loyalty in the United States* (The Hague, 1966), and the survey research conducted by Andrew Greeley and his associates.
3. By East Asian I mean immigrants from the Indian subcontinent east to the Philippines.
4. There is an analysis of these figures in Roger Daniels, *Racism and Immigration Restriction* (St. Charles, Mo., 1974).
5. Santa Barbara, 1976. This is an expanded version of *Pacific Historical Review* 43 (1974).
6. *A History of the American People* (New York, 1902), 5: 213–14.
7. Hilary Conroy, *The Japanese Frontier in Hawaii, 1869–1898* (Berkeley and Los Angeles, 1953), p. 140.
8. Hugh Tinker, *A New System of Slavery* (London, 1974).
9. For a more detailed analysis of the activities of the Japanese consuls see Roger Daniels, "Japanese Immigrants on a Western Frontier: The Issei in California, 1890–1940," in *East Across the Pacific: Historical and Sociological Studies of Japanese Immigration and Assimilation*, ed. H. Conroy and T. S. Miyakawa (Santa Barbara, 1972), pp. 80–84, and Donald T. Hata, "Undesirables: Unsavory Elements among Japanese in America Prior to 1893 and their Influence on the first Anti-Japanese Movement in California" (Ph.D. diss., University of Southern California, 1970).
10. For details see Roger Daniels, *The Politics of Prejudice: The Anti-Japanese Movement in California and the Struggle for Japanese Exclusion* (Berkeley and Los Angeles, 1962), pp. 31–45.
11. *Journal of the Senate of the State of California, 1905* (Sacramento, 1905), pp. 1164–65.
12. This material on the Japanese Associations is based largely on interviews over two decades and the published sources listed in n. 13 below. Since writing it I have read a draft of an essay on the subject by Yuji Ichioka, "Japanese Associations and the

Japanese Government: Their Special Relationship, 1909–1926," which is superior to any previous treatment.

13. M. Fujita, "The Japanese Associations in America," *Sociology and Social Research* 14 (1929):211–17; Yamoto Ichihashi, *Japanese in the United States* (Stanford, 1932), pp. 224–26, and Valentine Stuart McClatchy, *The Germany of Asia* (Sacramento, 1919).

14. The Associations subsidized the publication of such works as Albert H. Elliot and Guy C. Calden, *The Law Affecting Japanese Residing in the State of California* (San Francisco, 1929).

15. For details of the Alien Land Acts see Daniels, *Politics of Prejudice*, pp. 46–64, 87–92.

16. This is graphically illustrated in Dorothy S. Thomas and Richard S. Nishimoto, *The Spoilage* (Berkeley and Los Angeles, 1946), p. 31.

17. For a first class study of minority education see Irving G. Hendrick, *Public Policy Toward the Education of Non-White Minority Group Children in California, 1849–1970* (Riverside, Calif., 1975), National Institute of Education Project No. NE-G-00-3-0082.

18. John Modell, "Class or Ethnic Solidarity: The Japanese American Company Union," *Pacific Historical Review* 38 (1969):193.

19. Taishi Matsumoto, "The Protest of a Professional Carrot Washer," *Kashu Mainichi* (Los Angeles), April 4, 1937.

20. Gunnar Myrdal et al., *An American Dilemma: The Negro Problem and Modern Democracy* (New York, 1944), p. 310; Ivan H. Light, *Ethnic Enterprise in America: Business and Welfare Among Chinese, Japanese, and Blacks* (Berkeley and Los Angeles, 1972).

21. Japanese Chamber of Commerce, *The Present Situation in Manchuria and Shanghai* (Los Angeles, [1931?]).

22. *Campanile Review* (Berkeley) (Fall, 1937).

23. Much of this activity by the Treasury is documented in Vol. 470 of the "Diary" of Henry Morgenthau, Jr., Franklin D. Roosevelt Library, Hyde Park.

24. Arthur A. Hansen and David A. Hacker, "The Manzanar 'Riot': An Ethnic Perspective," in *Voices Long Silent: An Oral Inquiry into the Japanese American Evacuation*, ed. Hansen and Mitson (Fullerton, Calif., 1974), p. 60.

25. Minutes of the Japanese American Citizens League Anti-Axis Committee, 1941–42, John Anson Ford Mss., Box 64, Huntington Library. Tanaka denies ever having made this remark (see Hansen and Hacker, "The Manzanar 'Riot,' " p. 58) but both contemporary evidence and the memory of one participant in the anti-Axis committee argue for its authenticity.

26. Los Angeles *Times*, December 8, 1941.

27. For details of the evacuation see Daniels, *Concentration Camps, USA: Japanese Americans and World War II* (New York, 1972).

28. The best account of the Manzanar Affair is Hansen and Hacker, cited in n. 22 above. See also Dorothy S. Thomas and Richard S. Nishimoto, *The Spoilage*, pp. 49–52; Allan R. Bosworth, *America's Concentration Camps* (New York, 1967), pp. 157–62; Edward H. Spicer et al., *Impounded People* (Tucson, 1969), pp. 135–38; Bill Hosokawa, *Nisei: The Quiet Americans* (New York, 1969), pp. 361–62; Audrie Girdner and Anne Loftis, *The Great Betrayal* (New York, 1969), pp. 263–66; and War Relocation Authority, *WRA: The Story of Human Conservation* (Washington, 1945), pp. 49–51.

29. Tamotsu Shibutani, "Rumors in a Crisis Situation" (Master's thesis, University of Chicago, 1944), pp. 115–16.

30. Ibid., pp. 66–67.

31. As cited in letter, Monroe Deutsch to John W. Nason, April 27, 1943, President's Files, University of California Archives, Berkeley.

32. As cited by Hansen and Hacker, "The Manzanar 'Riot,' " p. 64.

33. Hosokawa, *Nisei*, p. 362.

34. I have described the Heart Mountain resistance at greater length in *Concentration Camps, USA*, pp. 117–29. A deeper exploration is Douglas W. Nelson, *Heart*

Mountain: The Story of an American Concentration Camp, (Madison, 1976). Japanese American Communists, of whom there were a few, essentially supported the JACL-WRA line. Their major dissident activity consisted of circulating petitions for a second front.

35. Letter, K.O. to Monroe Deutsch, March 15, 1943, President's Files, University of California Archives, Berkeley.

36. The classic statement is William Petersen, "Success Story, Japanese American Style," *New York Times Magazine* (January 9, 1966), pp. 20 ff. This article also represents one of the earliest examples of the retreat from advanced positions of racial egalitarianism by social scientists under the impact of the social turmoil of the later sixties. For example: "For all the well meaning programs and countless scholarly studies focused on the Negro, we barely know how to repair the damage that the slave traders started" (p. 21). "On a campus [Berkeley] where to be a bohemian slob is a mark of distinction, [Japanese American students] wash themselves and dress with unostentatious neatness." (p. 40). Warning against the argument by analogy, I have maintained elsewhere that the Issei "were a small, self-confident group entering a fertile region with a rapidly expanding population. They came with almost all the skills and technological know-how necessary to reach the bottom rungs of the ladder of success. They brought with them the ethnic pride of a successfully emerging nation about to assume the leadership of a continent. They came at a unique time in the history of their two countries: their experience cannot be repeated." Daniels, "Japanese Immigrants . . . ," p. 87. For an example of misuse of the immigrant analogy from within the community, see a story in the Los Angeles *Times,* July 6, 1963: "Nisei Tells Negroes to Better Themselves."

37. The most recent figures show Japanese American family income divided as follows:

Below $ 4,000	9.5%
$ 4,000– 7,999	15.0%
8,000– 11,999	22.5%
12,000– 14,999	17.4%
15,000– 24,999	28.3%
25,000+	7.3%

Bureau of the Census, *Japanese, Chinese, and Filipinos in the United States* (Washington, 1973), table 9, p. 42. Percentage figures my computation.

38. Daniels, "Westerners from the East . . . ," pp. 381–82.

39. Akemi Kikumura and Harry H. L. Kitano, "Interracial Marriage: A Picture of the Japanese Americans," *Journal of Social Issues* 29 (1973):67–81, have found startlingly high rates of intermarriage—about 50 percent—in three key localities.

40. JACL Iva Toguri Committee, *Iva Toguri (d'Aquino): Victim of a Legend,* (San Francisco, 1975), and the references there cited provide a good summary of the case.

41. I am sure that many in the community, especially young intellectuals, will disagree strongly with this conclusion. There is a great deal more ethnic self-consciousness among such intellectuals today than at any previous time. Much of this, I am convinced, is a mimetic response to the "success" of some black groups. There is also a great deal of serious probing of the ethnic past by third and fourth generation students and scholars. This heightened consciousness of the past—which is shared by many in the community—is, at least in part, social nostalgia and has not been conducive to heightened social action. For an example of the kinds of extreme rhetoric some Asian intellectuals are capable of, see the introduction (pp. xxi–xlviii) to Frank Chin et al., *AIIIEEEEE!: An Anthology of Asian-American Writers* (Washington, D.C., 1974).

The Germans

Frederick Luebke

IN 1928, MIDWAY BETWEEN the two world wars, H. L. Mencken observed that with few exceptions the leaders of the Germans in America were an undistinguished and unintelligent lot, a collection of mediocrities, most of whom had something to sell. The few national German ethnic organizations still in existence, he noted, were led by entirely unimportant men. Moreover, the leaders of German immigrant churches were nonentities, unknown to the general public. The blame for this lamentable dearth of leadership, in Mencken's view, rested upon the German Americans themselves, who displayed an unfortunate tendency to follow inferior men. As Catholics they are slaves of their priests, he said; as Protestants they are slaves of their pastors; and when they leave the church they become slaves of the first political buffoon they encounter. During World War I, in Mencken's judgment, they had turned almost instinctively to fools for leadership.[1]

Mencken's surpassing skill in verbal hatchetry tends to overshadow the perceptive qualities of his analysis. Though he was a prisoner of his elitist prejudices, Mencken described circumstances that were typical of most immigrant groups in America. The vast majority of persons had emigrated in search of a better life. Coming from the lower classes of Europe, they were culturally backward persons who inevitably devoted their energies in America to material advancement. This worked against the emergence of wise and able leaders. When an educated and cultured person attempts to lead the apathetic masses of immigrants, Mencken wrote, he quickly becomes discouraged and succumbs to despair as his place is taken by demagogues, self-servers, and other third-rate noisemakers.

Yet, because of World War I, the experience of Germans in America was qualitatively different from that of any other immigrant group. The

64

largest non-English-speaking group in the country, the Germans had already begun to arrive in the eighteenth century. They prospered in this country and were well received. They were proud of their language and culture; while many Germans assimilated with remarkable speed, others labored mightily to erect a complex of institutions that served to sustain ethnic culture. When German immigration dropped off sharply at the end of the nineteenth century, ethnic leaders sought to inhibit the inevitable disintegration of the group by espousing a new cultural chauvinism. Later, when Germany experienced its early successes in World War I, the leaders of German America were encouraged to exploit the Kaiser as a symbol around which to rally the group, thereby bolstering a considerable financial investment in ethnic newspapers and a variety of other business establishments. An unprecedented measure of support seemed to unify the German Americans and to stimulate their leaders ever more boldly to flaunt partisanship for Germany. At the same time this behavior was infinitely offensive to persons whose emotional attachments were with the Allies. The advocates of the Allied cause, led by President Woodrow Wilson and other champions of English culture, began to attack German-American leaders as disloyal and un-American. Unsure of the capacity of American society to assimilate ethnic diversities, they began a war on German culture in America as early as 1915. The German Americans, however, saw themselves as entirely loyal to the United States. In their view, strict neutrality was in the nation's best interest, while Wilson's policies would lead to war. That nonintervention worked to Germany's benefits was as incidental as the fact that Wilson's understanding of the national interest served to aid the Allies.[2]

The entry of the United States into the war in 1917 radically altered the circumstances of German Americans. Behavior that had been legal in the neutrality period was now tantamount to treason, and most persons of German birth or descent, regardless of citizenship, were suspected of nurturing some measure of loyalty for Germany. Although the spirit of oppression was not uniformly felt across the country, the German-American community generally experienced much persecution. Superpatriots delineated a new, narrowed conception of loyalty and demanded conformity from everyone. A fierce hatred for everything German pervaded the nation. German cultural symbols were debased; instruction in the language was practically eliminated in the schools; the use of the German language was restricted on the state and local levels; and German-language newspapers were harassed and censored. Gradually suspicion escalated to threats of violence, to forced sales of government war bonds, to liberal applications of yellow paint to churches, schools, and monuments, to vandalism, book-burnings, flag-kissing, tar-and-feather ceremonies, and, in one case, the lynching of an innocent German alien.

The German-American community was devastated by these events. For the majority of the seven million persons of German stock in the United States at that time, German ethnicity had become a source of social discomfort or deprivation. Countless families ceased conversing in the German language. Name changes were common among persons, businesses, and societies. Thousands stopped subscribing to German-language newspapers and periodicals. Memberships in ethnic organizations of all kinds plummeted. As a group, the German Americans were embittered, disillusioned, and demoralized, unsure of what appropriate behavior should be. For most of them, ethnicity had lost its savor. The injustices of World War I remained imprinted upon their memories, and they were eager to express their resentment in the polling booths. But above all they wanted to prevent a recurrence of the persecution. They were convinced that this could be accomplished best by avoiding obvious displays of German ethnicity. Few were ready to respond to a leader who promised to solve the problems of the Germans as an ethnic minority group. The majority were not interested in the promotion of ethnic consciousness or in the political defense of *das Deutschtum.*

At the core of the German ethnic group, however, were persons whose commitment to ethnicity was primary. They were convinced that the problems of the Germans in the United States were due to past failures of ethnic leadership. They believed that German Americans had been insufficiently aggressive during the prewar years, especially in politics, and that if German-American citizens would participate vigorously in political affairs at all levels their power would be such that no one would dare trample upon their rights. The most prominent of these ethnic chauvinists was George Sylvester Viereck, the notorious propagandist of Germany's cause during the neutrality period of 1914–17. In September, 1919, a time when German Americans still suffered from sporadic superpatriotic violence, Viereck published an editorial on German ethnic leadership in his periodical, the *American Monthly,* as he had renamed the *Fatherland* of the prewar years. Noting that the Germans were a numerous and powerful force in American politics, he observed that they were now floundering for the want of a national leader. The need, he wrote, was for a new Carl Schurz, a man whose record of loyalty and service to the nation was impeccable, someone above envy and petty intrigue who could combine the wrangling and conflicting subgroups of German Americans and lead them by inspiring word and courageous deed out of the wilderness of war to a promised land of respect and honor. He should have financial independence and mastery of the English language, announced Viereck, and he must not be a recent immigrant or a newspaper man. As a possibility, Viereck mentioned Charles Nagel, who was well known among German Americans as the secretary of commerce in former President Taft's cabinet. But judging from his subsequent behavior, Viereck had himself in mind as the new leader of his ethnic group.[3]

Viereck's editorial evoked a variety of responses over the next several months. Most reveal how deeply German Americans were wounded by the humiliations of the war period and how earnestly they desired a restoration to their former status. Moreover, most respondents called for some form of political organization as the means to unite the group and to articulate its goals. The names of many persons were naively suggested as potential leaders in these letters, which collectively demonstrate a shallow understanding of the German ethnic group, its characteristics, and its relationships to the larger American society.[4]

The fact was that there was no possibility of a national leader arising who would fit the mold that Viereck described. The Germans in America never had had one in the past, not even the revered Schurz. This was because they were so diverse socially, economically, culturally, and politically that there was no common interest strong enough to bind them together. They were as heterogeneous as the nation itself, with its rich and poor, its educated and undereducated persons, its urban and rural divisions, its occupational range from unskilled laborers to mightly industrialists and financiers. The Germans included people who organized their lives around religious values and those who were secular minded; there were pietists and ritualists, Catholics and Protestants, Democrats and Republicans.

Unlike blacks, Chicanos, or Japanese, the Germans had no serious social or economic problems to unite them in a struggle against oppression. They had never been discriminated against in a serious way except during the World War I era, and even then it had not been universal or uniform. When the Germans had been persecuted it was chiefly because of the tenacity with which they clung to their language and culture. Even though German language and culture were not in fact as uniform as they appeared, their defense was the only foundation upon which a potential leader could base his appeal. Because it was in the economic interest of the press to emphasize ethnic unity and cultural maintenance and because leaders had no choice but to stress it in their speeches, sentiment in favor of nurturing the German language and culture appeared to be strong. Yet it was rarely capable of overcoming the centrifugal forces of personal or subgroup interest.

The inadequacy of ethnicity as a cohesive force was due also to the fact that the Germans, in their physical, linguistic, and cultural characteristics, were close to Anglo-American norms. Indistinguishable in appearance from dominant elements of American society, they were persons of Christian heritage who spoke a language closely related to English.

It was possible for them to assimilate with astonishing ease if they so chose. When the retention of obviously German behavior became a source of discomfort or deprivation, as during World War I, the proportion of those who consciously abandoned ethnicity was dramatically enlarged.

In their long history in the United States, the Germans acted in concert only in response to external threats or events that impinged upon their culture. Prohibition, legislative threats to parochial schools, and anti-German propaganda are examples of issues that could temporarily stimulate German Americans to unity. When the threat disappeared, possibilities for strong leadership also vanished. If the defense of ethnic culture was the only basis for leadership, it was inevitable that when German-American voices were heard in the land, they sounded negative, harsh, and unattractive to old-stock Americans.

The alternative lay in the kind of leadership exemplified by Carl Schurz. As a politician, Schurz had not pursued specifically German-American interests. Even though he was willing enough to exploit German-American votes, he was essentially an American statesman who happened to have been born and educated in Germany. While his cultural heritage certainly influenced his goals and methods, his political appeal was rarely circumscribed by ethnicity. It was the quality of leadership in national affairs that gave him status and position. When he spoke on the issues, the nation as well as German Americans listened, even though they often did not agree with him. Thus Schurz's role as spokesman for his ethnic group was almost incidental—a by-product of his national leadership.

In the years following World War I, however, there was no one of German birth or descent of comparable stature on the national scene. Nagel probably came the closest. But he, like most men of modest fame in the political, business, or academic worlds, had no desire to be identified as the leader of the Germans. As for those persons who were closely tied to ethnic organizations, most were unknown to the public at large or were broken in spirit by the events of the World War—men such as Dr. Charles Hexamer, the former president of the defunct National German-American Alliance. There remained the vainglorious Viereck. Though his notoriety as a propagandist eliminated him from any substantial leadership role, Viereck saw himself in a different light.

The German immigrant churches in particular would have nothing to do with Viereck and his ilk. They had been the chief victims of superpatriotism, and superpatriotism had been stimulated by the verbal excesses of the German ethnic chauvinists. For the churches, ethnicity had been primarily a means to achieve religious ends; when it tended to hinder rather than to ease the attainment of their goals, they readily abandoned programs of language and culture maintenance. Most church leaders distrusted political activity as a way to accomplish their objectives, and they remained deeply suspicious of the ethnic political organizations, perceiving them as the heirs of the liberal, anticlerical traditions brought to America by the refugees of the revolutions of 1848.[5]

In most denominations there was a remarkably swift transition to English-language services in the first postwar decade, a mandatory step if the loyalty of the younger generation was to be retained. German-language church periodicals were gradually replaced by English equivalents. Most parochial schools converted to instruction in the English language. In the Evangelical Synod and in several Lutheran synods, notably the Iowa and Ohio synods, these alleged "nurseries of Kaiserism" virtually disappeared. Meanwhile, dozens of German Methodist congregations withdrew from German conferences and merged with parent organizations. Transition to English usage was especially dramatic in German Catholic parishes, and membership in the German Catholic Central-Verein, the national layman's organization, dropped to one-half of its prewar figure during the 1920s. Even the isolationist, pacifistic Mennonites, though slower to give up the use of German, developed extraordinary benevolence programs and voluntary relief work to demonstrate in positive ways their worth as American citizens.[6]

John Baltzer, president of the Evangelical Synod during the early 1920s, was typical of many German-American church leaders of the time. He repeatedly declared that his church, though German in origin, was thoroughly American in spirit and constitution. Yet he opposed the movement led by the great American theologian Reinhold Niebuhr, then a young parish pastor in Detroit, to merge the Evangelical Synod with other denominations. As a moderate, Baltzer admitted the inevitability and even the desirability of the transition to English, but he pleaded for a slowing of the process for the sake of clergymen and parishioners who could not accommodate themselves to an abrupt change. At the same time, some denominations, notably the Lutheran Church—Missouri Synod, inaugurated broad programs to equip the faithful for life in an English-speaking church. Sermons, instructional materials, religious literature, hymns, and prayers were published in English in the hope that orthodoxy could be sustained as linguistic barriers fell.[7]

In some respects the traditionally anticlerical Amerikanische Turnerbund acted much like the churches. Its leaders also believed survival depended upon transition to a nonethnic basis. By the 1920s, its political radicalism was only a memory, its name had been legally changed to the American Gymnastic Union, its periodical, the Amerikanische Turnzeitung, included many columns of English-language articles, and its adult male membership dwindled to about 30,000 persons. Its national chairman, Theodore Stempfel, strongly objected to German ethnic politics and disapproved of mass protest meetings. The assimilationist drift of the

Turnerbund was not unopposed, of course, and its leaders were bitterly attacked by the faithful, both within and without the organization.[8]

On the local level, thousands of ethnic clubs, societies, and associations of all kinds continued to exist, despite the corrosive effects of the anti-German hysteria. Some of their members advocated the conversion of their *Vereine* to "American" institutions, but most hoped to enjoy unobtrusively the pleasures of ethnic sociability, to celebrate their culture with drink and song, and to reap the economic rewards of ethnic contacts within the privacy of their organizational quarters.[9] A few societies experienced a resurgence of life after the war, as they were strengthened by persons whose ethnic consciousness had been awakened by wartime persecutions.[10] In many of the large cities, dozens of these societies were united into an umbrella organization, such as the influential United German Societies of New York and Vicinity.[11] Orinarily not given to political activity, the umbrella organizations often coordinated charitable endeavors, such as relief programs for war sufferers in Germany, and promoted annual German Day cultural festivals, which by 1920 had begun to revive. Some members of the *Vereine* feared that organized political involvement was a senseless rocking of a leaky boat. But others attacked such attitudes as promoting self-indulgence, complacency, and a deceptive spirit of security. They urged participation in the activities of the two national organizations for German ethnic political action that had emerged in the immediate postwar period.[12]

The first of these was the Deutsch-Amerikanische Bürgerbund, or the German-American Citizen's League, which had its origin in Chicago under the leadership of Ferdinand Walther. It was deliberately patterned on the discredited National German-American Alliance, with state and local branches organized wherever sufficient interest could be generated. The Bürgerbund was dedicated to the revival of German language and culture and was motivated by a spirit of revenge. George Sylvester Viereck found such militancy to his liking and, for a time, served as its eastern regional director. Its leadership consisted largely of former National Alliance officers, but, unlike that organization, it was openly and avowedly political. In August, 1920, when it sponsored a national conference to support the presidential candidacy of Republican Warren G. Harding, it resolved "to sweep from office all miscreants, irrespective of party, who abused the authority conferred upon them by the people for the prosecution of the war, to make war upon their fellow citizens, who hounded and persecuted Americans of German descent, . . . who, contemptuous of any hyphen except the one which binds them to Great Britain, unmindful of the supreme sacrifice of Americans of German blood in the late war, attempt even now to deprive our children of the noble heritage of speech and song and prayer that has come down to us from our sires beyond the sea."[13]

The Bürgerbund was formally organized as a national body at a poorly attended meeting in Chicago in January, 1921, when it adopted a series of resolutions defining its policies and commenting on current national and international issues.[14] Never very successful on the national level, the Bürgerbund was influential chiefly in Chicago and the Midwest, but even there it lacked the support of the German-language press. No German ethnic leaders of importance emerged from the organization. Its strategy was excessively chauvinistic; it spelled trouble in an intolerant age.[15]

The second national organization was the Steuben Society of America. Founded originally as a secret society in 1919, it was no less committed to political action than the Bürgerbund. It also sought to protest against the treatment which Americans of German descent had suffered during the war, and it accepted the theory that if the Germans could unite they could hold the balance of political power in the United States. But this organization recognized that German Americans also had to establish their credentials for civic virtue and patriotism. Instead of screaming for its rights to be recognized, the Steuben Society hoped to demonstrate that it deserved respect. Hence, it constantly urged energetic participation by its members in the political life of America and, as its name suggests, publicized the contributions of Germans to the greatness of America from colonial times to the present. Its defense of Germany in international affairs was less strident than what was typical of the Bürgerbund, and to the disgust of the chauvinist radicals, it chose English as its official language. The Steubenites believed that this strategy would bring sufficient status and power to prevent the German Americans from being persecuted or ignored politically in the future.[16]

Although the Steuben Society became the best-known national German-American organization in the two decades between the wars, it also produced no significant leaders. Carl E. Schmidt of Detroit, an aging businessman of moderate wealth and culture who had played a minor role in Michigan politics, consented to serve as national chairman, but he never gave more than symbolic leadership to the society, which was centered in New York City. Thus, leadership fell by default to Theodore H. Hoffmann, who was hobbled by acting chairman status until Schmidt's death in 1934.[17] As an instrument of German-American unity, the Steuben Society was also a failure. Throughout the interwar period it suffered from indecisive leadership, internal dissension, and severe criticism from German Americans outside the organization. Despite the respectability it enjoyed, its membership never exceeded twenty thousand.[18]

Even so, the Steuben Society's strategy was consonant with the advice of the historian Ferdinand Schevill, who had urged, in response to Viereck's 1919 editorial on the lack of German ethnic leadership, that any action the Germans took should be preceded by a self-examination "to discover

the qualities . . . which have invited hostility and contempt." Such dispassionate reflection was difficult for the chauvinists; it was impossible for
Viereck, who seemed to have learned nothing from the war. Eagerly seeking distinction as the leader of the German Americans, Viereck plunged
into the political waters as the presidential election of 1920 approached.
He exhorted his fellows to unified political activity in order to force
decision-makers in the national government to recognize German-American political power and to reward it when used to their advantage. He
energetically supported the candidacy of Republican Warren G. Harding
with every means at his disposal. First he tried to establish a German-
American political action group which he called the Committee of 96.
When it failed to catch on, he shifted to the Bürgerbund which, like
almost all the German-language newspapers, endorsed Harding, not
because they regarded him highly, but rather as a means to defeat Democrat James Cox, whom they despised as the political heir of Woodrow
Wilson. Everywhere Viereck preached boldness to the intimidated German Americans, and everywhere the press, to his delight, identified him
as their leading spokesman. Indeed, as the campaign drew to a close,
Cox singled out Viereck as his whipping-boy, as he denounced the return
of hyphenism to American politics. But Viereck was not dismayed; such
treatment was to be expected if he was to project himself successfully as
the dauntless leader of all German Americans who were properly conscious of their ethnicity.[19]

Viereck's claim to ethnic leadership had little substance. The *New
York Times* and other newspapers gave him much publicity because he
was articulate and arrogant; apparently they assumed that he was also
influential. But most German Americans, including the publishers of the
German-language press, ignored or disputed his claims to leadership;
many found his extremism appalling.[20] It is true that in the election of
1920 the majority voted overwhelmingly for Harding, as did the elector-
ate generally, but they would have done so even if Viereck had remained
silent.[21]

Viereck pressed on. Remembering Schurz's alleged delivery of the
German-American vote to Abraham Lincoln in 1860 and his subsequent
reward of the ministry to Spain, Viereck dispatched a congratulatory
telegram to Harding with a reminder that six million Americans of German descent had voted Republican as he had predicted.[22] In January the
Bürgerbund resolved to send a five-man delegation, including Viereck,
to visit Harding before he took office and urge him to consider the great
contributions of Germans to America when he made his cabinet appointments.[23]

Harding politely received the Bürgerbund delegation on February 16,
1921, while vacationing in Saint Augustine, Florida. The president-elect

understood fully that he owed no debts to Viereck or, indeed, to the German-American voting population as a group. He assured the delegation that no candidate for high appointive office would be discriminated against because of German birth or descent. The effect of Viereck's well publicized visit was to make it politically impossible for Harding to appoint a German American to any significant position, regardless of the candidate's qualifications. Ethnic politics, especially German, was simply repugnant to large numbers of native-stock voters. The Buffalo *Express*, for example, denounced the Viereck visitation as "ridiculously impudent," and in Kansas the Salina *Journal* called it "insolent stupidity." The American Legion protested against what it perceived as a German-American demand to receive an appointment to the cabinet. In Texas the state legislature adopted a resolution endorsing the stand taken by the Legion.[24]

Viereck and the chauvinists were disappointed with Harding's refusal to appoint a German American to high office. Even though it was apparent that their tactic was bound to be counterproductive, given the xenophobic tendencies of the times, they continued to pressure the President, especially in autumn, 1921, when the position of ambassador to Austria fell vacant. Instead of agreeing on a single candidate, each of several activist elements within the German community, mainly in New York, lobbied for their own men. In the end Harding appointed a non-German.[25]

The whole affair resulted in laying bare a deep division within the ranks of Germans who were committed to united ethnic action. The Viereck clique believed in the open organization of raw political power; some even seemed to think that a frankly German political party would be ideal. They were opposed by persons, usually German-language newspaper editors and publishers, who were influential as leaders in local umbrella organizations. Fearful of renewed nativistic recriminations against the Germans, this group of leaders espoused a more covert strategy. They preferred to limit the public display of German ethnicity to cultural and social affairs such as German Day celebrations, bazaars, and benefit concerts. Meanwhile, they hoped to negotiate privately with leaders of the major political parties, trading German ethnic support for promises to pursue policies they favored. They wanted to bargain under circumstances where rationality and discretion could prevail, without the extremism of either Viereck and his followers or of latter-day super-patriots such as the leaders of the American Legion. No less committed to German ethnic goals than the extremists, these moderates believed they could gain more for the Germans at less risk. Chief among them were the Ridder brothers, Bernard and Victor, the owners and publishers of the *New Yorker Staats-Zeitung*, one of the largest and most influential of the German-language newspapers in the United States.[26]

Once it was apparent that no German American would get the Vienna post, Viereck began a sustained attack on the Ridders, Paul Mueller of the *Chicagoer Abendpost*, F. W. Elven of the *Cincinnati Freie Presse*, and the German-language press generally. Incensed by their refusal to publicize, much less support, the activities of the Bürgerbund and other chauvinist groups, Viereck denounced them in January, 1922, as "renegade Judases" of "supine docility" and "bovine passivity" who meet "in secret conclave" with log-rolling politicians. In April he published his version of how the Ridder brothers, by their meddling, had prevented Bernard Heyn, a German-American attorney of New York, who had been a member of the delegation that had visited Harding, from getting the Austrian ambassadorship. The Ridders, charged Viereck, had inherited, not earned, their positions of leadership and were motivated solely by desire for financial gain. He complained that any potential leader who failed to concur in their dictation could expect to be punished by being denied publicity in the German-language press. Viereck pointed out that the Ridders' alleged manipulation had led to their banishment from the halls of the socially prestigious Liederkranz, whose president, William O. C. Kiene, had also become tangled in the Austrian imbroglio. Viereck dragged out what he considered to be dirty laundry from the war period to incriminate the Ridders. Finally, he reported that "throughout the country, Americans of German descent, desirous of bringing about harmony, are in open revolt against such individuals claiming leadership."[27]

Viereck's outbursts inevitably alienated intelligent men of good will among the German Americans. Frustrated by his failure to attract a substantial number of followers, Viereck next broadened his verbal attack to include his chief journalist rivals, the editors of *Issues of To-Day*, George Abel Schreiner and Frederick Franklin Schrader. Their periodical, closely tied to the Steuben Society of America, was strongly pro-German, like the *American Monthly*, but was better edited and more moderate in tone. In Viereck's indictment, Schreiner committed the crime of defending the French on one occasion, and Schrader had expressed some doubt about the truth of all the stories then circulating about forced prostitution of German women for black French soldiers then occupying the Rhineland.[28] But Viereck continued to suffer a steady erosion of support. Ultimately he was unable to command publicity in either the American or German-language press.

During the next two years the German ethnic group seemed to acquire a new sense of community. The storm-cellar mentality of the immediate postwar period faded as German-American leaders became more openly assertive of their rights and hopes. They made frequent references in their speeches and editorials to the wartime persecution their people had endured, and fresh voices were heard in favor of political organization. The Amerikanische Turnerbund, for example, received new, aggressive leadership in the person of George Seibel. He urged German Americans to ignore their differences, to unite in order to fight prohibition and other forms of cultural imperialism, and to denounce such international injustices to Germany as the French invasion of the Ruhr. Similarly, the United German Societies of New York acquired a Lutheran clergyman, Dr. William Popcke, as its president; he also espoused political organization to prevent the disintegration of Germany.[29] The German-language press also waxed more aggressive. The *New Yorker Staats-Zeitung*, for example, agreed that the time had come for all German Americans to develop a powerful, united political organization for their own self-protection and self-interest.[30] The Steuben Society of America emerged as the dominant political organization as the more radical Bürgerbund faded from the national scene. The *New York Times*, as well as the *Staats-Zeitung*, frequently publicized Steuben Society leaders and activity. Meanwhile, sympathy in the United States for Germany grew as the Weimar Republic struggled with inflation and the occupation of the Rhineland and the Ruhr. At the same time, revisionist historians and journalists, building on the widespread disillusionment with the Peace of Versailles, explained the origins of the Great War in terms much less favorable to Britain and France than given in the "official" version. Thus, as the election of 1924 approached, it appeared that German ethnic political action could succeed, even though the nation continued to be troubled by excesses of racism, xenophobia, and superpatriotism.

Most German Americans were disappointed with the major party candidates for president in 1924. Calvin Coolidge meant only a continuation of a Republicanism that had done little for them. Democrat John W. Davis was a hopeless compromise candidate who, to the Germans, symbolized Wall Street and the kind of financial manipulations that had dragged the United States into the war. Thus, when Robert M. LaFollette, their battle-scarred hero from the days of the World War, ran as a third-party candidate, the majority of the German ethnic leaders rushed enthusiastically to his support. They loved him not so much for what he favored as for what he opposed. All they asked of any candidate was that he be against British and French dominance in international affairs, against the Versailles settlement and any arrangement, such as the Dawes Plan, that tended to perpetuate it, against the international bankers of Wall Street, and against the restrictive immigration legislation of 1924. If a candidate had a record of having opposed prohibition, woman suffrage, and American entry into the World War, so much the better. German ethnic politics thus rested on a foundation of negativism; positive goals were rarely defined. Since party loyalty did not exist, German ethnic leaders could shift easily from a conservative Harding in 1920 to a progressive LaFollette in 1924.

The Steuben Society of America was especially active in the election of 1924. Its Political Committee sponsored a conference of German-American leaders in Chicago early in June to hammer out a platform for the edification of the major parties in their national conventions.[31] In August the SSA met to endorse LaFollette, and in September it staged a great rally in Yankee Stadium in New York. LaFollette himself addressed the assembly of forty thousand and told them with his usual eloquence what they wanted to hear—that Germans were hardworking, valuable citizens who had, by their intelligence, thrift, and endurance, contributed immeasurably to America's greatness. Crowds heard similar speeches at meetings staged in many other cities, including Philadelphia, Buffalo, Chicago, San Francisco, and Portland. By these means the German leaders hoped to demonstrate that their people were good patriotic Americans who happened to speak the German language and to value German culture; they were determined to revise the image of the German American as being more interested in Germany than the United States.[32]

Still, memories of World War I remained vivid. No longer, announced the *New Yorker Staats-Zeitung*, will German Americans allow themselves to be muzzled, slandered, or harassed. The enemies of *Deutschtum* can be routed if German Americans will work together to present a united front.[33] "The German elements," wrote Frederick Franklin Schrader, "knows when it is insulted, ignored, and impugned. It has a whole register of grievances, and since the policy is to dampen the smoldering fires of discontent rather than to put out the fire, the explosion will take place in due time, and it will not be to the liking of the powers that be."[34] Viereck reminded his readers that "no official rebuke was ever administered to the wretches who were guilty of . . . outrages [against Americans of German descent] except in a mild Presidential protest, utterly inefficient in checking the tendency to declare American citizens of German blood beyond the protection of the law."[35] Meanwhile, the national press gave extensive coverage to the activities of the Steuben Society and reported in considerable detail the political preferences of German leaders in the various states.[36]

But even with the LaFollette candidacy, the Germans could not achieve unity; it was impossible to define the group interest to everyone's satisfaction. It is true that the majority of the German-language newspapers condemned both the Democrats and the Republicans as they endorsed LaFollette, but the old divisions between the extremists and the more cautious editors and publishers had not disappeared.[37] Fearing a repetition of Viereck's strategy of 1920, F. W. Elven, the publisher of the *Cincinnati Freie Presse*, authored a lengthy editorial in which he reviewed the "flagrant tactlessness" of the Bürgerbund with its policy of ethnic separatism and of making demands in return for concessions. The appropriate leaders of the German ethnic group, insisted Elven, were the publishers of the German-language press; it was their duty to prevent "persons who lack every qualification of leadership to force themselves into prominent positions and by their blunders compromise the cause of the German element." Elven argued that circumstances made ethnic political activity unwise. "We have our hands full at present to make amends for the sins of men of German blood who do not take their oath of allegiance too seriously and refuse to recognize the fact that we are not living in a German colony."[38] While Elven did not mention Viereck by name, it is clear whom he had in mind when he upbraided incompetent and impertinent political amateurs who "immurred themselves with their itching vanity and monumental self-esteem." Others shared Elven's view. Schrader, for example, urged that the *Steubenfest* in Yankee Stadium be divested of all suggestions of "hyphenism" that were so susceptible to exploitation by "Anglomaniacs, Ku Kluxers, and the New York Morgan Gazettes." Nothing, he said, must be done "to suggest that our citizens of German origin expect either privileges or rewards in return for the solidarity they will manifest" on election day.[39] The *German American World* agreed with Elven that the Viereck visit to Harding was stupid and that German ethnic political segregation was the greatest of follies. Yet it adhered to the notion that if the German element was "to reassert its claim to that position of influence to which it is historically and economically entitled," it must remain neutral in the political contest until partisan lines are distinctly defined and then assign its weight to the candidate or party that is compatible with the German interest.[40]

Viereck was outraged by Elven's attack and published a lengthy defense of his own behavior. Later he countered with charges that German-language newspapers that supported Coolidge, such as Elven's *Freie Presse,* did so because they had been bribed with lucrative advertising contracts arranged by the Republican campaign committee. Viereck associated such corruption with the tragic suicide of Hans Hackel of the Saint Louis *Westliche Post;* but he reserved special scorn for Val J. Peter, publisher of the Omaha *Tribüne,* who, according to testimony given before a congressional investigating committee, had flipped to Coolidge late in the campaign in return for $12,500.[41]

Any prominent German who disagreed with the dominant pro-LaFollette position was severely criticized in the German-American press. When Charles Nagel, whose loyalty to the Republican party was above reproach, announced that he intended to vote for Coolidge on the basis of nonethnic issues, the Steuben Society prepared a long rebuttal. The society charged that Nagel, though proud of his German heritage, chose Coolidge because he was the Saint Louis representative of the Republican powers of Wall Street.[42]

The failure of LaFollette to win election in 1924 underscores the inability of the German-American leaders to marshal the ethnic vote. They obviously had not wielded the balance of political power, even though a substantial portion of his five million votes was cast by persons of German birth or descent. Many thousands had also voted for the major party candidates, especially Coolidge. It was apparent that either major party could ignore the Germans if such a course were otherwise in their interest. Nevertheless, the German ethnic leaders continued to delude themselves. Carl Schmidt wrote that his Steuben Society had finally shed the party yolk. "If we continue to throw our vote whichever way our conscience may dictate, we will compel the respect of all parties, and will henceforth receive consideration by whatever party may be in power." Viereck insisted that support for LaFollette had cut across all German ethnic classes and group divisions; he even toyed with the idea of a third party "recruited largely from the German element."[43] Viereck, Schmidt, and other leaders knew that German Americans generally were still bitter about their wartime treatment; they erroneously assumed that the masses would translate their resentment into unified political action. This capacity to misinterpret experience and to believe only that which conformed to preconceptions gives substance to Mencken's observation that the Germans in America were led by mediocrities. Yet the actual voting behavior of German American citizens belies his charge that they almost instinctively followed fools.

There was no way that the strategy urged by the Steuben Society of America could produce strong political leadership among the Germans. In this view, party loyalty was an evil; support was to go to the party that would cater to the ethnic group interest. Such a policy precluded the possibility of a German ethnic leader achieving prominence in one of the major parties.[44] Election to important political office was therefore impossible. The only remaining avenue to a leadership position was to work through ethnic organizations such as the Steuben Society. But this alternative offered no long-term promise, for the Germans constituted a disintegrating constituency—a melting iceberg, in the words of one observer. Moreover, the Steuben Society as a matter of policy played down the leadership of its officers. Despite his many years of service at the head of the Steuben Society, Theodore Hoffmann was not even well known among German Americans.

The bankruptcy of the idea that the Germans held the balance of political power in the United States, provided they could unite, was made manifest by the presidential election of 1928, when they were hopelessly split by the candidacies of Herbert Hoover and Al Smith. One group insisted that Smith's Democratic party was still the party of Woodrow Wilson, William McAdoo, and A. Mitchell Palmer and that the hated prohibition amendment had been foisted upon the American people by

Southern Democrats. Hoover, they said, was of German descent and proud of it; besides, he had saved thousands of Germans from starvation in his relief work after the war. But others saw Hoover as a pro-British conservative and a prohibitionist. They much preferred the Irish-Catholic Smith, with his open record of opposition to prohibition, his distrust of England, and his support for liberal, progressive measures. Capitalizing on this sentiment, the Democratic National Committee flaunted the names of persons who endorsed Smith, including the well-known former Republican Congressman Richard Bartholdt of Missouri, Theodore Hoffmann of the Steuben Society, Charles Korz of the Catholic Central-Verein, Val Peter of the Omaha *Tribüne*, baseball players Babe Ruth and Lou Gehrig, and even the disdainful H. L. Mencken.[45] But there were still other Americans of German descent, chiefly pietistic Protestants, who favored Hoover precisely because he was "dry." After the election, the usually apolitical *Christliche Apologete*, a Methodist periodical, hailed the new chief with a full-page portrait. Meanwhile Lutherans rejected Smith simply because he was Catholic.[46]

The German-American press was similarly divided. A few newspapers, including Elven's *Cincinnati Freie Presse*, endorsed Hoover. A few more, such as Paul Mueller's *Chicagoer Abendpost*, supported Smith. But the great majority, the *New Yorker Staats-Zeitung* among them, were reluctant to offend any significant number of their subscribers and remained independent or even ignored the election entirely.[47]

The Steuben Society of America was incapable of providing leadership under these conditions. At first its organ, the *Progressive*, edited by Frederick Franklin Schrader, dismissed Hoover as pro-British and praised Smith as the champion of all that was dear to German Americans. In August, however, Schrader made a sudden switch, offered apologies to Hoover, and recommended his election. Certain local branches of the SSA also publicly announced for Hoover, but the national organization, wracked by internal dissension, finally endorsed Smith in mid-October. It severed its ties to the *Progressive* and declared the *Steuben News*, the publication of the New York council, to be its official voice in the future.[48]

After the fiasco of 1928, German Americans spoke less of what could be accomplished through political unity. References to World War I became less frequent. Viereck abandoned all pretense of ethnic leadership as he surrendered the editorship of the *American Monthly* to others. The Steuben Society of America continued to exist, of course, but its effectiveness was scorned in many quarters. Unable to agree on presidential candidates, it unintentionally abdicated a national leadership role as it concentrated on state and local politics. Meanwhile, the *Steuben News* larded its pages with glowing accounts of the heroic deeds of the ethnic fathers. Sanitized tales of Steuben, Schurz, De Kalb, Lieber, Sigel, and many others were repeated ad nauseam, as ever more obscure Americans of German origins were discovered and publicized in this effort to lay claim to authentic Americanness.

But the number of German Americans who were attracted by such unrelieved filiopietism diminished steadily. By the end of the 1920s the Americanizers were firmly in control of most German immigrant churches. The number of German-language publications, including church periodicals and trade journals, dwindled to one hundred seventy-two, only a fourth of the prewar figure, and the multifarious *Vereine* continued to atrophy and die. In 1930, Oscar Illing, editor of *Die Neue Zeit* of Chicago and an old-time German-American journalist in the Viereck mold, delivered an extended lamentation on the impending fate of German America. Illing saw betrayal everywhere. No ethnic institutions, least of all the German-language press, escaped his jeremiads: all were led by fearful, self-serving cowards who avoided controversy and gave lip service only to the maintenance of language and culture. In his view, singing societies, for example, had degenerated into English-speaking businessmen's clubs where German songs could sometimes be heard, but were sung by hired singers. Illing could offer no remedy for the dissolution of ethnicity; he repeated the threadbare lines about political unity, but admitted it was impossible of attainment. He refused to understand that for the ethnic masses, immigrant language and culture could not be perpetuated beyond the point of their social or psychological utility. Illing wanted German Americans to organize in order "to cultivate the imponderable properties of German culture," and he resented it fiercely when ordinary people could not share his elitist values. The only bright spot in Illing's ethnic world was the new Carl Schurz Memorial Foundation, which he understood to be a great German-American cultural institute of imposing character and financial power sure to compel respect.[49]

Although the Schurz Foundation never became quite what Illing imagined, it was symbolic of a new emphasis in German ethnic life at the beginning of the 1930s. The futility of the political strategy having finally become obvious, leadership fell increasingly to the moderates, led by the editors and publishers who stressed the importance of cultural education programs.[50] Still, new efforts were made to create national organizations capable of serving the interests of Germans in America. One of these, the German-American Federation of the U.S.A., embodied all the cultural goals of the Steuben Society but specifically rejected politics as a means to achieve them. Merely a revival of the old prewar National German-American Alliance, it had difficulty attracting supporters, partly because of the interest shown in it by several American proto-Nazi organizations.[51] More important was the National Congress of Americans of German Descent, an informal conference which met in New York in October,

1932, under the auspices of the German-American Conference of Greater New York and Vicinity. The guidance of the Ridder brothers was much in evidence at this meeting. Cynically interpreted, the congress was an attempt by the German-language press to sustain and revive the ethnic community in a time of economic distress, just as the officers of participating ethnic organizations hoped thereby to preserve their positions of authority and respect.

The United States was approaching the depth of the Great Depression at the time of the first National Congress of Americans of German Descent. It was surprisingly well attended. Most delegates represented national, regional, and city organizations and alliances, but ethnic craft unions, socialist workers groups, and church bodies had no interest in such an affair. At the core of the congress were cultural chauvinists whose prosperity and education permitted them the luxury of cherishing ethnic heritage for its own sake. Many speakers urged the assembly to lead the German element to its rightful place in American society. Their repeated use of such words as "recognition" and "respect" demonstrate that they were still troubled by the status deprivation engendered by World War I. The congress seemed to flounder about in search of some device or some institution that promised to preserve ethnic culture. It supported proposals to create an institute for research in ethnic language and culture, and to establish German houses at universities, German-language instruction programs, information bureaus, and cultural exchanges with Germany. The least realistic was a proposal to create a German-American university.[52]

Meanwhile, the Schurz Foundation had been established in Philadelphia. Supported by substantial contributions from several wealthy German-American businessmen and industrialists, it made no pretense to ethnic leadership per se. Instead, the foundation promoted cultural exchange programs and sought to acquaint Americans with German cultural achievements through its beautifully edited magazine, *American-German Review*, which started in 1934.[53]

Philadelphia was also the scene of the second National Congress of Americans of German Descent, held in October, 1933, in commemoration of the 250th anniversary of the first German settlement in America in 1683 at Germantown. Devoid of new ideas and unable to overcome the constrictions of economic depression, the congress movement died thereafter. Quite sensibly, neither the first nor the second congress had shown any concern for Germany, possibly out of fear of being identified with Nazism. But both congresses also tended to ignore the problems of the approximately four hundred thousand immigrants from Germany who entered the United States during the 1920s.[54]

When the older generation of immigrants (or "Grays," as they were traditionally called) commented at all on the postwar arrivals from Germany ("Greens"), it was usually in uncomplimentary terms. They were distressed chiefly because the latter showed little interest in the preservation of *Deutschtum* and often formed organizations of their own rather than supporting older, established institutions, most of which desperately needed the backing of the newcomers. In one instance, the Greens were even criticized for joining the liberal Evangelical Synod, which was presumably less committed to German-language maintenance, rather than the conservative, orthodox Missouri and Wisconsin Lutheran synods. Observers in Germany also disparaged the postwar emigrants as having an unprecedented proportion of complainers and renegades who, after one year in America, preferred to speak bad English rather than good German.[55]

The Greens themselves saw their circumstances differently. One of their most eloquent spokesmen was Dr. Fritz Schlesinger of New York, who addressed the first National Congress of Americans of German Descent in 1932. He reminded the assembled Grays that the postwar immigrants had come seeking a new life, believing that America offered them more opportunities and better security than did Germany. Unlike the earlier immigrants, most of whom were farmers and workers who had arrived before 1895, the Greens were representative of all levels of German society, including a disproportionate number of intellectuals. The majority, said Schlesinger, were interested in a rapid acculturation and hence tended to regard the use of the German language as a necessary evil during the transition period. They had not pursued *Deutschtum* in America and generally considered it a hindrance to a successful adjustment. Schlesinger explained that soon after their arrival these immigrants discovered that most ethnic associations were interested in perpetuating an outmoded form of German culture. Moreover, the *Vereine* seemed both unprepared and unwilling to serve the needs of the newcomers. Forced to be self-reliant, the Greens therefore used the societies for the only thing they were good for—convenient social contacts. The idea that the immigrant had a duty of some kind to preserve *Deutschtum* in America never occurred to them. Schlesinger further pointed out that most of the agencies for cultural preservation, such as the Carl Schurz Memorial Foundation, the Goethe Society of America, the many singing societies, and the great umbrella organizations like the United German Societies and the German-American Conference, were almost exclusively run by second- and third-generation German Americans.[56]

The problem of German-American unity, according to Schlesinger, concerned social class much more than people were willing to believe. Americans of German descent completely overlooked the fact that Germany was a land sharply divided into social strata and that in their private social relationships Germans rarely crossed the traditional lines. Upon his arrival in America, the newcomer found persons of all classes and occupations mixed together in the *Vereine;* furthermore, the leaders seemed chiefly to be "self-made" men, economically successful but culturally deficient. Thus, the immigrant intellectuals—academics and professional people, many with language problems that forced them to accept work beneath their educational level—felt economically inferior but culturally superior to most of the German Americans. Made uncomfortable by this anomaly, they often preferred to seek admission to American circles rather than to ethnic organizations. Yet these persons were precisely the ones who were expected to be the new champions of German *Geistesgüte.* Even the simpler people among the Greens, Schlesinger observed, sensed a provincialism or the lack of progressive or modern spirit among the German-American leaders. Finally, Schlesinger pleaded for a deeper involvement in American political affairs, not in terms of the German ethnic group interest, but in the service of the entire American society. Ties to German political parties must be severed, he said, and preoccupation with daily political events in Germany must end, if German American unity was to be achieved.

Schlesinger, a Jew, was obviously thinking of the Nazi party and the advent of Adolf Hitler, who came to power in Germany three months later. Other postwar immigrants were also thinking of Hitler, but in rather more favorable terms. American Nazi organizations were formed as early as 1924. Their memberships consisted almost exclusively of urban workers or proletarianized members of the German middle class who found few of their American dreams fulfilled. In their frustration, they consciously rejected assimilation, disparaged American life, and embraced fascism. At no time did the Nazi organizations attract a collective membership of more than a few thousand persons.[57] But because of their ideology of authoritarianism, racism, and extreme nationalism, they crowded the staid, bourgeois German-American societies from the stage of public attention, beginning with Hitler's rise to power in 1933. From then until the American entry into World War II, the activities of the Friends of the New Germany and its successor, the so-called German-American Bund, were daily fare in the *New York Times* and other major metropolitan newspapers. By the end of the decade, Fritz Kuhn, the leader of the Bund, was the best-known German in America.[58]

American Nazi organizations, like the older ethnic societies, were also concerned with German-American unity and leadership. But instead of basing their appeal on culture, the Nazis used race. In their view, all Germans everywhere were united by blood and were thereby bound in loyalty to the Fatherland. Anti-Semitic and anti-Communist propaganda was spread to attract popular support; brutal methods and threats of violence were employed in a series of efforts, most of them unsuccessful, to take over or to discredit the old umbrella organizations and the Steuben Society.

The leaders of the German-American Bund repeatedly demonstrated ignorance of American society and of the place of German immigrants in it. They understood nothing of American ideals and values or of the extent to which the masses of German Americans shared them. The efforts of Kuhn and his coterie to assume the leadership of German America on dictatorship principles must be written off as an abject failure. Even the German foreign ministry was frequently embarrassed by Bundist blunders and took all steps short of outright repudiation to control the organization.

Yet the American Nazis succeeded in keeping the established leaders of the ethnic group off balance. This was partly due, of course, to the apparent success of the Hitler government in both domestic and foreign affairs during the 1930s. Few prominent old-line German-American leaders were willing to speak out forcefully and consistently against Nazi outrages, so proud were they of the positive accomplishments of the new regime. They took delight in the way Hitler violated the detested Treaty of Versailles. The leaders of the Americanized German churches likewise refrained from condemning Hitlerism.[59] Indeed, some of the churchmen seem to have been encouraged to indulge in their own versions of anti-Semitism.[60] Unlike secular societies, the churches did not count Jews among their members. Thus, only German-Jewish and Socialist organizations fought vigorously and relentlessly against American Nazism from 1933 to World War II.[61]

As a matter of policy, the leaders of the old organizations generally avoided commenting on Nazi excesses. In the cases of the churchmen, silence was partly the consequence of their *Weltanschauung;* disposed to divide human affairs into two separate worlds of the sacred and the profane, they rarely discussed contemporary issues of any kind. But the leaders of the secular organizations were fearful of losing their positions of prestige. Their societies had already been enervated by depression and assimilation, and they were reluctant to risk alienating even small parts of their constituencies. Some leaders were practically driven to take strong anti-Nazi stands by the Bundists, whose bully tactics left them no choice. Their moral perceptions dulled by ethnocentrism, the leaders of the German-American Conference of New York and the Steuben Society of America refrained from taking a forthright anti-Nazi stand until 1938, when the insolence and contempt of the Nazi challenge to their leadership was so general it could no longer be ignored.[62]

Two other events in 1938 stimulated a somewhat more general and open criticism among German Americans of Hitler and National Socialism. One was the imprisonment in a concentration camp of Pastor Martin

Niemöller, a special hero of German Protestants who had been a commander of a German submarine in World War I. The other was the *Kristallnacht* pogrom of November 1938, touched off by the assassination in Paris of a German diplomat by a young Polish Jew. These acts finally goaded both the *Kirchendeutsche* and the *Vereinsdeutsche* into condemning Nazism.[63] But even thereafter, muted pride in Hitler's deeds was more common in the German-language press than was consistent condemnation.[64] Some small-town newspapers, such as the *Fredericksburg* [Texas] *Wochenblatt*, concentrated on local news and ignored the world crisis generally; a great many papers, among them the *Sheboygan* [Wisconsin] *Amerika*, tried to present a neutral or objective reporting of the news; a few, such as the *Iowa Reform* [Davenport] and the *Dakota Freie Presse* [Bismarck], were clearly pro-German, anti-Semitic, isolationist, and intensely anti-Roosevelt.

Just before World War II began in 1939, Carl Wittke, the eminent historian of German America, who was then a dean at Oberlin College, encapsulated the moral problem faced by the leadership in his own ethnic group. It was apparent, Wittke wrote, that newspaper accounts of Nazi atrocities against the Jews were not exaggerated and that there were millions of persons in Germany who were appalled by the policies of the Hitler regime. But instead of giving moral support to honorable men who were fighting against fearful odds for decency, humanity, and brotherhood, the leaders of the German element preferred to extol the glories of the "Forty-eighters" and their flaming liberalism while excusing Nazi excesses as a passing phase or characterizing "the noble fuehrer" as an unfortunate "victim of an ignorant or brutal minority of his party."[65]

While H. L. Mencken had been disdainful of German ethnic group leadership, Wittke was simply disgusted. He was offended by their moral obtuseness and narrow chauvinism. It is clear, moreover, that their record over the two decades of the interwar period is distinguished by neither insight nor foresight. Most spokesmen for the group, self-appointed or otherwise, were deficient in understanding their constituencies and how they, as leaders, might relate to the great masses of Americans of German origins or descent. Remarkably various in economic status, religious belief, and even in language and culture, most German Americans, unlike the core of leaders, were not moved primarily by ethnic considerations. Hundreds of thousands of persons who were technically counted as German Americans had no significant measure of identification with the ethnic group. Indeed, some were antagonistic to programs for the preservation of ethnic identity. Others perceived ethnicity as inhibiting the attainment of other goals deemed more important. Church Germans, for example, abandoned ethnicity at an accelerated pace during the 1920s and 1930s.

But even those leaders who shared the desire for ethnic unity could not agree on how it should be attained. Some persisted in strategies that were inevitably counterproductive, given the character of the times, and thus stimulated further fragmentation of the ethnic group. Filled with bitterness and resentment over their treatment in World War I and perturbed by an enduring sense of having lost status, they first hoped to regain respect through united ethnic political action. Some advocated the use of raw political power; others preferred persuasion. After the political strategy had failed repeatedly during the 1920s, they shifted to an emphasis on culture. But their programs were based upon elitist values at variance with those of the masses. The leaders refused to believe that immigrant language and culture could not be effectively perpetuated beyond the period of social or psychological utility. Vitiated by the Great Depression, cultural programs faded as the American Nazis, ever bold and arrogant, captured public attention with their strategy of blood. This racist quest for German-American unity, appealing chiefly to recent, postwar immigrants, was so antipathetic to American ideals and habits of thought and attitude that it eventually drove most traditional German-American leaders into opposition. This meant that, except on the local or personal levels, the attainment of ethnic group goals by means of organized activity was abandoned with the advent of World War II.

One may scarcely speak of German ethnic leadership in the United States since World War II. The Steuben Society of America, the Catholic Central-Verein, the Carl Schurz Memorial Foundation, the American Turners, and more than a dozen other national organizations continued to exist, sustained by large numbers of German-speaking refugees from central and eastern Europe who arrived during the 1940s and 1950s.[66] Old patterns persist. The attitudes of the old Bürgerbund are presently reincarnated in the Deutsche-Americanische National Kongress and in the Federation of American Citizens of German Descent. Their rhetoric and strategies often seem unchanged from what they were in the 1920s.[67] But no one listens; these organizations, united chiefly by a hatred of Communism, are unknown to the general public and ignored by most German Americans who may have heard of them. Meanwhile, German ethnicity thrives in many hundreds of local *Vereine* throughout the land, but especially in major centers of German population, such as New York, Cleveland, and Chicago, plus Florida and California. They gather together persons whose attachment to the German language and culture is more emotional than intellectual, more social than political, who are interested chiefly in maintaining an associational environment in which they may converse, dine, play, sing, and dance with others who share their values and attitudes.[68] Ironically, it is this dimension of German life in America that the chauvinists of half a century ago predicted could not survive without their leadership.

NOTES

1. H. L. Mencken, "Die Deutschamerikaner," *Die Neue Rundschau* 39 (Band II, November 1928):486–95.

2. This and the following several paragraphs are summarized from my book, *Bonds of Loyalty: German-Americans and World War I* (DeKalb: Northern Illinois University Press, 1974).

3. *Viereck's The American Monthly* 11 (September 1919):5. Cf. George Seibel, "German-Americanism," *American Monthly* 25 (March 1932):9 ff.

4. *Viereck's The American Monthly* 11 (October, November, December 1919):42, 76, 107.

5. *German American World* 7 (15 February 1924):224; Rudolf Cronau, *Drei Jahrhunderte Deutschen Lebens in Amerika*, 2d rev. ed. (Berlin: Dietrich Reimer, 1924), p. 661; J. Eiselmeier, *Das Deutschtum in Angloamerika* (Berlin: Deutschen Schutzbund Verlag, n.d.), p. 30; Heinz Kloss, "Deutschamerikanische Querschnitt: Vereinsdeutsche, Nationalsozialisten, Kirchendeutsche," *Die evangelische Diaspora* 16 (1934):170 f.

6. See my more extended treatment of this development in *Bonds of Loyalty*, pp. 314–18. See also James C. Juhnke, *A People of Two Kingdoms: The Political Acculturation of the Kansas Mennonites* (Newton, Kans.: Faith and Life Press, 1975), pp. 113–16; H. Kamphausen, *Geschichte des religiösen Lebens in der Deutschen Evangelischen Synode von Nordamerika* (Saint Louis: Eden Publishing House, 1924), pp. 300–333; Heinz Koss, *Um die Einigung des Deutschamerikanertums: Die Geschichte einer unvollendeten Volksgruppe* (Berlin: Volk und Reich Verlag, 1937), pp. 164–66.

7. Kamphausen, *Geschichte des religiösen Lebens*, p. 313; Alan N. Graebner, "The Acculturation of an Immigrant Church: The Lutheran Church—Missouri Synod, 1917–1929" (Ph.D. diss., Columbia University, 1965), pp. 83–161.

8. *Amerikanische Turnzeitung* (New Ulm, Minnesota), 1 May 1921, 14 January 1923, 27 May 1923; *American Monthly* 13 (March, May, 1922):15, 85; Kloss, *Um die Einigung*, p. 302 f. See also Noel Iverson, *Germania, U.S.A.* (Minneapolis: University of Minnesota Press, 1966), pp. 32–35, 91–120.

9. *New Yorker Staats-Zeitung*, 22 September 1924.

10. Ibid., 21 December 1920, 6 September 1920; [Paul G. Kreutz], *Ein Gedenkwerk zum Goldenen Jubiläum des Plattdeutschen Volksfest-Verein von New York und Umgebung* (New York: Plattdeutsche Volksfest-Verein, 1925), pp. 174–76.

11. *New Yorker Staats-Zeitung*, 10 November 1920. In the early 1920s, the Plattdeutsche Volksfest-Verein listed eighty-three member organizations. Kreutz, *Gedenkwerk*, pp. 275–80.

12. For examples, see Kreutz, *Gedenkwerk*, pp. 171–80; *History of the Liederkranz of the City of New York, 1847–1947* (New York: Drechsel Printing Co., 1948), pp. 48–53.

13. *Viereck's The American Monthly* 12 (September 1920): 199; *American Monthly* 13 (August 1921):169, 175; 14 (September 1922):205; Niel M. Johnson, *George Sylvester Viereck: German-American Propagandist* (Urbana: University of Illinois Press, 1972), p. 82; Kloss, *Um die Einigung*, pp. 295–300.

14. *New York Times*, 11, 12 January 1921; *American Monthly* 12 (February 1921): 359 f.

15. See the scathing editorial from the *Cincinnati Freie Presse*, reprinted in English in *German American World* 7 (15 March 1924):281 f.

16. *Steuben News* 11 (May 1939):2–4; Cronau, *Drei Jahrhunderte*, p. 661; "The German-American Element and the Next Election," *Issues of To-Day* 6 (29 September 1923); "The German-American in Politics," ibid., 5 (21 October 1922):4–5.

17. Dr. Franz Koempel, "On the Twentieth Anniversary of the Steuben Society of America," *Steuben News* 11 (May 1939).

18. In addition to numerous articles in *American Monthly*, *Issues of To-Day*, *German American World*, see the *Steuben News*, which began in 1929. Cf. Kloss, *Um die Einigung*, p. 287.

19. *Viereck's The American Monthly* 11 (October 1919, February 1920):42, 181; *American Monthly* 12 (March, April, July, August 1920):4, 46, 133, 165; *New York Times*, 5 September, 17 October 1920; *Literary Digest* 66 (18 September 1920):11–12; Johnson, *Viereck*, pp. 82–87.

20. Ibid., p. 82.

21. Luebke, *Bonds of Loyalty*, pp. 325–28.

22. Johnson, *Viereck*, p. 88.

23. *New York Times*, 11, 12 January 1921.

24. *American Monthly* 12 (February 1921):359 f; 13 (March 1921):9; Johnson, *Viereck*, p. 89; *New York Times*, 15 January, 17 February 1921. Viereck later published a lengthy article defending his role in the affair and included lengthy excerpts from his correspondence with President Harding. See Alexander Harvey, "German-American Unity and the President," *American Monthly* 16 (July 1924):136–43.

25. See the convenient summary of this affair in Johnson, *Viereck*, p. 90 f. Viereck's version appears in *American Monthly* 16 (July 1924):141–43.

26. Viereck assailed the German-language press as early as February 1921, when it became clear that the editors refused to support the Harding visitation. See *American Monthly* 12:357.

27. *American Monthly* 13 (January 1922):344; 14 (April 1922):40–42. Viereck continued his "exposure" of the Ridders in the May issue of *American Monthly* 14:74–76. An extraordinary display of hypocrisy, this article accused the Ridders of being "professional German Americans" who "aim to build up their own prestige and the power of their newspaper at the expense of their fellows" by "shrewdly utilizing every political break, every personal spite and every personal vanity." No one was more intimately acquainted with such behavior than Viereck himself.

28. *American Monthly* 14 (June 1922):104 ff.

29. *Amerikanische Turnzeitung*, 16 September 1923; *New York Times*, 22 October 1923. Viereck applauded the selection of Seibel, whom he described as "just the man to lead the Turnerbund back to its true ideals which had been deserted so ignominiously by its former president, the unspeakable Stempfel." *American Monthly* 15 (September 1923):213. See also ibid., 15 (August 1923):183.

30. *New Yorker Staats-Zeitung*, 16 September 1924.

31. *German American World* 7 (1 July 1924):440.

32. *New Yorker Staats-Zeitung*, 16, 22 September; 9, 14, 15 October 1924.

33. Ibid., 16 September 1924.

34. "The Potentiality of 'the German Vote,'" *German American World* 7 (1 February 1924):199–200.

35. *American Monthly* 16 (September 1924):225. See also ibid., 16 (October 1924):250.

36. *New York Times*, 15, 30, 31 August; 11, 21, 22 September; 1, 5, 9, 10, 13, 22, 23, 25, 26 October 1924.

37. "Voice of the German Language Press," *German American World* 7 (1924): 442–43, 473, 495–96, 547.

38. Reprinted in translation in *German American World* 7 (15 March 1924):280–81.

39. *American Monthly* 16 (October 1924):255.

40. *German American World* 7 (1 April 1924):298.

41. *American Monthly* 16 (June, July, August, December 1924):105, 136–43, 158, 311.

42. *New Yorker Staats-Zeitung*, 17 October 1924; 24 October 1924.

43. *American Monthly* 16 (December 1924):312, 318. See also Alexander Harvey, "The German-Americans and the LaFollette Vote," ibid., pp. 318–19, 330.

44. Senator Robert Wagner of New York, who was born in Germany, never ran as a German-American candidate and carefully avoided identification with German-American political organizations, save the German-American Roland Society, which was staunchly loyal to the Democratic party.

45. *New York Times*, 22 October 1928; *New Yorker Staats-Zeitung*, 23, 25 October

1928; Richard Bartholdt, *From Steerage to Congress* (Philadelphia: Dorrance, 1930), p. 422. See also Sander Diamond, *The Nazi Movement in the United States, 1924–1941* (Ithaca: Cornell University Press, 1974), p. 76 ff.

46. *Der Christliche Apologete* 90 (14 November 1928):1083; Douglas C. Stange, "Al Smith and the Republican Party at Prayer: The Lutheran Vote—1928," *Review of Politics* 32 (July 1970):347–64.

47. *New Yorker Staats-Zeitung*, 26 October 1928; *New York Times*, 25 October 1928.

48. Mencken, "Die Deutsch-Amerikaner," p. 490; Kloss, *Um die Einigung*, p. 288; *New York Times*, 8, 14, 17, 19, 20 October 1928; *Steuben News* 1 (November 1928):4.

49. *American Monthly* 23 (May, June, July 1930).

50. For an impassioned plea for the cultural strategy and a rejection of ethnic political action by a distinguished German-American academician, see Kuno Francke, *Deutsche Arbeit in Amerika* (Leipzig: Felix Meiner, 1930), p. 91.

51. Deutschamerikanischen Bürgerbund von Nebraska, *Protokoll der fünften Jahres-Versammlung* (Omaha, December 1931), pp. 17–19; Kloss, "Deutschamerikanische Querschnitt," p. 167; *Steuben News* 4 (November 1931):1, 4; 4 (December 1931):2.

52. *Erster National-Kongress der Amerikaner Deutschen Stammes. Sitzungsberichte und Erläuterungen. New York City, October 27–30, 1932* (New York: Deutsch-Amerikanische Konferenz von Gross-New York und Umgebung, n.d.). See also *New York Times*, 28, 29, 30 October 1932.

53. Eugene E. Doll, *Twenty-five Years of Service, 1930–1955* (Philadelphia: Carl Schurz Memorial Foundation, n.d.), pp. 3–9; *American Monthly* 23 (November 1930): 34 f; *American-German Review* 1 (September 1934):56.

54. *Steuben News* 6 (November 1933):2; Kloss, "Deutschamerikanische Querschnitt," p. 168.

55. George Seibel, "German-Americanism," *American Monthly* 25 (March 1932):10, 14; Oscar Illing, "The Americans of German Blood, II," *American Monthly* 23 (June 1930):44; Kloss, "Deutschamerikanische Querschnitt," p. 173.

56. *Erster National-Kongress*, p. 50 ff.

57. Diamond, *Nazi Movement*, pp. 146, 169; Klaus Kipphan, *Deutsche Propaganda in den Vereinigten Staaten, 1933–1941* (Heidelberg: Carl Winter Universitätsverlag, 1971), pp. 51–55; O. John Rogge, *The Official German Report* (New York and London: Thomas Yoseloff, 1961), p. 129.

58. In addition to the books by Diamond and Kipphan, see Leland B. Bell, *In Hitler's Shadow: The Anatomy of American Nazism* (Port Washington: Kennikat, 1973); Alton Frye, *Nazi Germany and the American Hemisphere, 1933–1941* (New Haven: Yale University Press, 1967); and Arthur L. Smith, Jr., *The Deutschtum of Nazi Germany and the United States* (The Hague: Martinus Nijhoff, 1965).

59. *Steuben News* 6 (July 1934): 3; *Die Abendschule* (Saint Louis) 79 (4 May 1933):709; ibid., 80 (14 June 1934):796 f.

60. See several articles in *Der Christliche Apologete* (Methodist) 101 (1939), but especially "Verfolgung und Ausweisung der Juden" by John C. Guenther, p. 57 f. For other examples, see *Kirchenzeitung* (Reformed) 103 (11 January 1933):6; ibid., 108 (17 May 1938):16; *Kirchenblatt* (American Lutheran), 12 August 1939, p. 9; ibid., 26 August 1939, p. 3; *Die Abendschule* 80 (21 September 1933):167; and ibid. (14 December 1933):371.

61. *New York Times*, 4, 8–11 April 1938; *New Yorker Staats-Zeitung*, 16 September 1939; *Sonntagsblatt* [New York] *Staats-Zeitung und Herold*, 15 September 1940; Robert E. Cazden, *German Exile Literature in America 1933–1950* (Chicago: American Library Association, 1970), pp. 42, 44.

62. Kipphan, *Deutsche Propaganda*, p. 93. A detailed account of the fight is given in *Steuben News* 11 (October 1938):3, 5, and 7; see also ibid., June 1938, p. 8; August 1938, p. 3; and September 1938, p. 3.

63. *Kirchenzeitung* 108 (22 February 1938): 11; ibid. (12 April 1938):14–15; ibid. (3 May 1938):14; ibid. (6 December 1938):15; *Kirchenblatt* 81 (19 March 1938):6; ibid. (16 April 1938):11; *Der Christliche Apologete* 101 (4 January 1939); *New York*

Times, 3, 9 October, 23 November 1938; Dieter Cunz, *The Maryland Germans, A History* (Princeton: Princeton University Press, 1948), pp. 414, 437; Johnson, *Viereck*, p. 193; Diamond, *Nazi Movement*, pp. 276–77.

64. "Foreign-language Press: 1047 Immigrant Newspapers," *Fortune* 22 (November 1940):92–93. Even after *Kristellnacht*, the Ridders' *New Yorker Staats-Zeitung* refrained from strong criticism of Hitlerism.

65. *Cleveland Plain Dealer*, reprinted in *American Turner*, 13 August 1939, p. 6.

66. *Die Vereinswelt: Wegweiser der Deutschamerikaner*, *Sonderbeilage New Yorker Staats-Zeitung und Herold*, 13 May 1973. See especially the article by the publisher Erwin Single, "Aus der Werkstatt der Verlager," p. 3.

67. *Die Vereinswelt*, 1954, p. 3; *Der Deutsch-Amerikaner: D.A.N.K. Mitteilungen* 8 (January 1966):2; 8 (April 1966):9; 8 (August 1966):6; 8 (October 1966):3.

68. *Die Vereinswelt*, 1973; *Deutsch-Amerikanische Jahreskalender des Staates Ohio, 1963* (Cleveland: Ernst Printing and Calendar Co., [1962]); *78. Jahres-Bericht und Mitglieder-Verzeichnis, Schwaben-Verein Chicago* (1956); *20. Jahre-Vereinigung der Donauschwaben von Chicago* (1973); see especially the article by Christ N. Herr, "Die Vereinigung der Donauschwaben in Chicago: Entstehung und Werdegung," pp. 17–35.

Afro-Americans

Nathan Irvin Huggins

NINETEEN FORTY-FOUR—it was a good year for Americans to reassess social values and ideals. The Allies' cause in their war against fascism seemed at last destined to triumph. With the defeat of fascism —defined as much in terms of racist ideology as totalitarianism—what would be the conditions under which the world would be reordered, the ideals to which people would be asked to give assent? Clearly, racism and fascism were evil, not only because they were self-serving and corrupt ideologies, but because, as the war had testified, they were ultimately destructive of humanity. So, if the war with its awful costs was to have any redeeming qualities, they would have to be found in life-supporting principles which dignified all mankind, regardless of race or culture.

Sensitive Americans could not reflect on such matters without being aware of their own society's culpability. For the racism that left blacks defenseless against mobs, violence, and murder; that effectively excluded them from the commonweal through social, political, and economic discrimination; that framed legal and customary instruments, engendering a deep social corruption, maintaining one law and practice for whites and another for blacks; such racism was akin to what had inspired the Brownshirts and led to concentration camps and the ultimate "solution" of the holocaust. They were different to be sure, related not identical. The mind that could conceptutalize "our Negro problem" was bound in sympathy with the one that could speak of "our Jewish problem," and such minds could find attraction in the same solutions. So, it would be hard to imagine "winning the peace" that was to follow the war, and the bright new world that was to be redemptive, without contemplating how such wartime ideals, as comprised in the Four Freedoms of the Atlantic Charter, would be applied to race relations in the United States.

92   NATHAN IRVIN HUGGINS

The times called for a hard and dispassionate view of American racial realities as well as a rededication to American ideals for the future. This preoccupation suggests that the timing of Gunnar Myrdal's *An American Dilemma*—that "definitive scientific study" of American race relations—was not fortuitous.[1]

It was in 1944, also, the same year as Myrdal's study, that Edwin R. Embree, president of Julius Rosenwald Fund, wrote a book comprising the biographies of the thirteen "Negroes who are tops today."[2] His intent was to show Afro-American achievement in various fields, to celebrate individual victory over adversity, and to suggest the potential social benefits of a future of racial justice. To write his book, Embree had queried more than two hundred Americans, white and black, "who know the group best," giving them no guidelines. He asked them merely to use their own judgments in listing the black leaders of the day. He derived from this canvas a consensus of thirteen names, an interesting and strangely mixed group. There were two women, three educators, one research scientist, two writers of poetry and fiction, one labor organizer and leader, one "elder statesman" and intellectual, one composer of "classical" music, two singers (of "classical" and spiritual repertoire), the executive secretary of a protest organization, and one professional athlete. No professional politicians, clergymen, or businessmen made the list.[3] It was Embree's assumption, which was shared by many others, that these thirteen names constituted the top leadership of the race.

In the same year Rayford Logan edited a book of essays by notable Afro-Americans, assessing the status of race relations in the United States and defining some of the contours of that "new world" that must follow the war.[4] Unlike Embree, Logan collected the statements of prominent black Americans. He sought to make the book representative by offering a range of opinions from "conservative" to "radical." While only four of those in Embree's book reappear in Logan's, the lists are nevertheless remarkably similar in the occupations represented. Professional politicians and businessmen are conspicuous by their absence, and clergymen appear only in the guise of university and college administrators.

There would have been little argument that Embree's and Logan's lists constituted the recognized "leaders" of the Afro-American community, at least in one sense of the term. They were men and women who had achieved greatness, as Embree said, against the odds, or who were assumed to stand for some point of view that was shared by a significant number of black Americans. Leaders perhaps, but only three, those attached to labor organizations, could be said to represent an actual constituency.

These books were signs of the times in the kinds of leaders they identified. Similar canvasses at other times would have had quite different results. In 1900, for instance, almost everyone would have agreed on Booker T. Washington, but beyond him most white people would have been ignorant and most black people would have disagreed. Or, in the mid-1970s, it would be impossible to draw up such a list without including those with precise constituencies—politicians and leaders of community-based organizations—while intellectuals, artists, and ministers-as-college-presidents would have lost status. These differences reflect several things: the changed perceptions of Afro-Americans and the society in general, the changes brought by experience in politics and social interaction, the changed self-definition of blacks, their changed goals and strategies, and the changed realities—political, economic, and demographic—of the Afro-American people.

At best it is a difficult matter to identify a group's leadership. We are seldom certain what we are looking for. As for the Afro-American, much of the historical leadership is lost to us because we have not been much interested in the process by which individuals such as Harriet Tubman— or the numberless anonymous black men and women who helped to organize the underground railroad or to disrupt the administration of the antebellum fugitive slave laws—were identified and accepted by others as leaders. We have focused on the *hero* rather than on the *process*. Thus, even the names of the courageous men and women who formed the Loyalty Leagues during Reconstruction and the "Redemption," who tried to keep alive the political voice of blacks in the South, braving the violence of the Klan, are lost to us. Their fate was generally an early grave, unknown and unsung. We have not, even with the arrival of sophisticated social science techniques, chosen to examine the "little community" with an eye to discovering how and under what circumstances leadership emerges on a neighborhood level. The Afro-American leader has almost always been thought of as one who had weight in the "large community." That is why books like Embree's and Logan's made sense.

We are never clear in distinguishing between leadership and achievement. Edwin Embree's thirteen were certainly "tops" in their fields, they had made it against great odds, but only a few of them could be considered leaders in any programmatic sense. Successful black men and women were naturally applauded by Afro-Americans in general, because they showed possibilities that might otherwise have been in doubt and because they stood as symbols of the race. Thus, a black millionaire in the early decades of the twentieth century, like Madame C. J. Walker, could generate the same respect as a hero of atheletic contests. But, like Jack Johnson, Joe Louis, and Mohammed Ali, such respect did not imply goals or strategies for the race's betterment nor a group that was willing to follow.[5] We should not be surprised that achievement evoked resentment as well as respect. Much was expected of black men and women of prominence. They were to "lead," to be agents of change. But in reality their influence was quite limited and their efforts for the race frustrated, resulting in the appearance of empty pretensions. Thus black people might applaud them as leaders of the race at one moment and dismiss them as "dicty" at the next.

We have assumed that a significant black leadership began to emerge in the antebellum period—centering in the convention and abolitionist movements—and came to maturity in four decades between 1890 and 1930. We have thought of a personal leadership, the mantle shifting from Frederick Douglass to Booker T. Washington to W. E. B. DuBois as each leader passed. And, despite the problems to such a model posed by the development of national protest organizations such as the NAACP and the Urban League, in which policy necessarily became corporate and not individual, we have identified the black chief administrators (the Walter Whites, the Roy Wilkinses, the Whitney Youngs) by virtue of their places in the organizations, ignoring the question of the base of their support in the Afro-American population. Of course, the advent of Dr. Martin Luther King, Jr., reminds us that an individual may personify so completely and perfectly the spirit and ideals of a movement or epoch that he becomes leader by common consent. Twentieth century developments have made it more difficult for us to personify leadership. Activities on behalf of the race have become the province of organizations. Government, local and national, has become so highly bureaucratized, and blacks have become so dispersed within government, that it is impossible to imagine a single "Negro advisor" to the President. Thus, we can hardly expect to find, after World War I, a personality to dominate the age as Booker T. Washington did his.

Scanning the past, searching for the personal leader, historians have focused on the era dominated by Booker T. Washington and W. E. B. DuBois as the coming-of-age of Afro-American leadership. Since the two men articulated so clearly (in full respect of complexity) the Afro-American psychological, social, economic, and political predicament, we have been satisfied by that assessment. But from the point of view of the generation of the 1970s, which does not share those men's faith that ultimate justice is available within the system, their leadership between 1890 and 1930 appears as an interlude of great indulgence and good will (albeit forced), breaking a dominant current of distrust in the system's ability to reform itself without the force of power coming into play. Seen in this light, the attitudes, tactics, and style of black protest from the depression years, culminating in the civil rights movement in the 1960s, has more in common with the convention movements of the 1840s and 1850s, the underground railroad, and the obstruction of the fugitive slave laws than they do with the Washington-DuBois era.[6] Of course, the mid-twentieth century movements have been informed and affected by the interlude of "soft" protest, but they returned more and more to antebellum views on the need for power and direct action to bring about necessary changes in the American society.

It is useful, nevertheless, to focus on the roles of Booker T. Washington and W. E. B. DuBois, for they and the era in which they dominated serve to illustrate the predicament of all Afro-American leadership, whatever the time or assumptions. All leaders have had to contend with a caste-like arrangement separating the races, defying all strategies. That is to say, race relations in the United States presumed a system of a dominant white and a subordinate black group, where there might be parallel social stratification but where the bar would remain immutable along racial lines. In practice it meant that blacks were not accepted as part of the political process; even where they were allowed to vote they were not given entrée to the political machinery. Their participation as citizens was so circumscribed that the instruments of neither political nor economic power would be in their hands. It is in this caste-like reality that the styles and strategies of black leadership have been defined over time.

Although caste has been used by others to define the special relationship of the Afro-American to the white society,[7] it is well to make clear that there are differences between American racial practices and the classical caste arrangements such as have existed in India. The most important difference is that in the United States there has always been a presumption of equality, which is not the case in classical caste societies.

All Americans would deny that constitutional inequality characterized their society, and blacks, quite unlike the classical low-caste person, have accepted an inferior status as neither just nor permanent. Nevertheless, the difference between principle and practice in American history in regard to white-black relations is too dramatic to ignore. It has only been in the last twenty years that the laws and official practices that sustained inequality as custom have been rescinded. Presumptions of inequality in social practice (in one guise or another) persist. Throughout our history, blacks have been considered "outlaws" in the sense that they could become victims of violence and vigilante groups without any expectation of protection from established peace officers. Until World War II, thirty-one of the states had laws prohibiting intermarriage, protecting the dominant group from loss of identity.[8] Even in northern cities, where blacks had the vote, the major political machines have preferred to leave them unorganized rather than share power with them.[9] While it can be said that caste, as one thinks of it in India, cannot be used to define the black American's position, the word does help to make important distinctions between the experiences of white and black Americans. And it marks the crucial difference between the experiences of Afro-Americans and white ethnics. Ignoring these distinctions, some scholars have been too sanguine about the ease with which blacks could move into the mainstream of American life.[10] Caste, as I use it, is not mere rhetoric; it denotes the special and persistent subordination of Afro-Americans which has made certain leadership styles inescapable. Barring the word "caste," we would have to invent a new word.

Caste is the principal determinant of any discussion of historical Afro-American leadership. It defined the styles and possible strategies. The white and black groups were separate to be sure, the one dominant and the other subordinate, but they were not independent. While the separation suggested the possibility of a kind of "nationalism" on the part of blacks, the system would not tolerate the development of racial power blocks. Thus, in whatever other ways the dominated caste might mirror the dominant, separate political machinery was not one of them.[11]

Despite differences of class and culture, blacks were easily viewed by whites as a monolith and, for practical purposes, outside the body politic. It was convenient to imagine an individual or two who might be called the "Negro Leadership." They might be persons of notable achievement, respect, and reputation who could be understood to speak for the race. Lacking mechanism for popular choice, such people simply "rose to the top." This pattern is in many ways suggestive of styles of management by colonial powers. Some have referred to such leadership style as clientage or patron-client politics.[12] There was no expectation that a black leadership would arise from the people and be selected and sustained by them.

Between 1890 and 1930, the interlude of "soft" protest, caste imposed two styles on black leadership. From his position in schools, church, or journalism, the spokesman for the race could be an advocate of social change, envisioning a caste-less society where all artificial and arbitrary barriers were removed and all men and women would be able to rise according to merit. Such leaders were of a reformist mode, leaders more of a movement than of a race. While the focus of their reform was racial, the audience was understood to be all right-thinking men and women, regardless of race. Such reform leaders were not uniformly applauded by whites. Monroe Trotter, of Boston, was thought too outspoken and "radical." W. E. B. DuBois was seldom on good terms even with his white colleagues in the NAACP. Others, like James Weldon Johnson or Walter White, seemed more congenial. Regardless of how whites felt about them, prominent black reformers were acknowledged as "spokesmen."

There were those, on the other hand, who attained prominence and respect, often by remarkable personal achievement, whose principal concern was not reform but the effective manipulation of the system. Caste patterns, and the continued subordination of blacks to whites, was accepted as real, perhaps inevitable. One needed to find ways to serve oneself and one's race in terms of that reality. Such men, who were to serve as leaders, had first to be recognized by white men of power as exceptional persons who had influence in the black caste. Such leaders became conduits through which whites channeled their patronage and philanthropy to blacks. It was much easier and more efficient to deal with one such spokesman than it would be to respond to the multiple interests that actually comprised the group.

To act on the assumption that there was one "Negro leader" was, in effect, to capsulate, externalize, and alienate the group from the body politic. Such leaders, who were so identified and used, necessarily became influential and powerful figures among blacks. But they were not products of popular choice, and what power they wielded was that of the white politicians and philanthropists they served. They were, thus, emblems of the black caste, and I call their style emblematic as opposed to reformist.[13] The capital example of this mode was Booker T. Washington, who combined genius, character, great personal vision, and opportunism to bring the emblematic style to perfection. But every city and town having a black population was likely to have its own such figure, most often lacking in Washington's redeeming features.[14]

Seldom was any leader exclusively reformist or emblematic throughout his career. Frederick Douglass, for instance, had both charateristics, reformist predominating the antebellum years and emblematic toward the end of his life. And men of compellingly reformist bent, such as W. E. B. DuBois, showed evidence of being open to invitation to advise white men of power. While not mutually exclusive styles, they do characterize black leadership from Reconstruction to the onset of World War II.[15]

This was a leadership of personality. Never did such men work to organize black voters. While many talked of a time when the "Negro vote" would make a difference, few wanted to solicit that vote, and most were distrustful of those, like Marcus Garvey, who appealed directly to black masses.[16] They were something of an anomaly in an age of urban political machines, when the spoils of political office were being parcelled among white ethnics, and when ethnocentric and caste patterns were being institutionalized into public and civil service cadres and labor unions. Lacking power, excepting that of their white patrons, there was no basis for the kind of coalition politics fondly imagined by those who speak of an American pluralism. Caste does not make coalitions. The best that could be expected was antagonistic cooperation across caste lines. The situation was fraught with contradictions and dilemmas for the black leader.

Three characteristics marked the black leader: he did not derive his power from a democratic source, he was a self-styled exemplar, and his position was tenuous and vulnerable. This last feature resulted from the other two, but it was his role as paragon that was to place special limits on the Afro-American leader. He had to be acceptable in polite society, not threatening to decorum and order. He was to illustrate to whites that blacks could be respected and successful citizens and set an example to blacks of propriety, decency, and achievement.

After the Civil War there would have certainly been a consensus that Frederick Douglass was the single black leader of national stature, even though there were several blacks who held, for a time, important public office. Douglass had played a forceful and assertive role in the abolitionist movement. The Union victory, tied as it was to emancipation, was the ultimate triumph of Douglass's position. He was an extraordinary man; his life comprised slavery, escape, freedom, and public renown as a speaker and writer. He symbolized the dreams and hopes of the freedman. When American presidents, from Grant through Harrison, wanted to demonstrate their administration's recognition of blacks and their obeisance to the ideals of the war, they found a good symbol in Douglass. Of course, other blacks got political jobs, but with Douglass it was something more than mere political appointments.

After Douglass's death, the consensus passed to Booker T. Washington. There might have been other claimants, but Washington had special virtues.[17] As principal and founder of Tuskegee Institute, he was clearly working for the uplift of the freedman; he was a demonstrated builder, leader, and administrator. Furthermore, Tuskegee was a black institution (although supported by white funds), and its principles and goals seemed to accept and validate the de facto system of racial castes. In fund-raising for Tuskegee, Washington was in useful contact with very wealthy, powerful, and influential white men and women. While Washington did not have a power base in a political sense, he had in Tuskegee an institutional base which freed him from a primary dependency on anyone's political fortunes. Washington always, indeed, declared himself to be free of political motives and ambitions—keeping Tuskegee away from overt partisanship. Washington was also a southerner, his place and future was to be in the South where the bulk of the black population was to remain for decades and where one imagined the locus of the "Negro problem." Time also worked to Washington's advantage. With the death of Douglass, February 20, 1895, the representative of that generation of abolitionists and antebellum activists had passed. The resulting question of succession came at precisely the moment of Booker T. Washington's ascendency as an important national figure. Tuskegee had already proved successful, and Washington was already spending much time away on speaking and fund-raising tours. But the single most important event in Washington's career was to occur in September of the year of Douglass's death. It was then that he delivered his famous address at the Atlanta Exposition, affirming a prosperous New South based on caste arrangements. It would have been, from the moment of that speech, impossible to have challenged his claim as successor to Douglass. And, finally, Washington had the ability, despite controversy among blacks, to keep their loyalty and support.

Neither Douglass nor Washington were products of a democratic process, nor were they chosen by their people to be spokesmen. Rather, it was as if one day Afro-Americans awoke to find someone everyone concurred was their leader and whom no one in his right mind would challenge. Since there was no effective political apparatus for blacks, how could it have been otherwise?

Few would have expected a different kind of leadership from the one that emerged. Their role was the uplifting of a downtrodden people. Thus, it was a leadership of aristocratic and elitist assumptions, not democratic ones. The black leader should not be one of his people; he should, alas, be better than his people. "It is not enough to have rights, but one must deserve and earn them," was a sentiment repeated so much by Washington and his white and black contemporaries as to become cant. It cast onto the Afro-American the task—required of no immigrant from Europe—that he prove himself deserving of the rights which the revolutionary fathers had declared to be natural and unalienable to all men.

It was in this context that black leaders served as exemplars, presenting themselves as living proof that blacks could perform as citizens in ways that were above reproach. They could, thus, serve as agents of white society's philanthropy and good will, and they could serve blacks as a symbol of racial pride and self-esteem. This exemplary characteristic of black leadership made for very limited possibilities.

An exemplar could not make the mistakes of normal men or democratic leaders. Consider Frederick Douglass's problems with the Freedmen's Bank.[18] As one of the trustees of the bank (he was made president in its final weeks), he had seen it as a practical instrument for improving the condition of freedmen. The newly freed slaves had to be taught and encouraged to save, and this bank was an especially attractive opportunity because it would allow black men to serve as officers and to learn to manage finance. Even the bank's magnificent Washington offices were inspirational. The success of the bank would be both an example of and a means for black achievement. But, alas, the Freedmen's Bank fell in the wake of the bank failures set off by the collapse of Jay Cooke & Company in 1873. Like any other bank failure of the time, those with small savings were most vulnerable, but more was the pity that with this bank many of the savings were the freedmen's first meager efforts at accumulation. Most of the officers of the bank, seeing the coming collapse, were able to make timely withdrawals, thus, cutting their personal losses. Douglass could not. The loss of the bank, to him, was a personal and racial setback as well as an institutional failure. As a black man and president, he was embarrassed. He did not want to abandon his people; he had to try to preserve his honor.

It is also in this light that one understands Booker T. Washington's insistence that neither scandal nor criticism fall on Tuskegee. It explains the autocratic character of his administration at the school, where the staff and the students were forever on display to local and distant white visitors. And we see this quality when we read the autobiographies of Douglass and Washington. So much did they see their lives as *public* that there was little room in their imaginations for *private, personal* reflection and self-criticism.

The exemplary role also perpetuated assumptions of racial inferiority; not a constitutional or genetic inferiority of blacks to whites, but a recognition that the present status of blacks was marked by a lack in education, industrial skills, cultural refinements, and experience in government. It presumed the need for uplift. Necessarily, such leaders were cast as apologists for the race. "It may be true," they would say, "that our present status is lowly, but there will come a time when we will earn and, therefore, deserve our proper place in your respect."

Ultimately, the exemplary black leader was enmeshed in contradictions. He was assumed to be exceptional. Could a handful of such exceptional leaders do more than mark the distance between themselves and the masses? Often implied in their autobiographies (explicit in *Up from Slavery*) was the notion of the self-made man, who by dint of character and commitment overcame the odds; while the inequities and handicaps were real enough, sound character and methods had been surpassing. Doubtless Afro-Americans could be thrilled by the stories of such individual black achievement, but one could not help but suppose that those who remained lowly were lacking something in character. Thus, the blame for continued poverty could be turned inward and become personal or racial fault rather than remain outwardly focused on circumstances and the system. Such leaders were, therefore, speechless before the comments they invited: "You made it, so it isn't impossible; why not the others?" and "But you are an exception; one cannot expect much from the others."

Booker T. Washington's rise to prominence and influence epitomizes the mode of emblematic leadership. His teachers, those who had a shaping influence on his life such as Mrs. Viola Ruffner of Malden and General Samuel Chapman Armstrong of Hampton Institute, were strong-willed, tough, self-righteous Yankee missionaries who were certain of the proper formula for Negro uplift. This formula reduced itself to the familiar Protestant virtues: industry, frugality, cleanliness, temperance, order, decorum, and punctuality. With such traits, men and women (even freed-men) could do what they set out to do; or, failing, could at least be of good character. The message was attractive, even compelling, to men and women like Washington because it was so reasonable, clear, and simple; and it focused on self-improvement and self-reliance rather than on con-ditions of inequity which one might have been powerless to change. The characteristics that were celebrated were conveniently opposite to traits ascribed to the typical freedman. It was easy to assume that if the freed-man only learned these virtues, all would be well. The formula had mor-ality, almost a religious quality; success went to the deserving. And the ministers who preached this gospel to Washington were so certain and self-assured as to be truly overpowering.

It should be remembered that this gospel formed a major part of the conventional wisdom and lore of American culture. It was reiterated throughout: from McGuffey's readers, to Orison Swett Marsden, to Rev-erend Russell Conwell, to Horatio Alger, to Andrew Carnegie. It pre-empted any consideration of compensation for blacks or any other group that might have been exploited unfairly in the past. And, most impor-tantly as far as race was concerned, since any useful reform was personal and focused on character, this formula in no way challenged racial caste patterns.

The significance of this education and background is in the way it pre-pared Washington to function within the system of caste. His special suc-cess was in his ability, emotionally and ideologically, to make the most of it that anyone could, more than most would have dreamed possible. His was a schooling in the narrowest form of pragmatism, where even the smallest success and achievement became the object. There was little room for speculation or concern about what *should be*, rather one dis-ciplined one's mind to what *was* and what *was possible*. It was a training for a narrow maneuvering within given and unchallenged limits. Defer-ring ethical considerations, it appeared as opportunism.

One of the difficulties of assessing Washington's real character is the unquestioning and unself-conscious way he made himself an evangelist of the gospel of wealth and success. It would seem that he shaped himself to be a model of that prescription. Knowing the importance of appear-ance, we suspect that there was a private Booker, calculating his public image and managing himself to appear right before the world. The public Booker T. Washington was only a mask. But it is difficult to verify such suspicions. Recent scholarship has demonstrated that there was more to Washington than he allowed to meet the eye. He initiated and supported, anonymously and often in the most deceptive guises, court cases and projects designed to reverse trends of disfranchisement and racial vio-lence in the South. But he was forever careful to protect his public image, and true to the emblematic style, he was ruthless against those who took more forceful public positions, who were agitators likely to antagonize white friends and supporters.[19]

As an emblematic leader, Washington accepted caste patterns and was fundamentally in conflict with those of the reformist mode. There could, therefore, be little tolerance among the Washington loyalists for black leaders and organizations who were critical of caste. There were organizations and agitation for specific reforms, such as for federal antilynching legislation. There were those organizations, heirs to the antebellum convention movement, like the Afro-American League and the Afro-American Council, that would agitate for general reform. The Washington faction's style was to mute such agitation and to keep the appearance of a united black community under the leadership of Washington; one dare not frighten away white friends. In practice, the Washington faction, under the leader's specific instructions, worked within such organizations to see that nothing really happened. In effect, to disarm them.[20]

On the other hand, organizations that Washington thought might be useful, like the National Negro Business League, he was quick to take under his control and help support. Such practices had a deadening effect on black protest organizations into the twentieth century. Those who began the Niagra Movement criticized the Washington group not so much for philosophy as for the stultifying effects they had on others who would choose different paths. Many, including W. E. B. DuBois, thought it possible to have several different, coexisting strategies. But Washington's instincts were correct. The emblematic leader survives best in a world of peace and complacency, and, above all, a good emblematic leader must be peerless.

When W. E. B. DuBois criticized Booker T. Washington, it was in part for his tendency to stand mute before the great indignities against black people. But, more pointedly, DuBois attacked Washington's program of education because it lacked any sense of a need to train a black leadership. To compete in the work-a-day world, one need merely be fitted with a useful trade and with industrious habits and attitudes; the rest would take care of itself. And, since Washington presumed not to change caste patterns, he saw only mischief from the kind of leaders DuBois would have. As a reformist, antagonistic to caste arrangements, DuBois wanted a cadre of college- and university-trained men and women who would challenge customary racial attitudes.

It may have been unfortunate that DuBois used the term "talented tenth" to describe this group of leaders, because he has since been accused of elitism as against the assumed humility of Washington. Certainly, DuBois was elitist in that he expected that only highly intelligent and educated black leaders could design and bring about effective reform.

But Booker T. Washington was elitist in his own way, believing that blacks needed to be lifted up and that men like himself would be their models. Of the two, DuBois was the more at ease with notions of political democracy where even the unlettered and soiled would have the vote. When Washington wrote of rural blacks, his language was often heavy with condescension. On the other hand, some of the most moving passages of DuBois's *Souls of Black Folk*, are informed by his respect for the honor and dignity of a rural, unlettered people struggling futilely to better themselves. Both men were elitists, but whereas DuBois called forth superior black men and women, demanding that their superiority be respected by whites as well as blacks, Washington's superior black would be properly humble, acting in deference within the precincts of caste.

A product of nineteenth century higher education at Harvard and Berlin, DuBois fed on romanticism both from New England transcendentalism and the German source. It was, therefore, no contradiction to celebrate both the exceptional man and the immanent spirit in the souls of all black folk. It had been that spirit which sustained their humanity through generations of enslavement, and it would be its redemptive spark in the days of trial that followed freedom. That humanity had to be honored; there could be no compromise. DuBois saw the educated mind being able to transcend the mundane, ugly, and contentious circumstances so that one could feel a personal superiority whatever others thought. His dominant metaphor for the educational process in *Souls of Black Folk* is that of climbing a steep and rugged mountain. At the top, one would be buoyed and exhilarated by the experience of great personal achievement, and one would be open to the grand vistas of all past human experience and knowledge. That, in itself, would belie all superstitions and tendentious arguments justifying racial caste. Black men and women had to win at the white man's games—law, science, the arts, finance, business; it was not enough to be trained in useful trades.[21]

W. E. B. DuBois was correct in seeing the close relationship between questions of leadership for Afro-Americans and systems of training and higher education. Colleges defined leadership characteristics. In the years following World War I, several black colleges witnessed uprisings of students, faculty, and alumni protesting their schools' failure to promote black leaders.

Raymond Wolters has recently brought the stories of these campus struggles into a single volume.[22] Black schools, colleges, and universities had continued patterns of management and control from the late nineteenth century. Most were sustained by northern white philanthropy; some were church supported. Howard University was supported by yearly congressional appropriations, while Lincoln of Missouri received

state funds. Of the schools that Wolters discusses, Wilberforce, alone, was
in theory supported by a black organization, the A.M.E. Church. All of
these schools, to a greater or lesser extent, had the tutelage of the inferior as their institutional purpose. Most were little better than high schools.
It was strongly held that training for the liberal professions was likely
to be a waste of time, if not dangerous. All insisted that black students
needed the closest supervision in matters of morals and social discipline,
and, therefore, instituted regulations for student conduct considered
excessively strict even for that time. Except for Tuskegee, where Washington had maintained a tradition of a black-dominated staff, these
schools seemed to prefer white teachers and administrators and would
have presumed it unwise to have had a black president.

It makes little difference whether these habits were from genuinely
felt need or whether they were merely calculated to placate a white
society that was indifferent and even hostile to black pretentions to quality in education. The black faculty and administrators, students, and
alumni felt them to be holdovers from the Reconstruction era, vestiges of
a system of tutelage where the students were never expected to emerge
as men and women of real responsibility. Most of the protests were
against such a mentality, and for the most part they succeeded in opening
the way for the more general employment of black teachers and administrators, the eventual choice of black presidents at schools like Howard
and Fiske, and some easing of parental regulations.

The struggle at Tuskegee was different in an important way. The issue
there was the staffing and direction of the newly established Veterans'
Administration Hospital. Consistent with caste patterns, it had been difficult for black veterans ot receive care in normal facilities, especially in
the South. The government decided that a hospital for blacks should be
established, and that it should be in the South at Tuskegee. It was
assumed by President Robert Russa Moton and other black spokesmen
that blacks could, at least, reap the limited benefits of caste: employment
of black staff and administrators in top positions of responsibility as well
as in subordinate positions. The chief administrator certainly should be
black. This seemed even more likely as Tuskegee had always been under
black administration with a predominantly black staff.

But white Alabamans and other white southerners were caught in a
dilemma. They did not approve of blacks being cared for in white hospitals or by white nurses. Yet, they were not prepared to concede easily
to the presence among them of a highly professional cadre of black medical personnel. Whites were in the habit of assuming that such jobs
belonged to them. And while they might have been persuaded to accept
all of this as one of the realities of caste, they wanted at least to be pla-
cated by having a white man in charge of the institution. It was a class-

ical dilemma of American racial caste: separate institutions are fine, but it is extremely hard to allow the inferior caste the implied power and perogatives.

Tuskegee managed to win its point. Its medical and administrative staffs were to be black, and the chief administrator and medical officer was to be black as well. But the story of the Tuskegee Veterans' Hospital and the struggles on the black campuses in the 1920s illustrate the difficulties for the subordinated caste to find in separate institutions the means of developing and training a leadership cadre that would be free to manage those institutions independently.

The realities of racial caste patterns forced all who would aspire to black leadership to confront several dilemmas, those who would attack caste as reformers or those who would exploit caste as emblems. For to deny caste was likely to mean denying the potential power in race as well. It was difficult to imagine how one could achieve a society free from racial discrimination in which all had a fair chance on the basis of merit through the use of organized racial power. Yet any significant reform, from the elimination of discriminatory laws to an antilynching bill, was only likely to come as a result of organized political pressure. Reformist leaders tended to shy away from the political organization of the black vote, even in northern cities where that might have been possible. Rather, they tended to place themselves in reform-oriented organizations such as the NAACP and the Urban League, to work with white allies to improve conditions and bring about a better society. The favored tactic of legal tests in the courts was attractive because there seemed to be visible results and because it conformed to a notion of reform coming from justice rather than from power. For obvious reasons, reformers looked askance at those who would mobilize blacks along racial lines. Racialist leadership, after all, contradicted the ultimate goal of a society that was color blind.[23]

Emblematic leaders were no less victims of dilemma. Accepting the reality of caste, one had to accept the de facto supremacy and authority of whites. To the mind of the pragmatist-opportunist, de facto implies de jure. Even the presumed advantage of apartheid, where blacks are free to build and to control their own institutions, has to be qualified by the necessary white dominance. Nor could the emblematic leader be comfortable with the political organization of blacks, for his status depended upon a complacent "constituency." Even the most modest political organization would lead to pressure and demands for change that the emblematic leader would not be able to deliver.

These dilemmas could be torturous, as illustrated in the many twists and turns in the development of W. E. B. DuBois's political thought. He was fundamentally opposed to caste. He saw the capital problem of the twentieth century to be the "color line" and was certainly not tailored to the emblematic role. Yet, he could give his support to a segregated officer's training camp in World War I because it meant the possibility of commissioning black officers. He could applaud the establishment of the Veterans' Hospital at Tuskegee because it opened positions of authority to black professionals. And, frustrated by the intransigeance of race in America, he could articulate one of the earliest and clearest positions for black nationalism.[24] It wasn't easy to be a black leader.

There were men who attempted to defy these modes and, instead, would use black organization as an instrument of change. A. Philip Randolph saw his Brotherhood of Sleeping Car Porters as such a lever.[25] He tried to keep that organization free from white financial support and white dominance. He imagined that his Brotherhood, as an Afro-American union within the AFL, could bring about change. As a member of the AFL's councils, he imagined that he could prod the American labor movement to open itself to blacks. "A movement within a movement," he liked to say. At the session at which the Brotherhood was admitted into the Federation, Randolph warned its members that he intended to be a "spearhead which will make possible the organization of Negro workers." Without minimizing Randolph's influence, it is fair to say that by the 1960s the AFL was still the bastion of caste as well as of craft unionism.

Others, perceiving the intractibleness of race, took a different course. Numbers of Afro-Americans have advocated some form of expatriation or escape from American society with its castes and its dilemmas. Names like Paul Cuffee, the early Martin Delany, Bishop Alexander Crummel, Bishop Henry McNeil Turner, and Marcus Garvey come to mind. There are others, and we might place among them those "nationalists" who have dreamed of (and on occasion built) separate black communities in the United States.

While I have focused on the "large community" in this discussion of black leadership between 1890 and 1930, this analysis pertains to the "small community" as well. For no city or town, north or south, with a significant black population was without its emblematic or reform leaders. They might vary in effectiveness, competence, and character, but they played similar roles. During this interlude of "soft" protest, these leaders were not challenged by black political organization or by white politicians who wanted to win the black vote. Except for Chicago, where blacks were included in the political machine as early as 1915,[26] white bosses preferred the emblematic leader to an organized black constituency. It was only as late as 1944 that Adam Clayton Powell, taking advantage of the disarray of Tammany, was able to carve out for himself a stable political constituency which would keep him in office until his forced removal in 1968.

Doubtless this exceptional use of political power brought more services, amenities, and jobs to blacks than they might otherwise have received. Yet, by World War II, blacks in no way reflected their numbers in police and fire departments, and jobs in public transportation were all but closed to them. Even in New York and Chicago today, caste marks with unerring definition the civil service administrations and staffs. Regardless of their numbers in these cities, power and policy are not in the hands of blacks.

Local, emblematic leaders, those who would be most likely to affect the day-to-day lives of black people, would not be identified by such books as Edwin Embree's or Rayford Logan's. They were not likely to be known outside their communities, and they were not likely to be seen as being extraordinary achievers. Yet they were more typical of Afro-American leadership before World War II than those who would be named by a canvas of two hundred white and black "who know the group best." But as early as the 1930s we can detect changes in style and attitude that would challenge the reformist and emblematic modes and that would move ultimately to the assumption of power rather than prestige as the instrument of reform.

An attitude of defiance, which had been common among the abolitionists, was rekindled in the 1930s and marked an end to the era of "soft" protest. It was strikingly evident in the depression decade, persisted during the war years, and literally exploded in the 1960s. Since World War II the language of black politics has been amplified in crecendoes of *demands* rather than *hopes*. The word "demand" was hardly in the vocabulary of black leaders until the 1930s. Those who announced a "New Negro" in the 1920s spoke of black "militancy" and of fighting back against white violence, they often warned of dire consequences from continued neglect and duplicity on the part of white leaders, but none of them demanded anything.[27]

Demands imply power, and most black reformers knew that the little power they had was in the logic of their positions and the morality of their claim. It depended, therefore, upon the perception, moral sensitivity, and conscience of whites. Little changed in the real power of blacks in the 1960s, but there was a new attitude among Afro-Americans: a willingness, like their abolitionist forebears, to break the peace and to become agents of disorder.

The tactic of direct action brought into play a power always implicit in democratic politics. The ability to make a public display, to embarrass, to disrupt, to overburden jails and courts is power of a certain kind. It gives politicians who would otherwise be unmoved a sense of crisis and the excuse to act. It can persuade a normally complacent public to at least remain complacent while reforms are enacted which might restore the peace. With little actual political clout and a willingness to use direct action, a minority can win limited objectives.

The willingness of black leaders and reform organizations to take direct action was rather slow in coming. Until the 1940s the style and rhetoric was similar to that of other progressives, relying on the exposure of inequities, agitation through journals, alliances with influencial white liberals, and lobbying for favorable legislation. What was to become the prevalent tactic of court tests of discriminatory laws and practices was begun in the late nineteenth century, gaining dominance until its ultimate triumph in 1954. All the while, it was hoped that blacks would in time form a sufficient political weight to be effective in national and local politics. Little was done by black progressives, however, to organize the black voter. The closest that they would come to direct action were the various protest parades, calling attention to the rise in racial violence against blacks around World War I. But even these "demonstrations" were statements of moral outrage, were themselves quite circumspect, and were not at all intended as confrontations.[28]

While the organizers of the NAACP saw themselves as evoking the abolitionist tradition, while they shared the earlier sense of moral purpose and the racially mixed membership, they had a crucial element that their forebears lacked. The NAACP founders believed in the fundamental rightness of the American society and in the system's ability to reform itself. To them, racial inequities were a fault, but a sound system and essentially right-thinking people would ultimately correct them. Most of the abolitionists, on the other hand, knew that slavery was evil, that it was protected in the Constitution, that it corrupted the entire social fabric, and that it would not simply disappear. Abolitionists often claimed a "higher law" than the laws of the nation which sustained slavery, and most were prepared for direct action to defy those laws. Slaves, like Frederick Douglass, who ran away, stealing their freedom, blacks and whites who served the underground railroad, who defied federal officers enforcing fugitive slave statutes, who gave money (or their lives) for the raid on Harper's Ferry, these were agents of direct action. There was little of that in the NAACP.

Few blacks or whites by the 1930s were prepared to take the position that a corrupt nation and corrupt laws and practices deserve no respect, or that civil disobedience was the proper course for the righteous. Most would have insisted that the reformer not only be personally above reproach, but that he should not adopt tactics or language that would fail a test of propriety. Above all else, black people should be models of rationality, decorum; they must be the most unflinching supporters of law and order. It must be the racist opposition that would be cast as demagogues and law breakers. While this position could result in a sense of moral superiority and self-satisfaction, it did not move a nation to act against lynchers, rioters, or those who would deprive blacks of their citizenship rights. Neither did it open to Afro-Americans jobs, better housing, or schools. And while the legal tactic achieved striking and important victories in the courts, it was impotent to translate the de jure to de facto.

The narrowness of life in the 1930s sparked a different kind of black reaction. The riot in the urban ghetto, striking against merchants and police, was first evidenced in that decade. The Harlem riot of 1935 foreshadowed in style and character those which would erupt in the 1960s. The Harlem community had been deeply shaken by the Depression. Before the "crash," Harlem had been a symbol of Afro-American optimism and possibility. Despite the poverty that was there even in the 1920s, there were clear signs of a developing middle class of professionals and working people. Blacks had equity in over 35 percent of Harlem real estate. But with an unemployment rate that was as much as three times that of whites and a chronic difficulty of capital accumulation, most of that promise had been wiped away by the 1940s. The Harlem riot of 1935 seems too familiar to us now. It was spontaneous, as if the people just exploded into violence. It was hard to equate the apparent cause with the magnitude of the reaction. No one seemed responsible for it. Some wanted to blame the Communist Party, but in the end all agreed that people were just fed up. In that instance, as was to become the case in the 1960s, black leaders neither provoked, nor led, nor controlled, nor ended the outburst. Their role, at best, was to explain the phenomenon to white officials and the public.[29]

The Communist Party, in its efforts to organize blacks in Harlem, while by no means the instigators of changes in attitude and tactics, serves to illustrate the new mood. There were forms of direct action by blacks in several northern cities. For instance, the "buy black" campaigns were effective in Chicago and New York. Such efforts were lead by "nationalist" types like Sufi Abdul Hamid in uneasy alliance with some black ministers. They tended to be local, however, with little larger political importance. The Communist Party, however, tapped into such issues as employment for blacks in Harlem, attempting to make it a wedge of white-black cooperation in the labor movement. The Party used direct-action tactics to frustrate the evictions of blacks from their tenements, moving furniture and belongings back into the dwelling after they had been placed on the street by city or county officers. In such action, as well as in parades and demonstrations (often without a permit) black and white Communists were attacked and bloodied often enough by the police. It was the Communist organization and press, then, that joined in the standard and chronic black complaint against police brutality. In

all of this, the Communist Party seemed in the forefront of changing attitudes about proper and effective protest.[30]

The NAACP's embarrassment over the Scottsboro case illustrates
another aspect of this shift in attitude. The Communist Party took over
the defense of the Scottsboro boys from the outset. Despite acrimony
and repeated charges that the Party was cynically using the boys and
their parents, the NAACP was never able to wrest the case completely
from the Party's control. The NAACP was simply too slow in acting. It
was always very careful in the investigation of cases before taking them
on and equally careful in the choice of legal staff and preparation of
briefs. Generally, its cases were argued by conservative white lawyers
whose strength was in their prestige and experience and who were careful not to antagonize legal authority. The Communist Party, on the other
hand, was not burdened by such fastidiousness. It was a corrupt and
oppressive society that should be on trial, not the black youths. The speed
with which the Party's lawyers could act, the directness and simplicity of
its stand, was responsible for gaining the confidence of the boys and their
parents. And while the NAACP and other liberal forces persisted in trying to alienate the boys and their parents from the Party's lawyers, they
were never able to succeed. For even black officers, like William Pickens,
found it impossible to disguise a felt superiority to these southern black
peasant folk. After all, their principal argument was that the boys and
their parents were dupes of the Party; that was patronizing enough. So
it was easy to tag the reformists, black and white, as elitists and bourgeois.[31]

The Party's tactics in the case were also at issue. There was little hope
that the Scottsboro case could be won by legal brilliance in the court-
room. Unless the boys could be proved not to have been in the boxcar
with the white girls, or unless the girls could be made to recant (and
even then), there was no chance that the court in the little Alabama
town would move for acquittal. Given procedural correctness, one could
not depend on the United States Supreme Court to reverse the convictions. With the best legal talent in the world, the Scottsboro youths were
most likely to be executed. Unless, that is, it was made too embarrassing
to do so. So the trial and the case became an international *cause célèbre*,
exposing the ugliness of southern and American justice. The Party
wanted to put southern officials and courts, and the entire American system, on trial before the world. That was not the way the game was normally played. While the tactics justified the charge that the Party was
using the case to serve its larger political interests, it is true, nevertheless,
as many blacks observed, that without such tactics the Scottsboro boys
would have been dead. What was the price of propriety?

Such tactics were not new, nor were they exclusive to the Communist

Party. But they foreshadowed the spirit of direct action used by A. Philip Randolph in "demanding" of Franklin Roosevelt some federal fair employment instrumentation. Randolph threatened a march on Washington, which would certainly embarrass a nation fighting against Nazi racism and disrupt the war effort. In Randolph's March On Washington Movement was the kernel of the direct-action tactics later used by CORE, SNCC, and other groups in the 1960s. It was the same mood and spirit (perhaps with different motivations) that inspired Paul Robeson to announce at the height of the Cold War that Afro-Americans should not fight in a war against the Soviet Union, and for A. Philip Randolph to threaten President Truman with a national appeal for civil disobedience if blacks were drafted into a segregated army.[32] Congress and the President were deeply shaken by such threats. Lacking an emblematic leader of the national stature of Booker T. Washington, congressional committees called upon a wide assortment of "Negro spokesmen" to repudiate Robeson and later Randolph. True to the role, such a figure as Jackie Robinson (newly admitted into a major league system) could be counted on to testify that blacks had always been loyal to the United States and always would be. It was such pressure, nevertheless, that forced President Truman to desegregate the armed forces.[33]

The Brown Decision in 1954, by overturning *Plessy* v. *Fergusson* and the "separate-but-equal" doctrine, shattered the legal and constitutional rationale which had protected racial caste patterns. It would seem that one had only to wait for a law-abiding citizenry to comply for racial justice to be established in the land. But the defenders of caste had never been respectful of the law, as it applied to the rights of blacks. Defiance of the law, civil disobedience, and even mob rule had long been major weapons in their arsenal. Defiance seldom involved risk for them because the coercive power of the state was generally in their hands. Almost in tandem, the defiance and direct action of the protectors of caste provoked new and massive direct action by those who wanted change.

The genius of Martin Luther King and the early leaders of CORE and SNCC was their combining of direct action and civil disobedience with the high moral tone of those on the side of the law (the "higher law" at times) and justice. Nonviolence was the ligament that held these volatile forces in tension. With national TV coverage, even for the most complacent, it was always easy to tell the bad guys from the good guys. It was the bad guys who assassinated black and white, men and women, who burned churches and exploded bombs killing little children. The moral weight could never be questioned. Such direct action provoked crises, it obliged federal response. It is clear enough that the Justice Department, lacking any policy and itself supportive of maintaining caste, was in no way prepared to manage change in a peaceful way. In the vacuum of national leadership, the civil rights organizations were obliged to provoke crises in order to make federal officers approach their duty.[34]

Nonviolent, direct action brought victories but exacted a heavy toll on those in the movement. Lives were lost. There were beatings, harassments, and constant threats against life. It took extraordinary and sustained courage to persist. Certitude in one's moral correctness was hardly enough to feed on. While the action was dramatic, the changes seldom were clear or immediate. Little wonder that many black youths began to wonder if nonviolence was not ineffective and a sign of weakness. But direct action without nonviolence lost its claim to the public conscience and justified retaliation by means of overwhelming public force.

Young black leaders were understandably restive about a movement which was not black in its character and dependency. Like earlier reformist groups, the civil rights organizations, while having strong black leadership, were heavily dependent on white allies, influential whites, and white money. Seldom did these organizations tap down into any black constituency, except as they moved into voter registration in the South. The question could well be raised, Should not black goals and priorities be established by blacks themselves? What would happen if some other issue were to capture the imaginations and the enthusiasm of the white allies, as the Vietnam War was to do? Thus, the cry for "Black Power" reflected the historical need for the political organization of black masses, that their will be articulated though a black leadership. So leaders of the black revolution turned toward building a "positive black consciousness" and to organizing the "black community." The basic distrust of their white allies was merely an awareness that coalitions were impossible without a true power base. The organization of such a power base has been going on in the North and the South since the 1960s, sometimes with and sometimes without the young militants of the civil rights decade.

Direct-action tactics had their limitations. They could provoke complacent people and agencies into action; they could call up public funds to support the community and to keep the peace. Once the edge of moral superiority was lost, or once the public and officials became indifferent to moral appeal, legal force could be used with impunity. And once the threat behind the demands (escalating often to feed mass media's insatiable need for sensation) came to imply violence against police, these public forces could rationalize even preemptive violence against putative assassins. Northern police as well as southern sheriffs could become agents of official murder. And, of course, direct action and civil disobedience had always been the tactics of those who supported caste, and they would be again. Adopting slogans like "white power," "Irish power," "Italian power," and "Hard Hat power," northern whites were willing to use these tactics in northern cities to redraw caste lines in jobs, housing, and schools.

The vitality of caste, surviving the civil rights decade and the black revolution, has been remarkable. Nothing shows it more than the continuing struggle over civil service occupations and standards for employment, and, most of all, the struggle against de facto segregation in the public schools. White opponents of busing have not been subtle in their defense of caste lines. Many are quick to say that race is not an issue. In a way they are right. For it is not a question of whether or not blacks should be admitted into white schools; the question is how many? The term "tipping" is indicative, for at some point the character of the school stops being white and becomes something else. For as the numbers of blacks grow in the student body, they are able to affect the important nonacademic features of the school: its dances (the music and style), its athletics, and even its student government. In schools of small black populations, those blacks who play important roles reflect upon the liberality of the school and the community. But in schools with 35 percent or more, blacks become prominent because they have the power to be. These are often more important issues than academic excellence or the "quality of education" most often talked about.

It is hard to be persuaded that there is a meaningful difference in academic quality between South Boston High and Boston English. Both are pretty bad, as is most of the Boston public school system, victim of more than a decade of acrimonious conflict to protect caste and ethnic prerogatives. Black Bostonians do not have the alternative of accepting caste, saying, "let the Irish have their school, we will have ours under our community's leadership." That has been the argument of those who have placed themselves against "integration." Whites in Boston, in their school committee or in their unions, will be no more willing than their New York counterparts have been to permit the implications of caste which would allow control of institutions (and jobs) to fall into the hands of blacks. So the issue becomes the maintenance of caste under white subordination or the breaking of caste patterns; schools and jobs become the occasions. Blacks in Boston and other northern cities have no alternative but to destroy caste as it is manifested in primary public institutions, even if it means a continued white and middle-class exodus and decline of the cities. Alternatives to that result are not in the hands of blacks at all.

The "tipping" metaphor applies equally to cities as well as to schools. We have seen the exodus of whites (and many middle-class blacks) from cities as the non-white population has increased. Such demographical factors have been said to be central in the general decay of the cities, although there are other factors. But the result in many northern cities has been that blacks have come into their own as an effective political force at a time to inherit growing problems and costs and fewer rewards and opportunities. Be that as it may, the evidence is clear that in the cities, as in the South, black political organization is coming into maturity. Black reformers and those who would be emblems, or stand for the Afro-American people, must give way to the black leader who has popular support and a power base among black people.

Such a result is to be preferred over a leadership of prestige and pretense, but it has problems nevertheless. As the history of ethnically dominated city machines illustrates, political leaders whose power has come from a popular base have not always been equitable or wise in delivering service to their constitutency. That is why white ethnics, although organized and represented for a long time, still feel disaffected, alienated, and powerless. Sophisticated political machinery, as we have good reason to know, is no protection against venality and opportunism of leaders. And as events since the 1950s, and especially Watergate, indicate, real power in the United States has become corporate and plutocratic and is likely to continue to be so. The much awaited advent of political maturity among Afro-Americans may have arrived in time to be an anachronism.

After a century of experience struggling with the reality of caste, where leaders of the black community were only so effective as their reputations, connections, and influence with whites would permit, we are beginning to see evidence of something new. Black officials, elected to local and national office appointed to the high places in state and national administrations, reflect power rather than prestige. The Black Caucus in Congress indicates a consciousness and willingness to use that power as a lever with which to bargain. We will see in the next few years whether caste is sufficiently weakened to allow more than token power in the hands of blacks. Whether or not, or rather to what extent, coalition politics can work across racial lines remains to be seen. Antagonistic cooperation may remain a better description of interracial politics. But the true test of theories of coalition politics had to wait until blacks had the organized political power that could be measured in the balance.

It is well that we applaud the advent of political maturity among Afro-Americans. Yet we must be attentive lest a quality be lost in the process of change. Those leaders who lacked political clout—Booker T. Washington, W. E. B. DuBois, A. Philip Randolph, Martin Luther King, Malcolm X—embodied a vision, passion, and integrity that are generally lacking in the political mechanic. However much we might denigrate the notion of leader as exemplar—as well we should when it is empty of power, pretentious, self-righteous—Americans, white and black, in this post-Watergate era, can only pray for leaders who see their role as public figures to be examples of dignity, honor, and the selflessness of genuine statesmanship. But that is a problem and challenge for the national community, not merely for Afro-Americans.

The analysis of Afro-American leadership in terms of caste patterns illuminates the fundamental difference that race has made in American life. In very few ways can it be said that the Afro-American experience is analogous to that of white ethnics. While all have shared some forms of discrimination, and most may have felt the contempt of their fellow Americans, blacks alone, as a native population, have been systematically excluded from effective political coalitions. If spokesmen for white ethnic groups complain today that their people's aspirations are not being realized, that they feel powerless to control their futures, that they are victims of social and demographic flux, it is not because their groups have been historically excluded from political machines, from labor unions, from power in civil service and government. It may be that their leaders have delivered only superficially, that their definition of group interests has been so parochial and self-serving as to be indifferent to class or community interests. In any case, white ethnics have been all too willing to find primary identity in race and color (even prior to ethnic identity), strongly defending caste and failing to invite linkages where interracial coalitions might be effective.

The standard preoccupations of ethnic leaders have been quite different from those of Afro-Americans. White ethnic leaders have been mainly concerned with the defense of the group—its identity, its culture, its neighborhood—against the acculturating and assimilating vortex of American society. They have also had to struggle with the problems of dual loyalties, to the United States and to the motherland. These problems have never been central to black Americans.

Ironically, ethnic defensiveness is often caused by the ease with which certain groups can assimilate into American society. Foreign language disappears, young people move into the suburbs, customs and the old ways are lost. In a society where class loyalties have been weak, a perceived loss of ethnic coherence can produce anxiety, especially for those who are immobile because of poverty or age and, therefore, unable to move as the neighborhood changes. The sense of a cultural vacuum at the center of American life has provoked what some have called a romantic ethnicity[35] which tries to recapture some elusive quality that has given the group meaning in the past.

The defensive concern of some ethnic leaders sometimes comes from the possibility that the group may disappear. Some Jewish leaders have, therefore, struggled against the trend toward intermarriage. A relatively small ethnic population with a small birthrate, Jews might well imagine that the group may lose numbers and cultural integrity if intermarriage continues at a high rate.

This kind of ethnic defensiveness has not been a major element in the programs of Afro-American leaders. Color, itself, has been a safeguard against the fear that black Americans would disappear. Afro-Americans have made much of having a distinctive culture, but few have worried that it was losing its vitality or integrity. And caste has worked in such a way in America that even the children of intermarriages are additions to the group rather than losses from it. While mulattoes were a distinct category in the United States' censuses from 1850 to 1910, they never had in this country the semiofficial social status enjoyed by their counterparts in the West Indies, Haiti, and Latin America. In the United States, for all practical purposes, one was either black or white. So, while black Americans have had conflicting views about intermarriage (often negative), they have not been motivated the same as white ethnic leaders.[36]

Often, white ethnic leadership has been most pronounced about issues regarding dual loyalties. Events in the motherland naturally inspire sentiment and emotion among those who have migrated and their children. At such times, ethnic leaders have wanted to resolve conflict by identifying with American interests, or, as has been far more often the case, insisting that American interests are identical with the perceived interests of the motherland. Thus, ethnic leadership has been enmeshed in struggles for the Irish Republic, for the German and Allied side in World War I, against communist regimes in Eastern Europe, against Castro in Cuba, and for Israel against its Arab antagonists. It is fair to say that the United States has found it impossible to design a foreign policy since World War II independent of particular ethnic interests.

Black American leaders have been free of this kind of dual loyalty. Like it or not, Afro-Americans' single national identity is with the United States. It is true that there is a propensity to be in sympathy with Third World countries. But Afro-Americans have so far not insisted that the United States' interests are identical with any given nation. There has been strong support for African nationalism, but until the recent events in Rhodesia and the Union of South Africa there has been little effort to affect American-African policy. Perhaps, until now, the issues in Africa have been too ambiguous and Afro-Americans have been without effective leadership. But the conflicts in southern Africa have ripened at a moment when black Americans have the kind of political leverage to affect policy. It remains to be seen whether an American mentality, habituated to a tradition of caste, can adapt itself so as to promote a smooth transition of power from the hands of white men to those of black men.

NOTES

1. Gunnar Myrdal, *An American Dilemma: The Negro Problem and Modern Democracy* (New York, 1944).

2. Edwin R. Embree, *Thirteen against the Odds* (New York, 1944).

3. They were: Mary McLeod Bethune, Richard Wright, Charles S. Johnson, Walter White, George Washington Carver, Langston Hughes, Marion Anderson, W. E. B. DuBois, Mordecai W. Johnson, William Grant Still, A. Philip Randolph, Joe Louis, Paul Robeson.

4. Rayford Logan, ed., *What the Negro Wants* (Chapel Hill, 1944), includes essays by Mary McLeod Bethune, Sterling Brown, W. E. B. DuBois, Gordon B. Hancock, Leslie P. Hill, Langston Hughes, Rayford Logan, Frederick D. Patterson, A. Philip Randolph, George S. Schuyler, Willard S. Townsend, Charles H. Wesley, Doxey A. Wilkerson, and Roy Wilkins. This volume also contains an academic defense of caste from the point of view of a white Southerner in the "Publisher's Introduction," written by W. T. Couch.

5. The hero as leader is at least suggestive. The three heavy-weight champions mentioned had different public images—reflective of their respective epochs. Jack Johnson was a black man who beat white men and consorted publicly with white women at a time when both were acts of audacious defiance. Joe Louis was the personified challenge to theories of Aryan superiority, a gentleman, and "a credit to his race." Mohammed Ali reflects the spirit of black pride and defiance of the 1960s—both in his rejection of Christianity and his refusal to fight in the Vietnam War—representing the "black" as opposed to the "Negro" image.

6. Comments by Professor William W. Freehling at the Schouler Symposium at The Johns Hopkins University, February 5, 1976, were suggestive of this thesis.

7. Myrdal, *An American Dilemma;* Allison Davis et al., *Deep South* (Chicago, 1941); John Dollard, *Caste and Class in a Southern Town* (London, 1937); Paul Lewinson, *Race, Class, and Party: A History of Negro Suffrage and White Politics in the South* (London, 1932); Robert Weaver, *The Negro Ghetto* (New York, 1948); W. Lloyd Warner and Paul S. Lunt, *The Social Life of a Modern Community* (London, 1941); Frank U. Quillin, *The Color Line in Ohio* (Ann Arbor, 1913); Leslie H. Fishel, Jr., "The Negro in Northern Politics, 1870–1900," *Mississippi Valley Historical Review* 42 (December, 1955): 466–89; St. Clair Drake and Horace R. Cayton, *Black Metropolis* (New York, 1945); Robert S. Lynd and Helen M. Lynd, *Middletown* (New York, 1929).

8. Aside from seventeen southern states, fourteen northern and western states had statutes prohibiting the marriage of whites with blacks. Arizona, California, Colorado, Idaho, Indiana, Michigan, Montana, Nebraska, Nevada, North Dakota, Oregon, South Dakota, Utah, and Wyoming abolished their laws after World War II. Such state laws were declared unconstitutional by the United States Supreme Court: *Loving et ux, Apellants v. Virginia* (1967). Cf. Harry A. Ploski and Ernest Kaiser, comp., *The Negro Almanac* (New York, 1971), pp. 252–63.

9. Martin Kilson, "Political Change in the Negro Ghetto, 1900—1940s," in *Key Issues in the Afro-American Experience*, ed. Nathan I. Huggins, Martin Kilson, and Daniel Fox (New York, 1971), 2:167–92; Ira Katznelson, *Black Men, White Cities* (London, 1973), chaps. 6 and 7.

10. Nathan Glazer and Daniel P. Moynihan, *Beyond the Melting Pot* (Cambridge, Mass., 1963), and also Glazer, "Blacks and the Ethnic Groups: The Difference and the Political Difference It Makes," in Huggins et al., eds., *Key Issues*, pp. 193–211; Oscar Handlin, *The Newcomers* (Cambridge, Mass., 1959).

11. Kilson, "Political Change"; Katznelson, *Black Men, White Cities*; James Q. Wilson, *Negro Politics* (Glencoe, Ill., 1960).

12. The term and image is that of Martin Kilson, "Political Change."

13. I prefer the dichotomy "Reformist-Emblematic" to Gunnar Myrdal's "Protest-Accommodation" because I think the former more descriptive of the actual roles and intent.

14. While the word "token" could serve the same meaning as "emblem," I do not intend the pejorative connotations with which the word "token" has become charged.

15. Frederick Douglass, *The Life and Times of Frederick Douglass* (London, 1962).

16. Frederick Douglass's refusal to enter elective politics is interesting and pertinent

118 NATHAN IRVIN HUGGINS

here. Douglass, *Life and Times*, pp. 398–99; the argument against Marcus Garvey often turned on his "manipulation" of the masses; cf. A. Philip Randolph, "Garveyism," *The Messenger* 3 (September, 1921), reprinted in *Voices from the Harlem Renaissance*, ed. Nathan I. Huggins (1976), pp. 27–35. It is too seldom remarked how often the political thought of Afro-Americans has reflected an antidemocratic distrust of the masses; cf. Louis Harlan, *Booker T. Washington* (New York, 1972), pp. 300–303.

17. Harlan, *Booker T. Washington*, pp. 222–23; Emma Lou Thornbrough, *T. Thomas Fortune* (Chicago, 1972), chaps. 5 and 6.

18. Douglass, *Life and Times*, pp. 399–406.

19. August Meier, *Negro Thought in America, 1880–1915*, (Ann Arbor, 1963), pp. 112–13; Harlan, *Booker T. Washington*, pp. 296–98, 300–303.

20. Thornbrough, *T. Thomas Fortune*, chaps. 5 and 6; Harlan, *Booker T. Washington*, pp. 263–67.

21. W. E. B. DuBois, *Souls of Black Folk* (Chicago, 1903), chaps. 1, 4, 6, and 8.

22. Raymond Wolters, *The New Negro on Campus* (Princeton, 1975).

23. Although W. E. B. DuBois on occasion supported the idea of a "Negro Party," he never worked to organize one.

24. W. E. B. DuBois, "A Negro Nation within the Nation," *Current History* 42 (June, 1934), reprinted in Huggins, ed., *Voices*, pp. 384–90; see also W. E. B. DuBois, *Dusk of Dawn* (New York, 1940), chap. 7.

25. A. Philip Randolph seemed always to have had mass organization in his mind. He was one of the few notable black leaders who worked to mobilize Harlem voters in the years before and after World War I. Significantly, however, his efforts were for the Socialist Party and not for major party organizations. Jervis Anderson, *A. Philip Randolph* (New York, 1973).

26. Ralph Bunche, "The Negro in Chicago Politics," *National Municipal Review* 17 (May, 1928): 261–64; Harold F. Gosnell, *Machine Politics: Chicago Model* (Chicago, 1939); Katznelson, *Black Men, White Cities*, chap. 4, n. 73, sees the black machine in Chicago to have been "co-opted" in the 1930s; for Adam Clayton Powell, see James Q. Wilson, "Two Negro Politicians," *Midwest Journal of Political Science* 4, no. 1 (1960).

27. Nathan I. Huggins, *Harlem Renaissance* (New York, 1971), chap. 2; Huggins, ed., *Voices*, part 1.

28. Charles F. Kellogg, *NAACP* (Baltimore, 1967), 1: 224–27, for that organization's response to the East St. Louis riots.

29. Claude McKay, "Harlem Runs Wild," *The Nation* 140 (April 1935), reprinted in Huggins, ed., *Voices*, pp. 381–84.

30. Claude McKay, "Sufi Abdul Hamid and Organized Labor," in his *Harlem, Negro Metropolis* (New York, 1940), pp. 143–81; Mark Naison, "The Communist Party in Harlem, 1928–1936" (Ph.D. diss., Columbia University), chap. 3.

31. Naison, "Communist Party in Harlem," chap. 4; Dan T. Carter, *Scottsboro* (Baton Rouge, 1971); for an interesting discussion of the NAACP's style in legal advocacy see, August Meier and Elliot Rudwick, "Attorneys Black and White: A Case Study of Race Relations Within the NAACP," *Journal of American History* 62 (March 1976): 913–46.

32. Anderson, *A. Philip Randolph;* Virginia Hamilton, *Paul Robeson* (New York, 1974), pp. 131–34.

33. Anderson, *A. Philip Randolph*, pp. 274–82.

34. Steven Lawson, *Black Ballots: Voting Rights in the South, 1944–1969* (New York, 1976), chaps. 9 and 10.

35. Gunnar Myrdal, "The Case Against Romantic Ethnicity," *Center Magazine* 7 (July/August, 1974): 26–30.

36. Especially if we consider Anglo-Saxon as an ethnic group.

Native Americans

Robert F. Berkhofer, Jr.

FISH-INS AND RED POWER SLOGANS, the occupation of Alcatraz
and the takeover of the Bureau of Indian Affairs in Washington, the second battle of Wounded Knee and the rise of urban Indian guerillas all
demonstrate a new militancy among American Indians and their leaders.
The spectacular sales of Vine Deloria's *Custer Died for Your Sins* and
Dee Brown's *Bury My Heart at Wounded Knee*, the popularity of the
teachings of Don Juan, the Yaqui sorcerer, the advocacy by Marlon
Brando of Indian rights, and President Nixon's return of Blue Lake to
the Taos Indians all appear to indicate a new sympathy for and even
understanding of the first Americans by white Americans in general and
a drastic change in government policy. At the same time the very complaints of Indian leaders about new land grabs, lack of consultation with
them about the future of Indian peoples, and the dominant society's
apathy to the murder of Indians and the denial of their civil rights all point
to the persistence of longtime white attitudes and official policies. Reports upon the conditions among Indians issued by government agencies
and foundations in the 1960s and 1970s catalogued the same problems
of health, education, housing, economy, and federal administration detailed in the famous Meriam Report of 1928. For fifty years, evidently,
the basic plight of the Indian has remained much the same.[1] On the
Indian side, factionalism within tribes looks as great as ever; the Indians
as an ethnic group appear as little united as always. But the rise of new
organizations such as the American Indian Movement, the survival of the
National Congress of American Indians for over three decades, and the
rhetoric of pan-Indianism and Indian nationalism suggest a new day has
dawned in American Indian leadership.

These recent events and actions raise fundamental questions about
continuity and change in American Indian leadership. Have tribal and

119

intertribal organization and leadership changed sufficiently to demonstrate that a new stage of American Indian history has been entered, or are the old factionalism and tribalism merely wearing new labels? Have state and federal policies and general white American attitudes and practices modified enough to assert that a new era of enlightened white approaches to Indian survival has dawned? Do Indian leaders as a result have new options in seeking those ends they think best for their peoples, instead of accepting what government bureaucrats and white do-gooders maintain is best for "Indians"? In other words, are white Americans willing to assist Indian leaders with the problems of American Indians as the latter see and understand their condition? Will the Bureau of Indian Affairs (BIA), for example, allow the Indians self-determination without determining the bases upon which Indian leaders must accept that boon or what they must do to court the continued favor and funds of the "great white father" under such a policy?

Scholarly monographs and articles upon the history of white attitudes and goals abound in comparison to the dearth of scholarship of the goals and policies of Indian leaders over time, the changing nature of tribal governments and leadership, and the history of tribal divisions and factions.[2] Although the specific genealogy of modern Indian leadership cannot therefore be traced readily, the overall evolution of political organization in tribal socieities is known sufficiently to suggest the persisting problems facing American Indian leadership in general. The histories we do possess reveal that most tribal societies changed in order to survive under altered conditions and that adaptation produced internal conflict within the society about the methods of survival. Leaders and factions formed about the various strategies of survival and change. Modifications therefore occurred in Indian political systems for internal as well as external reasons. The basic divisions and strategies in the past provide the background of the factionalism that disunites Indian leaders and their followers today.[3]

As a result of this factionalism, no one Indian or group of Indians can speak for all residents of a reservation or all members of a tribe, let alone for all Indians. While schism is common to the history of all ethnic groups in the United States, it is especially complicated for Indians by the unique relationship many of them bear to federal and state governments. Because Indians were the original Americans and therefore the first inhabitants of this nation's territory, Indian tribes were once treated as separate political entities under the laws and treaties of the United States. Although factional divisions often prevented tribal leaders from acting in a unified fashion, white laws and political practices in regard to the first Americans demanded nothing less. Thus at the same time as white pressures upon tribal peoples partly caused and certainly exploited factionalism, the legal and diplomatic customs designed to foster land sales and assimilation presumed that these divisions could and should be overcome in favor of white goals and policies.

The consequences of this special legal connection and status constitute the problems and opportunities peculiar to Indian leadership as opposed to that of other ethnic groups. This unique heritage underlies the repeated references by Indian leaders to tribal sovereignty and their demands for self-government. The differences among leaders in defining these terms and what constitutes their proper exercise reveals the continuing factional divisions among Indians.[4]

The conditions that produced and have sustained factionalism can only be suggested through a brief schematic history of tribal political developments. From the perspective of present-day Indian politics, one historic trend seems paramount to all others: the changing balance of power between various tribal governments and white governments over time. As the balance of power shifted from one side to the other time and time again, the issues facing tribal members and the strategies they attempted changed in roughly similar ways for many tribal societies. Under these transformed circumstances, the number and types of leaders, the nature of tribal government itself, and even the size of the political community altered.

Scholars dispute whether or not factionalism existed in aboriginal Indian societies, but political anthropologists and historians of tribal government agree with nativistic-minded, traditional leaders that subsequent political developments and tribal factionalsm must be measured against the (presumed) nature of tribal governments before or shortly after contact with whites. The numerous peoples living in the area now the United States never established a state comparable in extent or organziation to that of the Aztecs or the Incas. Although a few tribes approached statelike governments, for most tribal peoples the effective political community was far smaller than the cultural or linguistic areas and even less than the tribal territories shown on modern maps. In other words, ethnic and cultural similarities like feelings of in-group identity did not coincide with political jurisdiction in most so-called tribes. Political decision-making extended to a territory and group of people no larger than a few villages or bands at best. Even in the renowned League of the Iroquois, for example, political activity mainly occurred at the village rather than the tribal or confederation level.[5] As a result, aboriginal political systems generally embraced few people, and the ratio of leaders to people was low. Moreover, chiefs, whether the position was inherited or achieved, possessed authority on the basis of influence and continued efficacy more than upon power and hierarchy as the whites understood these conceptions.

According to the hierarchical relationships thought normal and necessary to white society and the concept of national sovereignty held by those whites invading the continent, most Indian societies appeared to have little or no government. Freedom and equality, even anarchy, prevailed among most tribal peoples from the view of the whites, because the degree of formalization, specialization, and centralization of the political relationships was so low in most Indian societies as to appear nonexistent. Although most tribes probably had some conception of socioeconomic strata, they lacked the words for the power relationships presumed normal in white societies. Tribal peoples were vitally concerned about power, but their conception of it was so different that modern-day scholars may wonder whether the white conception of government and politics is cross-culturally applicable and therefore conceptually valid in the discussion of most Indian societies. Tribal peoples did not differentiate power into religious, political, or economic categories. They saw unity where whites, particularly modern ones, compartmentalize the sectors of human life. This ideal of life's unity, whether always real or not in the past, shapes Indian political consciousness even today, particularly among those persons claiming to represent the old, traditional ways in Indian politics and religion.[6]

Not only did the Indian peoples presumably exhibit a nonhierarchical, nonbureaucratic, nondifferentiated sociopolitical unity compared to white societies, but they also professed to believe and to practice unanimity or consensus in decision-making. According to many scholars and Indian leaders, native political units before the coming of whites decided upon a course of action through consensus of the whole group or left the thing undone. Voting was presumably as unnecessary as it was undesirable. If factionalism existed and if it could not be contained through traditional methods of social control, dissenting leaders and their families and followers could remove to another place within the tribal territory and therefore restore political consensus in both the old and the new community under the rule of local autonomy that prevailed in most tribal societies. The ideal of consensus remains today like the ideal of unity— a principle espoused by many Indians, especially traditionalists, as the most desirable state of tribal political affairs. Even as such goals increasingly recede from any possible practice by Indian political units, some leaders espouse them ever more eagerly.

Most tribal histories subsequent to white contact can be divided for analytical purposes into four or five generalized phases: (1) the period of indirect contact with white trade goods, diseases, and ideas introduced into a tribal society through Indian intermediaries; (2) the early years of direct contact with various types of Europeans or Americans with their ways of life and values as well as material artifacts; (3) a time of intensive large-scale interaction between a tribe and whites who

demand diplomatic alliances, land cessions, and adoption of white religions and ways of life, leading to warfare, disruption of tribal life, and
dispossession of lands; (4) an era of a relatively stabilized conquest
society usually marked by the continued cession of lands, placement upon
one or more reservations, and a more intensive demand for social and
cultural change according to white models; and, lastly, (5) a modern
period that varies in length according to whether it is measured by a
"new" federal policy or by degree of change within a tribal society. Of
course, not all tribes passed through all phases or in such strict sequence.
Moreover, times varied for entrance into a phase and for the duration of
a phase in different tribes. Furthermore, for those tribes long beyond the
reservation stage, the modern period must be differentiated into additional phases.[7] In spite of these conceptual problems, however, such a
schematic periodization still makes sense in discussing political change
in a tribe, because it calls attention to the parity of power between a
tribe and the encroaching white society in each phase and the resultant
implications for self-determination and political autonomy for the tribal
society.

As the balance of power, or the real foundation of sovereignty,
changed, the usual social controls that supported the decision-making
process failed to contain factionalism. As the balance of power tilted in
the direction of white society, the urgency of coping with white demands
for cession of land and the adoption of Christianity and "civilization"
increased. But the ability to agree upon any one strategy declined under
the ever-larger number of white interests and the ever-stronger presence
of white force in tribal affairs. Traditional methods of social control
became harder to apply as factions formed around different options, and
some tribal leaders and their followers received white approbation and,
more importantly, support of funds or force at the expense of other
leaders and followers. Factionalism therefore flourished as tribal power
vis-à-vis white power diminished, partly because of the inherent nature
of tribal political systems and partly because of the increasing effectiveness of the whites in controlling the overall framework of Indian decision-
making. Traditional native governments based as they generally were
upon local autonomy and consensus rather than hierarchy and force
appeared particularly fertile ground for increasing factional division in
these changing circumstances.

Containment upon a reservation represented (some would say represents) the height of white political power in relation to a tribal society
and forms the immediate background to the modern period in many
tribes. The classic reservation originated as the federal government's solution to the Plains Indians' lifestyle, but the power relationship embodied in the concept of the reservation stretches back to colonial times.

Essentially the reservation subjected the basic direction of tribal affairs as well as residence to outside white decisions and control. Ultimately, white officials determined who would live upon a reserve, where, and how. Depending upon the time, they also decided upon the sale and leasing of tribal lands and other resources, the overall economic development of the reserves, the nature of educational facilities, and even at times the churches and religions, as well as whether or not to recognize tribal governments. The line of command stretched from officials and politicians in Washington to the BIA agents on the reservations who were expected to put these policies in effect and so were given power to call out the military to enforce their powers, to exercise judicial authority at times, to control rations and trust funds, to lease and sell lands, water rights, minerals, and forests, to remove children from their parents in order to send them to school, and to recognize or to sidestep traditional tribal political systems—all to further decisions made in the capital. Thus Indians became at best clients patronized by the agents sent to rule over them. So complete was the agents' legal authority that some analysts have likened the reservation to a colony; others have gone so far as to depict the reserves as the equivalent of concentration camps.[8]

Actual white control on the reservations was never so sweeping, however, as to destroy opposition to white policies or to suppress traditional religions and lifestyles. Various lifeways coexisted (and survived) in spite of white discouragement or encouragement. Previous factions coalesced or new factions formed around the divisions between newer and older ways of life. Such differences often were reflected in the place of residence on the reserve. Around the agent's buildings on larger reservations in the classic period grew up a small town composed of a school, churches and missions, perhaps a hospital, and the homes of white and Indian employees dependent upon white institutions for favor and power. Those Indians who chose assimilative lifestyles gathered there also for psychological support, while those traditional Indians who strove to retain the native ways resided in the more remote backcountry of the reservation. The locus of power and factional lines assumed on some reservations, therefore, a geographical form.[9]

As treaty negotiations shifted from diplomacy and alliance to land cessions and removal and/or concentration upon a reservation, as religious contact changed from isolated missionaries to concerted efforts to stamp out native religions, as the pressure to adopt white ways changed from exhortations to forced schooling and to manipulation of tribal monies and resources, the issues and options presented by whites switched from the periphery of tribal decision-making and politics to the center of the stage. As whites gained increasing control of the framework in which tribal existence had to be lived, their intervention became all the more persuasive and resistance to them all the more difficult. Nevertheless, two or more sides continued to exist on most issues. Should white wishes be resisted at the risk of warfare or retaliation with possible victory, or should they be acceded to in the hopes of gaining long-term benefits from agreeing to what some Indians saw as inevitable? If resistance was chosen, then what was the best strategy for obtaining the desired end and how far should such reistance go with what means? Was survival as a tribe better achieved through capitulation to some white demands or by resisting all white demands tooth and nail?

What the issues and strategies were that divided the people of a tribe changed over time as the parity of power between them and the whites altered. Accordingly, sides formed at first in favor of and against treaties of cession, conversion to Christianity, and the introduction of white agriculture, schools, and other acculturative elements into tribal life. To whites at that stage, these divisions became known as the friendlies and the hostiles, the pro- and antitreaty factions, or Christians and pagans. Further demands for cessions and concentration or removal, the coming of additional Christian denominations, and the establishment of more schools and other acculturative practices created new factions, divided old ones, or transformed the issues and strategies of previous factions. Upon the reservations, BIA agents saw these new factional developments in terms of progressives who favored the religions and ways of the whites versus the conservatives who retained the native religion and older ways. Sometimes they viewed these factions as dividing along lines of mixed "breeds" or mixed "bloods" versus full "breeds" or "bloods." From the viewpoint of the agent, these divisions indicated not only the degree of acculturation but also their receptivity to his policies.

How pervasive these factions were in how many areas of life in a tribe and how permanent their personnel over time is generally unknown because both historians and anthropologists have usually neglected tribal political genealogy. Did these factions form along hereditary lines, and did political association, religious affiliation, reserve residential location, and family connections correlate to a large degree? Or, were factions loose floating coalitions of interests rather than of persons that changed according to the circumstances? Were ends always in dispute, or just means? Although, we do not know the specific answers to these questions, we do know that factionalism has a long history in many tribes.[10]

Moreover, we know that what passed for traditional as well as progressive lifestyles and beliefs changed over time. Some conservative religions today, for example, originated as revitalized or syncretic faiths in the historic, reservation period, such as the Long House religion of the Iroquois or the Peyotism of the Plains. Thus what was defended by some tribal factions as traditionalist modified throughout the course of a tribe's history.

With this history in mind, the question of who was a tribal leader and to whom can be surveyed briefly from early contact times through the reservation period as prelude to the modern-day problem. Even before white contact in the so-called protohistoric period, widespread death from the diseases that swept through many tribes may have opened up leadership positions to those not normally eligible for such office in a tribe and may have raised the issue of legitimacy and authority of new-comers in those offices. During the early phases of contact, those who dealt with officials from white governments were frequently the war chiefs, who normally acted as go-betweens with outsiders, rather than the hereditary leaders. As white officials learned more about a tribe's political system, they might still have chosen to treat with those they designated chiefs rather than the legitimate leaders. The question of who was a chief became increasingly disputed, therefore, as white pressures for diplomatic alliances, land cessions, and conversion to white religions and ways increased. The treaties that whites demanded required signa-tures of Indian leaders from a specific tribe controlling a specific terri-tory. Just as white negotiators often designated certain Indian groups as tribes without fully understanding the actual political community as opposed to the ethnic territory, so too white negotiators chose those Indians friendly to their demands or liable to coercion or bribery who would sign the treaty or grant the concession, regardless of their actual status in the tribal political system.

On the other hand, the problem of who was a chief to whom may have become an issue because of internal tribal politics also. Rivalry between traditional leaders and those who sought leadership positions without the proper family connections or other background considered correct accord-ing to customary rules may have determined who sided with white demands for cessions and for assimilation or who led the resistance to such demands. Richard Metcalf hypothesizes in a recent article that those in positions of authority according to traditional ascription coped with white leaders through reconciliation of their fellow tribespeople to their policies, while the opposition to white requests came from those tribes-men who coveted leadership positions for which they could qualify only by resistance to white demands.[11] Certainly those whom the whites rec-ognized as friendly to their demands might benefit their followers as well as themselves. Such recognition discriminated between those who would lose and who would retain lands in cessions, who would have power through the control of political affairs in a newly emerging polit-ical arena, and whose authority would be enhanced through control of annuity distribution. Chiefs benefited personally from emoluments and prequisites that went with accession to white demands. In brief, faction-alism in many a tribe may have represented a struggle of ins versus outs, animated by the promise of patronage and personal benefits.

Although nearly every tribe went through a reservation phase, its effects on political organization, size of political community, amount of factionalism, and number of leaders varied from tribe to tribe. Partly the variation occurred because reservation boundaries restructured tribal relationships in so many divergent ways. Some tribes retained part of their native lands, while others were removed to areas distant from their ceded homelands. Sometimes the various political communities of a tribe were consolidated upon one reserve, while at other times they were distributed among various reservations. Or, in still other cases, political communities of more than one tribe were concentrated upon the same reservation. Since reservation formation was usually not a single event in a tribe's history, members of a tribe experienced more than one of these variations over time.

Each variation had different implications for the identification of chiefs and the shape of factionalism. Consolidation of bands and villages upon a reserve located upon original tribal lands meant the loss of lands by some tribespeople in favor of others, and the consequent movement of the losers into the traditional political jurisdiction of the other tribespeople. Relocation and consolidation upon lands distant from the ceded territory meant either the reestablishment of political communities along territorial or jurisdictional lines of old or the formation of new ones in the new locale. The scattering of bands, villages, or fractions of a tribe to different reservations preserved political autonomy of local political units in a sense. The combination of villages or bands from different tribes upon the same reserve fostered either conflict or separation along tribal lines. In some cases, tribal factions informally split reserves through residence; in other cases, one or more factions removed to new reserves, often at quite a distance from the old locale, to the glee of land-hungry local white citizens.

On some reservations and in some tribes, reservationwide or tribalwide political organizations formed for the first time in response to internal and external pressures. Factionalism fostered such a development in many cases because the progressive or acculturative faction frequently tried to establish a more centralized and formalized government upon a territorial basis in place of the traditional kinship system. Usually such a government borrowed white ideas of structure and power. Constitutions, law codes, and elections all indicated the new drift in political organization. In theory these governments asserted more power and authority over the members of a tribe than had the traditional political system in most cases. Traditional or conservative leaders, in opposing tendencies to a newer and wider political arena, counterorganized upon a reservationwide or tribal basis. Political decision-making was thereby transferred from the more localistic political community so traditional in most tribes to a structure embracing a larger population and usually emphasizing a more formal and specialized approach to power. White governmental agents or philanthropists often aided in this development through advice or through working with the faction promoting new tendencies in governance. Some agents from the Bureau of Indian Affairs, for example, treated the reserve as a whole and sought tribal approval for their policies from the faction favorable to their ideas and wishes or created a group of leaders outside the traditional political system. Traditional leaders might organize more formally to oppose this threat to their authority as well as to protect old ways of life, thought, and faith.

Continued factionalism frustrated the effective working of new political systems. It led to persistent, even formally institutionalized sides, which usually refused to recognize each other's authority and legitimacy. As a result the selection process for leaders was disputed as much as their jurisdiction; the method of arriving at rules and decisions for the tribe or reserve as whole was as unsettled as the rules themselves. To what extent this institutionalized but nonlegitimated conflict followed old politics of ins and outs, patronage distribution, and family affiliation remains to be discovered in most cases. Before the modern period very few tribes or reserves achieved a party system in which factional opposition became formally organized into competing parties operating within an electoral framework considered legitimate by the people it embraced.[12] The Indian Reorganization Act passed under the New Deal had as its purpose the organization or reorganization and election of such tribalwide governments. From the viewpoint of this chapter, the Indian Reorganization Act therefore tried to force many Indian tribes into the modern period. But such a new kind of government ran counter to ideas of proper leadership in many tribes; and that has produced the latest phase in their factional divisions.

To speak of the modern period of tribal history introduces an ambiguity. Is the modern period a phase in our generalized analytical schema, or is it the current status and very recent past of tribes regardless of their political evolution? In terms of the analytical scheme, the modern phase is the late reservation or postreservation period of detribalization. Under this definition, some tribes are just entering the modern phase while others passed that point long ago. The discrepancy between the modern phase of generalized tribal history and the modern day condition of specific tribes spotlights the diversity of tribal societies and political organizations among Indians today. Even when the modern period is given an absolute chronological beginning, a problem of dating the starting point remains. Should the point be seen in the context of white policy or in the light of Indian nationalism? Should the modern period, for example, commence with the general allotment of tribal lands in the late nineteenth century, when so many tribal membership rolls were constructed, or should the period begin with the Indian Reorganization Act with its reestablished tribal corporations and governments? Still other analysts suggest the period after World War II, when so many Indian veterans and factory workers returned to the reservations and when the United States government pursued a policy of terminating federal trust status for Indian lands and ending federal services based upon that relationship. In looking at Indian political and cultural developments, anthropologist Eleanor Leacock dates the modern period from "the emergence of a new sense of national consciousness and common purpose and by attempts to achieve effective political organization and viable social and cultural reintegration of Indian institutions within the context of contemporary industrial sociey."[13] Why each of these different criteria is significant for understanding the contemporary situation can be seen in the history of two quite different tribes.

The Narragansett entered the postreservation phase well over a century ago but still retain a sense of tribal identity. They occupied approximately the southern half of Rhode Island when the Puritans began settlement of New England in the seventeenth century. Conflict over white expansion led to the conquest of the tribe in King Philip's War (1675–76). In 1709 the chief sachem deeded all tribal land in Rhode Island to the colony, except for a reserve of sixty-four square miles. In the mid-eighteenth century a church and a school were built upon the reserve and marked the acculturative familiarity of the Narragansett with the economy, religion, language, and social institutions of the whites. By that time the authority of the traditional head chief was being replaced by that of a council, and when the last head chief died during the American Revolution he was not replaced. In 1792, the Rhode Island legislature specified the composition of the council, provided for annual elections, and stipulated the voting requirements.

By the 1880s the detribalization of the Narragansett was complete except for ethnic identification and an annual powwow. The reserve had dwindled to only a thousand acres of land held in common by the tribe. Apparently at the behest of the tribal members all but two acres of this reserved land was sold by the Rhode Island legislature, which passed an act abolishing the tribal status of the Narragansett under state law. To divide the sales money from the land, a legislative commission faced the perplexing problem of determining who was a tribal member, for membership was in dispute among the Narragansett themselves because of intermarriage, residence elsewhere, and nonparticipation in tribal affairs. After that decade, Narragansett tribal identification continued through the Indian church on the two acres of ground, the annual powwow, and the persistence of some kind of tribal organization which became incorporated under the Indian Reorganization Act of 1934. As of 1970, 424 Narragansett survived.[14]

The history of the Navajo contrasts in almost every way with that of the Narragansett. During the nominal jurisdiction of the Spanish and Mexican governments, the Navajo maintained almost complete independence. Although their culture was influenced by Spanish as well as Pueblo ways, they remained free of white military, political, and ecclesiastical control. Subjugation, however, came rapidly after the United States took over the area in the 1840s. At that time seven to ten thousand Navajo resided in small communities of ten to forty families scattered about the present-day states of Arizona and New Mexico. The power of the United States government and army became manifest in the still vividly remembered "Long Walk" and incarceration of most of the tribe at Fort Sumter from 1864 to 1868. During this period United States military officers tried to redirect the life of the tribe. As part of the experiment, the commander divided the tribe into twelve divisions with the headman of each division composing a council. Deeming the whole experiment unsuccessful, the whites permitted the Navajo to return to a reservation about a quarter of the size they had previously inhabited.

Release brought a return to the traditional decentralization of authority and decision-making as well as dispersion of the population to areas outside the official reserve boundaries. Over the years lands were added to the reserve. In 1915 the BIA divided the reserve into five separate jurisdictions, each with its own superintendent and staff. These superintendents soon after encouraged the formation of local community councils, called chapters. In 1923 the BIA set up a council of two Navajo from each of the five jurisdictions to advise on or to consent to mineral leases on tribal lands. Usually selected by the superintendents, these "advisors" constituted the Navajo Council. This council was enlarged in 1936 to seventy-four delegates elected from federal land management districts within the tribe. Though the Navajo never organized under the Indian Reorganization Act, the tribal council functioned like those established according to its guidelines. It too worked under a written constitution through elected representatives. Not until the 1950s, however, did this imposed tribal government structure become representative of the tribe in any real sense, for only during that decade was an effort made to integrate the chapter organization on the local level with the council on the tribalwide level. The Navajo Nation, as the tribe calls itself today, has a population of over 130,000 on a reserve the size of West Virginia, and its government functions with a large budget in new buildings at its capital in Window Rock. Thus the Navajo passed from local autonomy to nationalistic government only in the post-World War II period.[15]

The dissimilarities between the Navajo and the Narragansett hardly begin to suggest the great diversity among tribal groups today in size of population, place of residence, degree of acculturation, and the nature of tribal government. The Navajo are by far the most numerous tribe with the largest unitary reservation in the United States. The two next most populous tribes, the Sioux or Dakota and Chippewa or Ojibwa, do not together equal the Navajo in numbers and are scattered upon numerous reserves and throughout the general American society. For example, the over 50,000 members of the Sioux constituting the four Eastern Dakota bands or tribes, the two Middle Dakota tribes or bands, and the seven subbands or tribes of the Teton or Western Dakotas live on many reserves located mainly in the states of Minnesota, North and South Dakota, and Montana (and in the provinces of Manitoba and Saskatchewan) as well as in large and small cities throughout the United States (and Canada). The almost as numerous Chippewa live on reserves in Michigan, Wisconsin, Minnesota, North Dakota, and in cities and towns throughout the upper Midwest and elsewhere in the United States and in Canada as well.

The fourth largest tribe, the Cherokee, divide between North Carolina and Oklahoma primarily, although these people too can be found in cities throughout the United States. The Eastern band of Cherokee in North Carolina descend from those of the tribe who escaped forced removal under Andrew Jackson and numbered perhaps five thousand in 1970. The larger population of Cherokee in Oklahoma possess no reserved land in federal trust status, because all their property was divided in severalty and allotted in 1906 when the tribal government was dissolved. The so-called tribal or traditional Cherokee cluster in five counties of Oklahoma, while many other Cherokee live acculturated lives elsewhere in the state. The officially recognized Cherokee Nation represents the interests and activities of the latter more than the former, and the Principal Chief is appointed by the President of the United States. These four tribes constitute about a third of all Indians in the United States. Another eight to ten tribes may have as many as eight thousand members according to 1970 figures, but on the whole most tribal memberships are small.[16]

Reservation populations are also small, and as many Indians live off as on reserved lands these days. The BIA estimated in 1969 that of 255 reservations, for which it claimed some responsibility in the lower forty-eight states, seventy-eight (30.5 percent) contained less than one hundred people, another seventy-five (29.4 percent) had less than five hundred residents, and twenty-five (9.8 percent) accommodated less than a thousand persons. Only twenty-two reservations of the whole number had over five thousand residents, while fifty-five, or 21.5 percent, held from one to five thousand Indians.[17] Those Indians who reside off reservations may live in nearby rural areas, smaller cities and towns in the general area, or in large cities far away. Many Indians off and on the reservation live in rural circumstances. One authority estimated that in 1960 in the twenty-three states with the vast majority of the Indian population as many as 95 percent of the Indian population in North Carolina and Mississippi and 90 percent in Arizona, Wyoming, and North Dakota were rural but only 17 percent of the Iowa and 30 percent of the Kansas Indian population lived in rural areas. All of Arizona's rural Indian population he estimated lived on reservations, but only a mere 2 percent of California's rural Indian population resided upon reserves.[18]

Although the actual population figures of rural Indians probably rose since then, the proportion of rural to urban Indians has probably declined since 1960. Many Indians live in the towns and cities near reservations—Rapid City, South Dakota, and Gallup, New Mexico, come to mind immediately—or in the large industrial cities throughout the United States. Although urban Indian migration was already noted in the Meriam Report, the great movement from reservation to city began after World War II, partly at the behest of the BIA relocation program but more so on individual initiative. According to the 1970 census, nearly one-third of all Indians live in cities of over ten thousand inhabitants and another 15 percent dwell in towns of from twenty-five hundred to ten thousand population. For instance, the second largest aggregation of Indians in the United States outside of the Navajo reservation today is presumably in Los Angeles, but this Indian aggregation is composed of over one hundred different tribal affiliations, with Navajo, Sioux, and Cherokee believed most numerous.[19] Most of these urban Indians live in poorer dwellings and circumstances, but some reside in suburbs with middle-class attributes. Some of them are members of the many urban Indian centers that have arisen in recent decades, but others remain unattached to their fellow Indians. City life enhances the sense of tribe as well as being Indian for many of these urbanites, but others prefer to live as whites in the mainstream culture with little or no attachment to tribal heritage or pan-Indian association.[20]

Such statistics only hint at the diversity of location, lifestyle, and economic and political interests prevailing among present-day Indians. Perhaps half live on or near federal reservations and have close ties with the BIA and its services. Official figures on such affiliated tribes and reservations vary somewhat according to definition and service but no less than 270 groups seem included. Far fewer Indian groups live in some special relationship to state governments.[21] Many Indians do not live on reserve lands at all because they emigrated from them, lost such lands and services through termination at one time or another, or belong to groups who never had such recognition in their history. Some Indians live on lands once a part of their ancestors' native territory; others reside in places far removed from ancestral homes. Many reservations lie in isolated rural regions, but still others stand adjacent to urbanized areas. Along with the variety of location and residence goes a diversity of lifestyle on and off reservations, in and out of cities. Within as well as among tribes, individual cultures range from the traditional to the fully "assimilated." On reservations, differences in outlook as well as outer lifestyle exist between the traditional Indians, often called "country" or "full bloods," and the more acculturated "progressive" or "mixed blood" Indians living in reserve towns and working for the BIA or staffing the tribal government. Even in the cities, customs and attitudes range from the thoroughly assimilated middle-class suburbanites to the poverty-stricken Indians having difficulty with the English language as well as other general American habits and institutions.

Some Indians still speak only their ancestral tongue, while many others know only English. For some the regular everyday language is ancestral, but many more use English mainly and their tribal language but on occasion.[22] Educational levels vary greatly, with some having almost no formal training in white-type schools and some few others having college degrees. The vast majority among the young are in school today, but their chances of graduating from high school are slim but increasing. Religious faith among Indians on and off reservations exhibits the same diversity found in other areas of Indian life. On many larger reservations, churches for the standard Catholic and older Protestant denominations coexist with newer Protestant fundamentalist missions and the Native American Church or other nativist-oriented faiths. Some reserves have a population primarily younger, older, or more female and incapacitated than is typical of the Indian population in general. On some reservations and in the city, much intertribal marriage has taken place and even more outmarriage with white Americans. Whites, through intermarriage or through lease and sale of allotted lands, predominate over the tribal population on some reservations.[23] From such a variety of outlooks and residences comes the diversity of economic, political, social and cultural interests that constitute the internal problems of modern Indian leadership within tribal governments and within intertribal, or what some call pan-Indian, organizations.

Before considering how the diversity of interests among Indians today affects tribal political systems, a brief examination of the possible relationships between ethnic entities called tribes and those governments termed tribal is necessary. As a consequence of historical circumstances some ethnic tribes have more than one tribal government located in different places as a result of federal or state policies of relocation and consolidation upon reservations, while some tribal councils recognized by the federal government today represent a constituency comprised of peoples from more than one ethnic tribe. Some Sioux tribes or bands, for example, have a reservation and a council of their own, but some reservations are shared by Sioux from more than one band but with only one government.[24] The Seneca tribe basically divided after the Revolution into Canadian and New York segments. During a removal fight in the 1830s and 1840s, the New York Senecas further divided into two groups that both now possess tribal governments. The Seneca Nation of New York governs two Seneca reserves and the Tonawanda Band of Seneca live and have a council of their own for a third reservation. Those Cayuga who did not go to Canada after the Revolution are organized as the Cayuga Nation but live on one of the reserves of the Seneca Nation.[25] Members of three ethnic tribes were placed upon the Fort Berthold Reservation in Montana, and they now constitute the officially recognized Three Affiliated Tribes Council. Some small tribes have no government at all or not one that is officially recognized under federal or state law. Therefore tribal councils are usually reservation governments representing parts of the ethnic tribe, or a whole ethnic tribe, or members from several ethnic tribes. To the extent that such tribal councils are reservation governments recognized under federal law, then its members are under its jurisdiction in addition to those of local, state, and federal governments to which they are also subject as citizens of the United States.[26]

Given the history of tribal factionalism, small wonder that dispute still surrounds who are the legitimate leaders upon a reserve and what is the proper government for the tribe-reservation. Traditional or country Indians refuse to recognize the legitimacy or authority of the officially recognized tribal council in many instances, because they declare the council a creation if not also the creature of the BIA and surely not the descendent of the traditional manner of tribal governance. In some cases their boycott of the tribal council arises from the belief that the new tribalwide or reservationwide bureaucratic government asserts power that violates both the traditional allegiance to local autonomy and to equality of decision-making. In other cases, their boycott stems from the origins of the tribal government under the Indian Reorganization Act with its real or implied connection to the BIA. Often the persons running the official tribal councils are those progressive or mixed blood members of the reserve who have the more general outlook if not interests of the BIA in their vision of reservation policy. Thus the division over the legitimacy of the tribal council reflects different acculturative attitudes and vested interests, varying approaches to what is proper government for a reserve, and different persons claiming to represent the majority opinion upon a reserve.[27] Traditionals frequently abstain from voting or participating in tribal government at all in protest. Progressive leaders distribute among their followers the patronage of government programs, particularly under the Office of Economic Opportunity and other poverty programs in the last decade, or they decide how income from leases or other sources will be spent. Tribal election results are frequently disputed, for the different sides refuse to recognize that the other side represents a majority opinion. Still too often tribal politics seem governed in attitude if not in reality by the ideal of aboriginal consensus rather than the idea of party system and conflict.[28]

Off-reservation members of a tribal government may not question the legitimacy of the official tribal council so much as its policies and beneficiaries. Here the question is who will share in the tribal or corporate estate and how. Should the monies arising from leases or from successful claims litigation be distributed among the members of the tribe-reservation, or should the monies be invested in the long-term development of the reservation? Many off-reservation people have favored the immediate division of income and other tribal dollars on a per capita basis so they will benefit, while tribal council leaders wish to promote employment and resource development on the reservation for the benefit of those who remain (and presumably for their own reelection). Such disputes over the fate of the tribal income and estate have raged between off- and on-reservation factions among the Spokane, Flathead, and Blackfeet tribes. The fight on the Colville Reservation in Washington has been particularly bitter, for the off-reservation faction even went so far as to advocate the sale of the entire reservation and the distribution of the proceeds on a per capita basis to the members of the tribe no matter where they were located. Traditionals on many reservations, on the other hand, adjure claims awards from the Indian Claims Commission, for they argue that acceptance of these monies constitutes tribal recognition of the legitimacy of the fraudulent treaties of the past upon which the successful litigation was based or forestalls "reparations" for larger and more important claims against white governments. Leasing not only diminishes the land base of the tribe in their opinion but also encourages white economic practices violative of the sacred mother earth. Naturally, the sale of the reservation appears most heinous of all in their eyes, because it destroys the physical-spiritual foundations of the religious and cultural community that comprises the essence of the tribe in their belief. From their viewpoint, no tribal government possesses the legal authority to negotiate such a sale.

Such internal conflicts lead inevitably to disputes about who are the legitimate members of the reservation-tribe. Who is entitled to vote for the tribal council which decides these matters? Who can legally share in the tribal estate and assets? Who, in short, are the rightful members of the tribe-reservation and by what or whose criteria? Is membership measured by descent from officially registered members on a tribal roll constructed at the time of removal or allotment, or by blood quanta, by self-proclaimed tribal identity, by cultural affinity, or by interest in and residence on or near the reservation? All these criteria possess different implications for membership, hence benefits and responsibilities accuring to different persons. Should off-reservation as well as on-reservation members be allowed to vote for the tribal council or to decide the future of the reservation and its resources? Who will share in the tribal estate and in what form all rides on these criteria, and the problem of differential advantage and changing residence of tribal members produced the problem in the first place.

Allied to these conflicts and their implications for tribal governance is the contention over the tribe's relationship to the BIA and the federal government as a whole. Traditionals all too often want nothing to do with the agency they hold responsible for wrecking their lives and culture and for supporting the progressives at their expense. Outright assimilationists see no need for any special relationship with the federal government not applicable to all United States citizens. But the vast majority of those people claiming to be Indians probably prefer some special relationship, although they may disagree upon its exact form. Tribal council leaders, beyond their vested interest in the relationship, see more advantages than disadvantages accruing to the tribe from its connection to the federal government and the services of the BIA. While they feel that the white government must always be suspected, they also recognize that benefits do come from vigilance. As the Governor of the Zuni Pueblo commented:

Indian individuals and communities must work together with the local, State and Federal governments. We at the Zuni Pueblo in New Mexico have developed a Zuni Comprehensive Development Plan with the help of local, State, and private agencies. In this development we were aided by what some refer to as the "old time bureaucrats." These so-called bureaucrats are the best hope of the Indian tribes in obtaining the progress the tribes need through new programs and new policies.[29]

Traditionalists and militants see the tribal council members as too acquiescent in BIA policies even if these appeared to help the tribe.[30] Official tribal leaders themselves do not want to share BIA services and funds with off-reservation, particularly urban, Indians of the tribe, for fear that those services and funds will provide help for even fewer reservation people than at present. Urban Indians, on the other hand, feel discriminated against just because they have chosen to leave the reservation. The BIA, caught between the two sides, has increasingly come to recognize the claims of the urban Indians as their numbers rise in proportion to reservation residents.[31]

A new division over tribal governance may be arising as women claim formal office in tribal government. Although women possessed influence in many traditional tribal political systems, they did not have chieftanships as such. Among the Iroquois, for example, clan matrons had the power to bestow and remove the antlers of office on the hereditary sachems. In the actual modern government of the Seneca Nation, however, women did not receive the right to vote until 1964 and to hold office until 1966.[32] The conflict over women's role in tribal government came to a head among the Menominee after restoration of tribal status to them in 1973. The Menominee Restoration Committee was headed by a woman and contained a majority of female officers, which disturbed the male traditionals. In the occupation of the Alexian Brothers Novitiate in Gresham, Wisconsin, in early 1975, one of the demands of the Warriors Society of the Menominee was the reestablishment of the Menominee male's traditionally dominant leadership role in tribal affairs.[33] How much such conflict portends the future remains to be seen, but increasingly women are assuming leadership positions, particularly in urban Indian affairs.

Differing opinions about tribal political systems naturally transferred to efforts establishing intertribal political organizations upon a national scale. Could any one organization embrace all shades of the Indian political spectrum? Could on- and off-reservation, rural and urban, traditionalist and progressive, militant and moderate, young and old Indians join in the common cause to seek the welfare of all Indians as Indians? Or would they divide along the same lines as they had over tribal governments? Could land-based and non-land-based, Alaskan and continental, Eastern and Western, large and small tribes agree upon a joint program beneficial to all? Should an intertribal association work with the BIA, or even against the BIA but within the American political system, or should such an organization repudiate the whole white system and pursue goals disruptive of national and state governments? Could most Indians even be persuaded to see issues beyond those of immediate interest to their own reservation or tribal situation for ones faced by all Indians as Indians? Would different tribal peoples even recognize each other as Indian, or would they argue over the racial, cultural, and social characteristics of who was more truly Indian and who could more accurately represent all Indians? The answers to these questions are not yet in, but suggestions of possible answers come from the recent history of intertribal political organizations.

Although Indian nationalists of today point out the inspiration for such intertribal organization in the political confederacies of the Iroquois and other tribes or the diplomatic confederacies led by Pontiac, Tecumseh, and other famed Indian leaders, the modern phase of pan-Indian political association came only with the formation of the Society of American Indians (SAI) in 1911. The society was the first national Indian organization run by Indians in the name of Indians. Previous associations working for the benefit of the Indian were run by white philanthropists and reformers for the welfare of the Indian as they understood it. Although the SAI spoke for the Indian, most of its leaders had little or no connection to the tribal governments or peoples of the time. They were acculturated professionals who had achieved position in the white society, and as result often favored the assimilation of the Indian as the long-run solution to the problems foisted upon tribal people by the general allotment act. In other ways, however, they worked on issues that would command attention in later pan-Indian organizations: the status of Indians under law, the opening of the United States Claims Commission to tribal appeals, the reorganization of Indian education, the improvement of health conditions, and, after World War I, self-determination. Soon after that time, the society membership divided badly over assimilation, the relation between the SAI and the BIA, the peyote religion, and the place of tribal causes vis-à-vis pan-Indian welfare. The society faded away in the 1920s as new attitudes and approaches appeared in the formation of Indian policy. The movement toward cultural survival and tribal self-determination became part of the Indian New Deal under Commissioner of Indian Affairs John Collier.[34]

If the Society of American Indians was a response to the allotment act and Indian policy of the 1890s and early twentieth century, then the National Congress of American Indians (NCAI) arose from the policies of the 1930s. Founders of the NCAI, like those of the SAI, were young professionals from the BIA, religious bodies, anthropology, but, unlike the SAI, also from the tribes. Although acculturated, they saw value in the Indian way of life, and they sought leadership from the tribes. Since the leaders of the tribes frequently came from the newly organized and recognized tribal councils created under the IRA, the NCAI tended to look out for the interests of federally recognized and landed tribes, and so the congress came to be dominated by people from the Oklahoma and Plains tribes. The NCAI monitored federal legislation affecting the tribes as well as the policies of the Department of Interior and the BIA. As a result of this purpose, the NCAI moved from watchdog to advocate and lobbyist. Since the preservation of tribal status was foremost in the interests of the congress as set up, it particularly opposed termination of federal trust and services for the reserves during the 1950s. The congress tried to undo the whole termination program announced by House Concurrent Resolution 108 and in Public Law 280, both passed in 1953. (The latter authorized individual states to assume unilaterally jurisdiction over crimes committed on reserves.) Both policies destroyed the foundations of tribal government and eroded the last vestiges of treaty rights from the Indian point of view. Essentially NCAI sought to improve the position of Indians from within the given structure of federal relationships, and as a result tribal leaders and councils came to work against the BIA through working with it and knowing its ways. More and more issues came to be formulated narrowly in terms of tribal lands and treaties for the benefit of the landed tribes. By the end of the 1950s opponents of the established NCAI leadership saw them working too closely with the very persons and bureau they were supposed to fight so vigorously. The dissent from within spilled over into the 1960s as new rhetoric, new tactics, and new organizations.[35]

Many educated Indian youth finally found their formal organized voice in the National Indian Youth Council in 1960. Although these youth had been meeting throughout the previous decade, their dissatisfaction with the Indian "establishment" reached a head in the conflict over a "Declaration of Indian Purpose" that was to issue from the American Indian Chicago Conference organized in 1960 by anthropologist Sol Tax to get a united Indian voice to influence the new presidential administration. Twelve uninvited youths formed a caucus at the meeting to influence the final "Declaration of Indian Purpose" along the lines of their thinking.[36] Shortly thereafter these youths, alienated alike from general American society and from the established leadership in tribes and the NCAI, formed the National Indian Youth Council (NIYC). They expressed as much repulsion for the cautious tactics and right-wing politics of the "Uncle Tomahawks" and "middle-class Indians" as they did for the paternalism of the BIA "colonial office," as they called it. In their approach they chose to work outside of official tribal leadership and the structure of the BIA relationship. Probably inspired by the stance as well as the rhetoric of militant civil rights and black activist movements, the NIYC leaders spoke of "Red Power" and developed militant tactics appropriate in their opinion for Indian activism. In the name of tribal sovereignty and Indian nationalism, they employed new tactics to call attention to white violations of Indian treaties and civil rights. The American public first became aware of this force in Indian affairs through the Pacific Northwest fish-ins of 1964 that made the news media with the help of Marlon Brando. In the same year a NIYC member, Vine Deloria, Jr., became executive director of the NCAI. The militant tactics of the young, educated Indians began to define Indian issues for whites as their activities were picked up by the mass media. They hoped to outflank the tribal council as well through these tactics, for they thought their opinions represented the "real tribal people" better than those voiced by the "Indian Bureau Indians" filling official positions in the tribes. Their interpretation of tribalism and self-determination brought before the public the new approach to these traditional Indian outlooks.[37]

140 ROBERT F. BERKHOFER, JR.

Urban Indians also sought political ends through pan-Indian political organizations in the late 1960s. Urban Indian centers espoused political interests as well as the customary social and educational programs. In the Chicago American Indian Center, for instance, factionalism arose over support for the occupation of Alcatraz by young college-educated youth and urban Indians in 1969. From the dissent came a second Indian center.[38] The American Indian Movement (AIM)—so well known today for its urban guerilla tactics, its skillful manipulation of white mass media, and its dramatic causes—started as a patrol in Minneapolis to check police harassment of Indians. Founded by Indians with urban "smarts" and prison experience, the organization quickly spread among city Indians in the Midwest.[39] Although a coalition of urban Indian centers was attempted in the late 1960s and early 1970s, each attempt proved abortive. Nevertheless, urban Indian organizations lobbied for power in the NCAI, and an urban Indian was elected president in 1971.

The increasing power of the urban and Eastern Indians in the NCAI and the attention paid to activists by the federal government aroused the fear of politically conservative, nontraditionalist tribal leaders about the future of the old aims of the organization, especially taxation upon allotments, treaty rights as developed by the tribal councils, the autonomy of official tribal governments, heirship divisions and land consolidation, and the economic development of reserves. In 1971 fifty-one of these leaders formed a separate organization known as the National Tribal Chairmen's Association to protect reservation interests in general and to combat the urban and non-federally recognized Eastern Indian influence in the NCAI. Naturally this group opposed the extension of BIA services to urban and other non-reservation Indians.

In recent years a new alliance appears being forged between some college-educated youths and urban Indians on one side and traditionalist religious and tribal leaders on the other. Their common enemy is the official tribal government and the BIA connection that supports it. Their common ground has become the repudiation of the whole federal relationship as presently structured in favor of a return to tribal sovereignty defined as the kind of political autonomy Indian political communities enjoyed during the treaty-making period. They urge a return to bilateral negotiation for determining the status of all Indians, the conditions under which they would live, and their future relationships with state and federal governments. Evidence of the new alliance and program could be seen in the intertribal caravan that crossed the United States from Pacific coast cities to Washington, D.C., in 1972 to call attention to the "Trail of Broken Treaties." In a twenty-point program tribal traditionalists, AIM people, and Eastern Indians announced this radical view of tribal sovereignty through renewed treaty negotiation. In Washington on the eve of the presidential election the caravan culminated in the takeover of the BIA offices. Subsequently BIA officials and their Indian supporters and the caravan leaders and their supporters violently disagreed about the amount of damage done to the building during the occuption.[40]

Even more dramatic was the armed confrontation in Wounded Knee, South Dakota, between members of the new alliance on one side and the official tribal leaders and the federal government on the other. For AIM leaders the occupation in early 1973 of the tiny hamlet on the Pine Ridge Reservation of the Oglala Sioux continued a series of demonstrations they had staged to protest white murders of Indians in the Dakotas, but it took on an added dimension as a consequence of Oglala traditionals' complaints against the administration of Richard Wilson, the President of the Oglala Sioux Tribal Council. Not only did the traditionals accuse Wilson of being a pawn of the BIA but they also said he was guilty of corruption. Wilson was an acculturated plumber who lived in the assimilationist town of Pine Ridge; his accusers resided in the more isolated areas of the reservation. During the days of armed conflict and stalemate, AIM militants were joined by Oglala holy men, Indian youths, urban Indians, and Indian nationalists from around the country. They faced federal marshals called out by the BIA and the Wilson-directed tribal police. Manifestoes of Oglala national independence and sovereignty issued from the hamlet, while Dick Wilson threatened to crush the radicals violating his tribal authority. The occupation ended after seventy-two days, but the issues raised there for intertribal organization and tribal government continue to perplex and divide Indian leadership. Should Indian leaders work within the federal system as defined by congressional enactment and BIA policy to achieve tribal self-determination, or must they work outside the customary framework to establish a new kind of tribal sovereignty and independent status for all Indians?[41]

The effect of the new alliance is to bring isolated traditional leaders into the larger pan-Indian world and to link internal tribal division more firmly to national Indian organizations. By introducing college and urban Indians to tribal traditionals, the former gained (or thought they regained) a sense of lost heritage most had not possessed before. Many became militant, self-conscious traditionalists as a result of their new-found tribalism. Being tribal and being Indian, to these self-conscious traditionalists, meant learning the ancestral language and religion. For them the newly emerging Native American studies programs in universities ought to teach the native ways and languages so that modern Indian youths could return "home" once again.[42] History was of vital importance in conveying the sense of a lost world and in proving the autonomous status of tribal societies vis-à-vis the white world and government. Tribal traditionals, on the other hand, gained a new educated voice articulate in the language of the dominant society to express their longstanding grievances and feelings against the whites and the BIA Indians. From the merger has come an escalation in the rhetoric of sovereignty and a new sophistication in tactics to achieve traditional goals.

Like the factionalism of old, this modern alliance has brought about a broader and more formal level of organization. A new stage of pan-Indian traditionalism has emerged to counter pan-Indian progressivism. Will that in turn lead to a new level of assimilation and acculturation, in spite of the professed rhetoric and goals of the new alliance? How consistent is the rhetoric of tribalism with the imperatives of modern Indian political organization? Must the new traditional tribalism become bureaucratized to be effective, although its proponents espouse an ideology of Indianess that professes a value system just the opposite? Will legitimated party conflict emerge upon the pan-Indian level, as it has in some tribes? Does the new alliance portend the adoption of political modernization, in the name of old ways, as the means necessary to old goals? Or, will the new alliance fall apart because of a basic incompatibility between the tribal traditionalists who remain on the reservation and those urban and college-educated Indians they look upon as pseudotraditionalists at best?

Except for apathetic or active assimilationists, all Indians today espouse the self-determination by Indians of Indian affairs without the termination of some kind of federal relationship and services. Traditionals and their new-found allies push for de facto sovereignty as the only true protection for the survival of Indian societies and cultures. Official tribal leaders also favor self-determination, but to them it means their right to decide tribal affairs within the framework as now constituted. Both positions look back to a tribal sovereignty antedating the power of the white government to determine the framework of a tribe's destiny. Both positions see the continuance of a special place for American Indians in American society and their governance resting upon a special relationship with the federal government. Both rest their cases upon the history of treaties, but they interpret the significance of that history quite differently. One side states that the legal autonomy and actual sovereignty of the tribes was not impaired by conquest: their status remains what the bilateral negotiations once recognized and still imply. The other side accepts the de facto power of the federal government but nevertheless asserts its right to self-determination upon the grounds of custom as well as what the treaties promised. Both sides insist that the treaty obligations of the United States supersede all other laws and policies of the federal government under the supreme law of the land clause in the Constitution. Thus both sides contemplate some sort of continuing Indian separateness, sustained by either special services, special laws, or by a special homeland.

Under any interpretation self-determination leads to tribal control of federal monies and services. The BIA has started contracting with tribal governments to carry out the services it used to perform. Health care, education, and other programs are now being managed by a few tribal governments with federal connections, as the earlier quotation from the Zuni governor implied. None of these tasks is more important to ethnic persistence than control of the school system and its redirection to Indian ends.[43] Self-determination sharpens the old problem of who handles the money and for whose good. As a result continued political conflict may be expected upon the reserves and within tribal governments—a conflict complicated but not diminished by a continuing urban migration. Those Indians who have lived their adult lives off the reservation but return "home" for retirement only add fuel to the flames of such conflict. Tribal and intertribal organizations will have to accommodate or be superseded, just as the NCAI over time embraced a larger constituency and broader program.

In the end, however, the nature of Indian politics and the problems of Indian leaders must be viewed as much in terms of the framework established by white attitudes and government as by the internal pressures arising from diverse interests and outlooks of the Indian population. Many of the basic issues facing Indian peoples today depend, as in the past, upon what white Americans want and Congress legislates. Can Indian Americans achieve self-determination without white Americans' acquiescence? Will Congress permit the spending of federal funds without specifying how the monies will be spent? Since Congress has not allowed Indians as federally recognized tribes to determine the basic framework of their own destiny in the past, why should we expect any fundamental change in the years to come? Even the recent "therapeutic experience of responsible democracy," to us Henry Dobyn's phrase, comes from federal impetus, exists under its guidelines, and often receives funds from the federal treasury. The Indian Reorganization Act spurred the formation of many a tribal government. The use of lawyers to give added voice to the tribe originally stemmed in many instances from the aegis of the Indian Claims Act of 1946 and was increased by the funding and activities of the Office of Economic Opportunity (OEO) in the 1960s.[44] At times the OEO lawyers aided the opposition to the official leaders in addition to the tribal government itself. In those cases, white professionals supported by federal funds entered the delicate internal politics of the tribe or reservation to influence the direction of social and economic change.[45] Only total abandonment of their status as tribal

Indians finally frees Indian Americans from the paternalism of the BIA
and the ultimate supervision of Congress. The factionalism found today
within tribes and on the pan-Indian political scene stems partly from
trying to cope with the fluctuating policies of those two governmental
bodies.

Two basic aims dominated federal, state, and local Indian policy in
the past: the acquisition of Indian lands and resources and the acculturation and assimilation of Indian peoples. Whites sought to put Indian-
owned resources to "higher uses" according to the values of American
capitalism and tried to reshape Indian minds and habits to the "American Way of Life." Although many liberals may think the nation has
entered a new era of cultural pluralism and tolerance of ethnic differences, most Indian leaders are far from sure that such professions of
idealism are nothing more than the passing fancy of a few alienated
whites who talk one way while their many fellow whites think and act
quite another. White individuals and governments upon all levels still
seek Indian lands and resources as ardently as ever, now in the interest
of urban water supplies and farm irrigation, sports fishing and hunting,
tourism and parks, the necessity for oil or other minerals, conservation
and land management practices, or just about any use but an Indian
one.[46]

In most Americans' minds the Indian constitutes "America's unfinished
business," to use the subtitle of a recent foundation report that studied
the "problems" of American Indians. These now classic problems of
health, education, welfare, and economic development activate government policies that lead to assimilation in the minds of Indian leaders.
Today they suspect that the new policy of turning over federal services
to tribal direction is really aimed at terminating those services. Still other
tribal leaders see giving tribal members the same civil rights possessed
by other Americans as another way of destroying the authority of the
tribal government.[47] In the end, white Americans generally wish to help
"the poor Indian" by reforming him according to their understanding of
his problems rather than as Indians understand their problems—of which
the whites comprise a large part in their opinion.

Given the overwhelming preponderance of the white population and
the centuries-long drive to assimilation and dispossession, the endurance
of Indianness and the existence of any tribal resources is remarkable. In
light of the persistence of Indianness and even tribalness, anthropologists
as well as other whites are no longer certain of the ultimate assimilation
of the Indian into American society. The factional politics that preserves
that separateness so effectively is also responsible for fostering change as
well. In recent decades that fight has moved increasingly to the national
level of preserving Indianness as the best protection of individual tribes-

people. From a historical perspective, eternal vigilance seems the regular price of Indian survival; the cost is factional division among Indians.

NOTES

1. Compare Lewis Meriam et al., *The Problem of Indian Administration* (Baltimore: The Johns Hopkins Press, 1928), with, for example, William A. Brophy and Sophie D. Aberle et al., *The Indian: America's Unfinished Business* (Norman: University of Oklahoma Press, 1966); Sar A. Levitan and Barbara Hetrick, *Big Brother's Indian Programs—With Reservations* (New York: McGraw-Hill, 1971); and Alan L. Sorkin, *American Indians and Federal Aid* (Washington: D.C.: The Brookings Institution, 1971).

2. Some exceptions are Deward E. Walker, Jr., *Conflict and Schism in Nez Perce Acculturation: A Study of Religion and Politics* (Pullman: Washington State University Press, 1968); Thomas S. Abler, "Factional Dispute and Party Conflict in the Political System of the Seneca Nation (1845–1895): An Ethnohistorical Analysis" (Ph.D. diss., University of Toronto, 1969); and James A. Clifton, "Factional Conflict and the Indian Community: The Prairie Potawatomi Case," in *The American Indian Today*, ed. Stuart Levine and Nancy O. Lurie (Baltimore: Penguin Books, 1968), pp. 184–211. I owe much to these and similar studies for my analysis in this paper as I also do to personal conversations with my colleague Frances Svennson, who offered insight both as a Sioux and as a political scientist, and with Robert E. Bieder, assistant director of the Center for the History of the American Indian at the Newberry Library, Chicago, and the Fellows at the Center during the academic year 1974–75. The new scholarly emphasis on what I call Indian-centered history will, one hopes, produce numerous dissertations on native politics, for the sources exist in tribal archives and oral traditions as well as in manuscript depositories and libraries around the United States.

3. I offer an argument for such an approach to Indian politics in "The Political Context of a New Indian History," *Pacific Historical Review* 40 (August, 1971): 357–82. See also P. Richard Metcalf, "Who Should Rule at Home? Native American Politics and Indian-White Relations," *Journal of American History* 61 (December, 1974): 651–65.

4. Wilcomb E. Washburn, *Red Man's Land/White Man's Law: A Study of the Past and Present Status of the American Indian* (New York: Charles Scribner's Sons, 1971), offers a brief introduction to the legal definition of the status of Indians by an historian.

5. On the size of effective political community among the Iroquois, consult William N. Fenton, "Locality as a Basic Factor in the Development of Iroquois Social Structure," in *Symposium on Local Diversity in Iroquois Culture*, ed. William N. Fenton, Smithsonian Institution, Bureau of American Ethnology Bulletin, no. 149 (Washington, D.C., 1951), pp. 35–54, and Abler, "Factional Dispute and Party Conflict," pp. 35–62.

6. Marshall Sahlins provides an introduction to tribal political and social systems in general in *Tribesmen* (Englewood Cliffs, N.J.: Prentice-Hall, 1968). A brief overview of North American Indian political systems may be found in Harold E. Driver, *Indians of North America*, rev. ed. (Chicago: University of Chicago Press, 1961), chap. 17, but see also chaps. 15–16, 18–20. Some idea of the difference between Indian and white views of power and governance may be gained from Walter B. Miller, "Two Concepts of Authority," *American Anthropologist* 67 (April, 1955): 271–89. On the language of strata and power in nine Indian cultures, see Munro S. Edmundson, *Status Terminology and the Social Structure of North American Indians* (Seattle: University of Washington Press, 1958), particularly pp. 25–31, 34–36.

7. Some anthropologists sketch the histories of eleven tribes or culture areas according to such a generalized schema in Eleanor B. Leacock and Nancy O. Lurie, eds., *North American Indians in Historical Perspective* (New York: Random House, 1971).

8. Joseph G. Jorgensen argues the relation between Indian deprivation and neocolo-

146   ROBERT F. BERKHOFER, JR.

nialism in "Indians and the Metropolis" in Jack O. Waddell *The American Indian in Urban Society,* ed. Jack O. Waddell and O. Michael Watson (Boston: Little, Brown & Co., 1971), pp. 67–113, and *The Sun Dance Religion: Power for the Powerless* (Chicago: University of Chicago Press, 1972), pp. 89–173. The analogy to the concentration camp is drawn in the title of Carlos B. Embry, *America's Concentration Camps: The Facts about Our Indian Reservations Today* (New York: D. McKay, 1956). Compare Edgar S. Cahn, ed., *Our Brother's Keeper: The Indian in White America* (Washington, D.C.: New Community Press, 1969). Other "theories" of the reservation may be found in Henry F. Dobyns, "Therapeutic Experience of Responsible Democracy," in Levine and Lurie, eds., *The American Indian Today,* pp. 268–91, and George P. Castile, "Federal Indian Policy and the Sustained Enclave: An Anthropological Perspective," *Human Organization* 33 (Fall, 1974): 219–28.

9. On the modern geography of factionalism among Plains tribes, see Murray L. Wax, *Indian Americans: Unity and Diversity* (Englewood Cliffs, N.J.: Prentice-Hall, 1971), pp. 65–87.

10. In addition to Walker, *Conflict and Schism in New Perce Acculturation;* Abler, "Factional Dispute and Party Conflict"; and Clifton, "Factional Conflict and the Indian Community"; see, for example, the following works among others on the Cherokee: Frederick O. Gearing, *Priests and Warriors: Social Structures for Cherokee Politics in the 18th Century,* American Anthropological Association Memoir, no. 93 (1962); Henry T. Malone, *Cherokees of the Old South: A People in Transition* (Athens: University of Georgia Press, 1956); Marion L. Starkey, *The Cherokee Nation* (New York: Alfred A. Knopf, 1946); Morris L. Wardell, *A Political History of the Cherokee Nation, 1838–1907* (Norman: University of Oklahoma Press, 1938).

11. Metcalf, "Who Should Rule at Home?"

12. Compare the timing in various tribes for these developments as seen in Abler, "Factional Dispute and Party Conflict," and in Walker, *Conflict and Schism in Nez Perce Acculturation.*

13. Eleanor Leacock in Leacock and Lurie, eds., *North American Indians in Historical Perspective,* p. 12.

14. I follow Ethel Boissevain, "The Detribalization of the Narragansett Indians: A Case Study," *Ethnohistory* 3 (Summer, 1956): 225–45. The population today is given in Theodore W. Taylor, *The States and Their Indian Citizens* (Washington, D.C.: Government Printing Office, 1972), p. 230. The population in the early 1600s is variously estimated. Alden T. Vaughan, *New England Frontier: Puritans and Indians, 1620–1675* (Boston: Little, Brown & Co., 1965), p. 28, places the figure as low as four thousand including the Eastern Niantic. Francis Jennings estimates that the tribe mustered five thousand warriors alone in the same period, *The Invasion of America: Indians, Colonialism, and the Cant of Conquest* (Chapel Hill: University of North Carolina Press, 1975), p. 26.

15. Brief histories of the Navajo may be found in Edward H. Spicer, *Cycles of Conquest: The Impact of Spain, Mexico, and the United States on the Indians of the Southwest, 1533–1960* (Tucson: University of Arizona Press, 1962), pp. 210–28, but passim; Evon Z. Vogt, "Navajo," in *Perspectives in American Indian Culture Change,* ed. Edward H. Spicer (Chicago: University of Chicago Press, 1961), pp. 278–336. On political developments in particular, consult Mary Shepardson, *Navajo Ways in Government,* American Anthropological Monograph, no. 96 (1963); Peter J. Iverson, "The Evolving Navajo Nation: Diné Continuity Within Change" (Ph.D. diss., University of Wisconsin, Madison, 1975).

16. Even population figures for tribes today must be seen as rough estimates at best, for the census probably underenumerates Indians by a considerable margin. D'Arcy McNickle, *Native American Tribalism: Indian Survivals and Renewals* (London, Oxford, and New York: Oxford University Press, 1973), pp. 171–79, provides a convenient summary of tribal population figures and location. On the location and life of the present day Sioux, see Nurge, ed., *The Modern Sioux.* For Plains Indian and Cherokee life today, see Wax, *Indian Americans,* chaps. 4–5.

17. Reservation population sizes include Alaskan Indians and are derived from table no. 2 in Levitan and Hetrick, *Big Brother's Indian Programs*, p. 9.

18. Everett E. White's estimates as given in table no. 1 in Helen W. Johnson, "American Indians in Rural Poverty," in *Toward Economic Development for Native American Communities*, Joint Economic Committee of the United States Congress (Washington, D.C.: Government Printing Office, 1969), p. 38.

19. John A. Price, "The Migration and Adaptation of American Indians to Los Angeles," *Human Organization* 27 (Summer, 1968): 168–77.

20. Waddell and Watson, eds., *The American Indian in Urban Society*, provide a collection of articles on the topic of their title, which they have supplemented in *American Indian Urbanization*, ed. Jack O. Waddell and O. Michael Watson (Lafayette, Ind.: Institute for the Study of Social Change, 1973). For other views, see also the discussion of "The Urban Scene and the American Indian" in *Indian Voices: The First Convocation of American Indian Scholars* (San Francisco: Indian Historian Press, 1970), pp. 333–55.

21. Taylor, *The States and Their Indian Citizens*, discusses federal as well as state relationships with tribes.

22. Department of Labor analysts show some perplexity over the language situation in "Role of Manpower Programs in Assisting the American Indians," in *Toward Economic Development for Native American Communities*, pp. 129–31.

23. Both Wax, *Indian Americans*, chaps. 4–5, 7, and Estelle Fuchs and Robert J. Havighurst, *To Live on This Earth: American Indian Education* (New York: Doubleday & Co., 1972), chap. 3, try to convey some of the diversity of modern Indian life.

24. Some conception of the complexities of the Sioux situation can be gained from a comparison of James Howard's lists in Nurge, ed., *The Modern Sioux*, pp. xii-xv, with the list of governments in Taylor, *The States and Their Indian Citizens*, pp. 240, 242–43, or a list of "Governing Bodies of Federally Recognized Indian Groups" issued periodically by the BIA.

25. These developments in the Seneca Nation can be followed in Abler, "Factional Dispute and Party Conflict in the Political System of the Seneca Nation."

26. For the relationships between ethnic identity and tribal government today, compare the lists given in Taylor, *The States and Their Indian Citizens*, appendixes J, K; Barry T. Klein, ed., *Reference Encyclopedia of the American Indian*, 2d ed. (Rye, N.Y.: Todd Publications, 1973), 2: 147–213; Bureau of Indian Affairs, "Governing Bodies of Federally Recognized Indian Groups" (issued periodically).

27. See the strong feelings of Rupert Costo on the official tribal governments expressed in *Indian Voices*, pp. 286–87, but the whole section on "Forms and Uses of Tribal Government" is worth perusal.

28. Particularly virulent have been disputed elections among the Brule Sioux on the Rosebud Reservation and the Oglala Sioux on the Pine Ridge Reservation. For a participant's view of the dispute, see Robert Burnette and John Koster, *The Tortured Americans* (Englewood Cliffs, N.J.: Prentice-Hall, 1971), and *The Road to Wounded Knee* (New York: Bantam Books, 1974). Robert A. White provides some insights into Sioux politics in "Value Themes of the Native American Tribalistic Movement Among South Dakota Sioux," *Current Anthropology* 15 (September, 1974): 284–303. William O. Farber, "Representative Government: Application to the Sioux," in Nurge, ed., *The Modern Sioux*, pp. 123–39, surveys the electoral framework of recent Sioux tribal government.

29. Robert E. Lewis in introduction to Taylor, *The States and Their Indian Citizens*, p. xix.

30. A view of the BIA by a former Executive Director of the National Congress of American Indians is Vine Deloria, Jr., *Custer Died for Your Sins: An Indian Manifesto* (New York: Macmillan Co., 1969), pp. 128–47.

31. BIA administrator James E. Officer suggests the perplexity of his agency in Waddell and Watson, eds., *American Indian in Urban Society*, pp. 61–62, and Waddell and Watson, eds., *American Indian Urbanization*, pp. 7–10.

32. Abler, "Factional Dispute and Party Conflict," p. 17.

33. The takeover and the demands are presented and discussed in the *NCAI Sentinel Bulletin*, February 1975.

34. This paragraph is based upon Hazel W. Hertzberg, *The Search for an American Indian Identity: Modern Pan-Indian Movements* (Syracuse: Syracuse University Press, 1971), pp. 31–209.

35. There is at present no full-fledged history of the NCAI, but see the Vine Deloria supplement to Jennings C. Wise, *The Red Man in the New World Drama: A Politico-Legal Study with a Pageantry of American Indian History*, ed. Vine Deloria, Jr. (New York: Macmillan Co., 1971), pp. 372–75; Hertzberg, *Search for an American Indian Identity*, pp. 289–91; Wax, *Indian Americans*, pp. 145–48. The best place to trace the changing personnel and policies of the organization is through its own periodical *NCAI Sentinel*.

36. Some indication of the conflict among Indian groups at the AIIC can be glimpsed in Nancy O. Lurie, "The Voice of the American Indian: Report on the American Indian Chicago Conference," *Current Anthropology* 2 (December 1961): 478–500. The declaration may be located in *Great Documents in American Indian History*, ed. Wayne Moquin and Charles Van Doren (New York: Praeger Publishers, 1973), pp. 337–46.

37. The standard source on the background and formation of the NIYC is Stan Steiner, *The New Indians* (New York: Harper & Row, 1968), but some of the leaders of the movement repudiate the quotations according to Beatrice Medicine in *Indian Voices*, p. 300. In fact, the whole discussion by her and other participants at the convocation on "Red Power: Real or Potential," ibid., pp. 299–331, is interesting. Robert C. Day summarizes briefly the history of Indian activism during the 1960s in "The Emergence of Activism as a Social Movement," in *Native Americans Today: Sociological Perspectives*, ed. Howard M. Bahr, Bruce A. Chadwick, and Robert C. Day (New York: Harper & Row, 1972), pp. 506–32.

38. Merwyn S. Gabarino, "The Chicago Indian Center: Two Decades," in Waddell and Watson, eds., *American Indian Urbanization*, pp. 74–89. Documents issued from Alcatraz by the group calling themselves Indians of All Tribes have been reprinted in part in *Red Power: The American Indians' Fight for Freedom*, ed. Alvin M. Josephy, Jr. (New York: McGraw-Hill, 1971), pp. 187–89; Moquin and Van Doren, eds., *Great Documents*, pp. 374–79. See also Ruperto Costo, "Alcatraz," *The Indian Historian* 3 (Winter, 1970),; 1–12, 64–65.

39. On AIM, see the brief mentions in Wise-Deloria, *Red Man in the New World Drama*, pp. 377–78, 394–97; Frances Svensson, *The Ethnics in American Politics: American Indians* (Minneapolis: Burgess Publishing Co., 1973), pp. 39–43.

40. Vine Deloria, Jr., gives a short history of the caravan and the occupation of Wounded Knee as well as an exposition of the theory of treaty relationship and tribal sovereignty that came out of these demonstrations in *Behind the Trail of Broken Treaties: An Indian Declaration of Independence* (New York: Dell Publishing Co., 1974). Appendix 4 of his *God is Red* (New York: Grossett & Dunlap, 1973), gives the twenty points, the reply of the White House, and a further Indian response.

41. Alvin M. Josephy wrote of his impressions of "What the Indians Want," in the *New York Times Magazine* (March 18, 1973), pp. 18–19, 66–82.

42. Different views of the purposes of Native American Studies programs can be found scattered throughout the discussion of the subject in *Indian Voices*, pp. 161–90. Also see Frances Svensson, "Language as Ideology: The American Indian Case," *American Indian Culture and Research Journal* 1, no. 3 (1975): 29–35, for an analysis of the topic of her title.

43. Recent tribal control of educational institutions is described in Margaret Szasz, *Education and the American Indian: The Road to Self-Determination, 1928–1973* (Albuquerque: University of New Mexico Press, 1974), chaps. 12–13; Fuchs and Havighurst, *To Live on This Earth*, chap. 17. The rationale for such a movement is offered in David Adams, "Self-determination and Indian Education," in *American Indian Education*, ed. R. Merwin Deever et al. (Tempe: Arizona University Press, 1974), pp. 3–8.

44. The implications of tribal counsel for altering customary reservation relations with the federal government are pointed out in Dobyns, "Therapeutic Experience of Responsible Democracy."

45. The moral and legal dilemmas of lawyer intervention in tribal politics are considered in Monroe E. Price, "Lawyers on the Reservation: Some Implications for the Legal Profession," in *Toward Economic Development for Native American Communities*, pp. 191–222.

46. Recent white efforts to take Indian lands are detailed in Kirke Kickingbird and Karen Ducheneaux, *One Hundred Million Acres* (New York: Macmillan Co., 1973). Problems of fishing tribes in the state of Washington with white government agencies over sports uses and conservation are presented in American Friends Service Committee, *Uncommon Controversy: Fishing Rights of the Muckleshoot, Pyallup, and Nisqually Indians* (Seattle: University of Washington Press, 1970). A good survey of the subject of its title is Willian H. Veeder, "Federal Encroachment on Indian Water Rights and the Impairment of Reservation Development," in *Toward Economic Development for Native American Communities*, pp. 449–518.

47. Indian scholars discuss "Implications of the 1968 Civil Rights Act in Tribal Autonomy" in *Indian Voices*, pp. 85–104. Testimony before Congress against the Indian Civil Rights Act of 1968 is reprinted in *Of Utmost Good Faith*, ed. Vine Deloria, Jr. (San Francisco: Straight Arrow Books, 1971), pp. 221–27.

Eastern and
Southern Europeans

Josef J. Barton

THE EMERGENCE OF TRADITIONS of leadership was an important part of the building of ethnic communities. The expectations of immigrant peoples of Southern and Eastern Europe shaped the experiences of newcomers and the responses of leaders. The agricultural villages of Bohemia, Slovakia, Rumania, Slovenia, Croatia, and Italy, from which the newcomers whom I am here studying journeyed, imposed certain stringencies and encouraged certain aspirations. Patterns of immigration selected certain people and led them to settle in particular locales. The development of associations shaped the lives of young communities. Rearing children, learning to labor in an industrial economy, and watching sons and daughters leave the household to form their own families— these events, too, reveal the diverse meanings which urban life held for immigrants. Leaders were able to shape these new communities as they participated in these experiences, as they felt and articulated the distinctive memories of villages in dissolution and the hopes of urban communities in formation. In order to understand the leadership of Southern and Eastern European ethnic communities, then, we need to watch men and women over an adequate period of change, to see them as they define the boundaries of new communities.

In beginning a task of this sort, I have tried to start out afresh to produce the long-term and fine-comb research which can give palpable actuality to the story of ethnic leadership. Here I begin two tasks: first, to sketch the emergence of a little tradition of communal leadership and the development of a larger tradition of national leadership, and second, to outline features common to the development of these two kinds of leadership in several diverse groups. In going about this, I pursue four related themes. Emigrants left their villages, in the first place, having already learned something about leadership in communal life; the emergence of little traditions of leadership among newly arrived immigrants, then, was part of a longer story which began in the European countryside. In the second place, ethnic leaders created institutions of enduring function in the lives of families and communities; hence, the social context of newcomers' lives lay behind patterns of leadership. In the third place, even though much of this essay concentrates upon the development of nuclei of communal loyalties, at some point in the trajectories of every group the creation of boundaries became an important task. And, fourth, as this shift in strategies took place a new kind of ethnic leadership emerged. Sometimes continuous with communal leadership, more often this elite developed in organizational settings beyond the community; this new leadership came to dominate ethnic groups during the second generation. In carrying out research to illustrate these themes, I have worked in small settings, in households, parishes, communities. These small facts, when coaxed into a comparative setting, can be made to speak to larger issues.

Since ethnic communities are without formal definitions and structure, we cannot easily assume that position and influence are identical. Hence I have chosen to deal with traditions of leadership which took shape through a pattern of choices made as immigrants came to terms with American cities. It is important to note, then, what I do not do. I have made no complete census of positions, no collective biography of persons who filled political, social, and religious offices. To do so would require the assumption that the dignitaries were also the powers—a questionable assertion about a formal political system and unwarranted in speaking of so ill-defined a thing as an ethnic community. Nevertheless, ethnic groups clearly have leaders about whom we can speak in a disciplined way. Here I have followed the emergence of traditions of leadership and sketched some of their social and cultural contexts. I do not claim that these were the only kinds of leadership, only that these traditions had great importance in the making of ethnic communities.

Emigration was a symptom of important changes in the peasant villages of Eastern and Southern Europe, and it also hastened change. Peasants left a world on the wane, a society in disaggregation. The development of national markets for agricultural products and the transformation of land, especially communal pasture and forest, into just another commodity threatened the social order of the village and the status of peasants. These changes left the peasantry in perpetual ferment, but without the cohesion to give collective expression to its aspirations and

needs. So when faced with hardship, a large proportion of rural cultivators chose emigration as an alternative to the old order.[1]

The areas of heaviest emigration in Eastern and Southern Europe—
southern Bohemia and Moravia, eastern Slovakia, Transylvania, Slovenia
and Croatia, and Italy—were characterized by a relatively broad distribution of property and mixed agricultural systems. The redistribution of
property and the development of commercial agriculture had gone far
enough to create a countryside in which large and small holdings, ordinarily labor intensive, were ranged side by side. A few large proprietors
formed the upper stratum of rural society, while a second stratum of
middling cultivators enjoyed some growth as alienated estates and communal lands passed into the hands of a rural petite bourgeoisie. An even
larger group of small owner-operators who produced enough for their
own households and a tiny surplus for town markets occupied a third
stratum. Finally, a sizeable group of laborers made up the largest segment of the agricultural labor force. Traditional agricultural practices
and relatively broadly distributed property muted inequalities of income.[2]
Hence emigration affected most strongly those regions where agricultural
development was most backward but where an equality of misery characterized rural society.

The distinctive characteristic of the regions of heavy emigration, then,
was a diffusion of property rights which ordinarily provided land and
dowries for sons and daughters of peasants. By no means was this an
equalitarian society: my point is that the continuity of traditional agriculture and relatively broadly distributed property muted inequalities of
income. The practice of partible inheritance continued to fragment land
and to provide at least a scrap of land for a new generation; it was just
such miserable patrimonies which tied men and women to their villages.
The broad distribution of property rights, the use of sharefarming and
sharecropping, the division of holdings—these factors sustained peasant
agriculture. Emigration was symptomatic in these regions, then, not of
some general crisis in peasant agriculture, but of the growing imbalance
between the needs of peasant households and the opportunities of non-
agricultural employment. What had further contributed to the stability
of peasant households before the 1870s was the connection between
agriculture and household industry. But everywhere a spurt of agricultural modernization (and hence of specialization) and the decline of
household industry (because of the penetration of manufactured goods
into the countryside) restricted peasants' resources. Unable to find a
piece of land in already crowded villages, unable to support themselves
in household industries, young men and women abandoned the land
altogether. And as their chances of finding work in the villages narrowed,
they joined a world market of labor.[3]

The crowded railroad cars arriving at Bremerhaven or Naples or Trieste carried Czech, Rumanian, Croatian, and Italian villagers. It was through the villages that peasants were integrated into agrarian society, that laborers found daily employment, that artisans disposed of their products. Villages belonged also to the outside world and found continuous interaction with it. A steady pattern of population movement characterized villages in areas of heavy emigration. Small-holding peasants and day laborers of the Southern Italian village of San Pietro in Guarano depended upon seasonal migration during the nineteenth century for the little cash they needed to buy tools or seed. By the 1870s young men began to venture to Bari for construction work, young women to Salerno for a season in the textile mills, both eventually to Pittsburgh and Chicago in the 1890s. By 1900 every peasant household in the village had sent at least one member to some Italian or American city in search of work.[4] From Sibiel, a small village in the Carpathian foothills of Rumania, a steady stream of young men and women flowed first to sheep-raising areas of Rumania and Bulgaria, then to the industrial shops of Cleveland and Chicago.[5] After 1870, wherever one looks in these areas of Eastern and Southern Europe, a characteristic restlessness appears in a variety of villages—a seasonal movement first, then a search for small industries, finally a journey toward an European or American industrial city.[6] Few households escaped the effects of this mobility; all villages experienced the changes wrought by this rural exodus.

More than an unsettling restlessness, this mobility was symptomatic of a felt loss of mastery in the villages. The cycle of communal ceremony —the ritual observance of baptisms, funerals, namedays, Holy Week— enacted the shared sense of participation in a village community. The enormous variety of family and communal celebrations rendered tangible and predictable the interdependencies of the social order. But the erosion of the household economy and the astonishing mobility of villagers after 1870 began to weaken the hold of family and communal affiliations. Festival and ritual depended upon the active participation of all present, upon the breaking of boundaries between spectator and actor. When that participation shrank, a sense of dissonance entered the life of the community.[7]

The disaggregation of community life came slowly, sometimes imperceptibly, everywhere accompanied by a dissolution of the household economy and its rhythms. And nothing was more emblematic of this crisis than the peasants' and laborers' loss of communal lands. The slow but insistent usurpation of pasture and forest by a new rural bourgeoisie shut off access acre by acre, until by the 1870s the communal economy was weakened.[8] The resonance of this crisis was felt in every area of the peasant community but most acutely in the household. The pattern of work, once interwoven in the texture of communal life, became synchronized with the demands of commercial agriculture and wage labor. In San Pietro, for instance, at least one member of every peasant family was drawn into some sort of organized wage labor after 1870. Family life was governed less by collective rhytms, more by actions of an impersonal labor market.[9]

In this new situation in which families lived exposed to the vicissitudes of an external economy, peasants adopted two strategies of defense. First, they developed an enlarged network of kinship ties outside the household, ties which were important sources of aid. In the Italian village of San Pietro and the Rumanian hamlet of Sibiel, these ties bound families through apprenticeship and foster parentage, through dowry and donation, through gifts of aid. There emerged, then, a cohesive and overlapping pattern of small groups, an informal collective life in which kinship linked a number of households in mutual assistance.[10]

Second, families formed voluntary associations to create organizations which gave collective response to their new vulnerability. There emerged an enormous variety of associations after 1870 to insure for illness and death, to supervise education, to form agricultural and artisan organizations, to pursue political aims. In Huslenky, a Moravian village of about 1200 inhabitants, at least fifteen associations flourished between 1870 and 1900. Masons formed a mutual benefit society, share tenants an agricultural society, carpenters and joiners a burial union.[11] The shepherds of the tiny Rumanian village of Sibiel organized a mutual benefit society in 1891, the sharecroppers an evening school in 1898, the whole commune a savings bank in 1901 which shortly before 1914 became also a cooperative store.[12] In Alcara Li Fusi, a Sicilian village of 1,800 inhabitants, a similar array of associations developed after 1890. An evening school for agricultural laborers, a mutual aid society for "honest workingmen," and several agricultural societies assured residents membership in one or another association.[13] As the cumulation of economic and social changes fragmented village communities into many competing groups, each concerned to secure its position by creating new coalitions, voluntary associations furnished a means of achieving a measure of stability in a changeful world.[14]

Within this context of fragmentation and partial integration, there emerged a characteristically segmented community. A proliferation of mutual benefit societies traced the lines of change in Calabrian and Sicilian societies, each association fulfilling in some particular way needs once met comprehensively. The mutual aid society of San Vincenzo, founded in Alcara Li Fusi in 1889, was joined by a religious confraternity in 1891, two more confraternities in 1895, yet two more in 1901, and three mutual benefit societies in 1907, each composed of allied family groups, each securing some measure of order in a changing community. This frenetic activity attracts one's attention wherever one turns in the Deep South of Italy.[15] Among the peasants of Sibiel, a similar web of voluntary affiliations grew in the 1890s that held families in an associational life of confraternities and sodalities, youth choirs and mutual aid societies. And here, too, one finds the same events in neighboring villages.[16] By the end of the nineteenth century, in those regions soon to be emptied by mass migration, peasants had achieved a partial yet enduring cohesion of household and community life in which voluntary associations played a large part. Within these crosscutting bonds of kinship and association, individuals and families constructed a tangible community identity.[17] After all other impressions fade, this one lasts: while there was a loss of any felt cohesion in the community, yet there remained the signs of a community which peasants, in response to a profound transformation of labor and social relations, built for themselves.

After the 1870s, both the form and the leadership of the collective life of Southern and Eastern European peasants changed decisively. The emergence of relatively complex associations of social and economic groups rather than communal groups meant a greater articulation of objectives and demands. A variety of rural peoples began to find ways to express their aspirations about the world. Not yet political, collective action remained a locally confined event. In the Rumanian villages under Hungarian rule, for example, rebellions might break out among day laborers or miners, and for a moment a whole village might galvanize into action; but the protest made, the village lapsed into quiescence. Only in the Banat did this endemic violence become epidemic, and there because the commercialization of agriculture had largely made over the old agrarian order. In areas of peasant emigration, however, even endemic local violence subsided after 1905. Observers noted an exhaustion, and the great peasant revolt of 1907 produced only faint echoes in Transylvania, the area of heaviest emigration.[18] A transformation had begun, then, but nowhere in the areas of mass emigration had it proceeded far enough to produce great collective protest.

The leadership of these new associations was drawn from remarkably varied sources. In Southern Italian villages, a petite rural bourgeoisie of small landholders, lawyers, and local officials led the early associations of the 1870s and remained important leaders into the early twentieth century. But a growing number of artisans and peasants moved into leadership roles after 1890, and by 1900 a sizeable group of ordinary villagers could claim leadership experience. In Alcara Li Fusi, for example, peasants and laborers took command of the San Vincenzo society, while a young group of carpenters, most in their twenties and early thirties, assumed control of another mutual benefit society. A similar development came in San Pietro, where a group of peasants organized a credit association which would eventually finance much of the emigration from and agricultural development of the Calabrian village.[19] In other villages as well—Sibiel, in Rumania, Smihel, in Slovenia—peasants came into the leadership of their own associations by the end of the nineteenth century. And as they did so, they created a group of men to which the emigrant community could look for leadership.

Now the mass emigration began, in the troubled time between the disaggregation of the communal economy and the consolidation of a new agrarian regime.[20] First to feel out of place in their own land were artisans, who often became pioneers of migration streams which emptied whole villages of their inhabitants. A settlement once established in Cleveland or Pittsburgh or Chicago, a community took shape. The pattern of migration itself—the predominance of migrants from a few villages or a few districts—ensured that most newcomers to a city would encounter familiar faces, dialects, and early established demographic and social hegemonies in settlements, partly through sheer numbers, but also because they tended to annex, through marriage or other means, large numbers of immigrants from sparsely represented areas. Traditional loyalties to village and district took hold in favorable demographic contexts during the lifetime of the first generation and shaped the communities' social life.[21]

The building of immigrant communities was in part a reconstruction of old models of order and in part an accomodation to the life of the city. Newcomers looked backward to a village past as well as forward to an urban future. Already familiar with the use of voluntary associations in community life, immigrants set about constructing a tangible organizational reality within which newcomers could identify themselves and declare their solidarity with a people. But since Czech and Slovak and Rumanian and Croatian and Italian immigrants were drawn from hundreds of villages, the urban communities were no mere transplanting of villages. Rather, they were made of specialized associations meeting partially the needs that peasant households and the villages of which they had been a part had fulfilled comprehensively. It was in this accomodation that immigrants developed distinctive orientations toward the problems and prospects of the city.[22]

The cities—especially those burgeoning giants on the bleak flatland of the midwest—assumed after 1870 the new patterns of the industrial metropolis. Chicago, Pittsburgh, Cleveland, Detroit—all counted a growing proportion of their inhabitants foreign-born after 1880. Work patterns changed also, for what had been cities of laborers and merchants in 1880 became filled with clerical and sales workers by 1950. The motley sources of population growth and the diversification of occupational structures created new social arrangements, the most important of which was residential segregation of racial, ethnic, and occupational groups. The laggard response of public institutions to urban problems meant that private institutions worked to structure the city. The family, the neighborhood, the voluntary association—these were the principal agencies of social control between 1890 and 1950. These characteristics, then, defined the new world of immigrants and directed the course of their lives.[23]

However unfriendly to rural life the modern city appears, the passage from village to metropolis was no sudden plunge into modernity. The very fragmentation of urban life created interstices in which local communities could create and sustain a humanly satisfying culture. It was here, in these discontinuous circles of urban life and work, that immigrants learned to live in the city. In so doing, they traced a pattern which defines our own urban inheritance.

This patrimony was a weave of small patterns, an outcome of thousands of decisions made in household and workplace. Crucial to an understanding of urban ethnic culture is that it was the possession of agricultural laborers, peasants, artisans—newcomers who took half a lifetime to learn to be industrial laborers, owners of city lots, skilled machinists.[24] I take for my motto here a Slovak laborer's ejaculation to a Hungarian consul: "A poor man stays a poor man, and the rest is nonsense."[25] Immigrants of elite background ordinarily came from an intellectual petite bourgeoisie who had even in the village put off any remnants of peasant culture. This tiny group of newspaper editors, barbers, and merchants were always eager to cash in on a fashionable nationalism, but their chance would not come until the 1920s. Working-class immigrants inherited the aging core of the cities, and they and their leaders built for themselves a distinctive culture. Mike Gold puts the case bluntly in *Jews without Money:* "The city was my world; it was my mother's world, too. We had to live in it, and learn what it chose to teach us."[26]

The fact that the bulk of peasant immigrants began their lives as unskilled laborers is a decisive one in interpreting their experiences, for their beginning at the bottom of the occupational hierarchy meant that most families would not escape manual labor. But newcomers did not remain in an identical class position. Even though mobility was largely within the working class, the movement of unskilled laborers into skilled jobs or their purchase of property represented significant gains over their origins.

Family social mobility, as recent work on cities between 1880 and 1960 shows, falls into three crude patterns.[27] As my study of Cleveland reports, slightly less than a fourth of the unskilled starters and their sons remained laborers for their whole lives. A static work experience characterized a third of Slovak families, while a slightly larger proportion of both Italians and Rumanians climbed out of their laboring origins. Some early returns from a similar study of 360 Czech families in Chicago illustrate a similar pattern, as do some crude results of my onging study of Croatian and Slovene immigrants. Both the fathers and their sons took such jobs as hod carriers or furnace stokers; the fortunate gained some skills as press operators or machine hands; the aristocrats became steel rollers or machinists. For the largest part of immigrant communities, however, wages left little margin to invest in property, and employment provided few opportunities to acquire status.

Nevertheless, many men who had begun in similar positions managed to gain skills and to acquire property. A little less than fifty percent of unskilled starters in Cleveland, for instance, moved into the skilled and propertied segment of the working class. In about half of this group, family members acquired skills, while in the other families advanced their position through the purchase of property. This kind of mobility was especially important in the Czech, Slovak, and Croatian communities; for it established a tradition of skill in about a third of the families whose fathers had started out as laborers. The sons of Italian laborers who gained skilled occupations, on the other hand, frequently had to begin again, as their fathers had, in unskilled jobs. Despite ethnic differences, the acquisition of skill and property made the largest part of immigrant communities a stable segment of the working class within a generation of arrival.

The workshops of this remarkable achievement were the subdivided houses of Chicago's Koven Avenue and the tiny cottages of Cleveland's Berg Street. Biographies convey this experience better than a sociological filter of finest mesh.[28] František and Maria Svádek came to Chicago from Zahradke, in Bohemia, in 1874. František had owned about an acre of land and knew carpentry as well. He and his wife had three children, Anton, born before they left Europe, and Jane and Frank, both born in Chicago, none of whom attended school beyond the fifth grade. The father worked as a laborer in a rail yard, earning between $360 and $450 a year; Anton, the oldest, began working in a planing mill at sixteen, earning about $250, while Jane became a tailor's apprentice at twelve, working twelve hours a day for $2 a week. When they pooled their earnings, there was enough to buy a tiny house on Twelfth Street and to set aside $10 a year in a savings account. Life was crowded but satisfying in this house, where all the sons lived into their thirties.

Look at the themes in the lives of another ordinary family. Francesco Sila left the Sicilian village of Alcara Li Fusi in 1899, married Anna Di Fazio of the same village in 1901; six children were born to them between 1904 and 1917. The father served as a plumber's helper for the first fifteen years of his career, then became a master plumber in 1924. None of his four boys got past the eighth grade, none of the girls past the sixth. Nevertheless, Luigi, the oldest, became a skilled machinist after a long apprenticeship, while Urban, the second son, worked most of his life as a bartender. The two youngest, however, Giovanni and Alberto, spent their lives in casual labor, waiting days on end in a hiring hall, then spending a few days on a construction job. Francesca, the oldest girl, worked for ten years as a clerk in a small grocery store, and Giovanna, the youngest daughter, as a seamstress in a laundry.

The need for roots, the search for stability and continuity: as the constitution of a Czech workers' society had it, family life depended on "diligence in duty, attendance at Mass, Catholic schooling, and frugality."[29] The story of Josef Hlavaty and his family, from Budišov, illustrates these themes. Josef and Katrina arrived in Chicago in 1881 with two children; they found a tiny apartment in a tenement occupied by ten Czech families. They searched for jobs. Josef finally found work as a construction laborer, while Kate took in washing. Josef, the oldest child, was apprenticed to a boilermaker at age thirteen in 1886, became a master of his trade in 1895, and set up his own shop in 1896. Rebecca went into service at fourteen, married a Polish ticket agent, and became head of an enormous household of her own children and her husband's relatives. Or another family, that of Milan Vukić, who left Bosenski Semac in Croatia, in 1902, to work in the steel mills of South Chicago. Milan and Antonia had seven children between 1904 and 1914, all of whom finished parochial school. The father remained a mill hand at Republic Steel all his life, but managed to acquire a small lot and a tiny house in 1921. All four sons became skilled steelworkers, while two of the daughters became school teachers. Three of the older sons and the youngest daughter continued to live in the parental household into their early thirties while the youngest, Martin, resided at home for ten years after his marriage.

Family life in such households took the form of connected networks of social relationships, first to relatives and second to friends. Immigrant families lived in this overlapping connection of kinship, of neighborhood, of association. Husband and wife brought to marriage an already closely knit network of ties; the birth of children, which brought godparents into the family, created new connections. Each family member, each relative, became a link not only with other kin but also with people outside the family as well. Across the open frontiers between households flowed relatives, boarders, mutual assistance. In these tangential circles of intimacy flourished a dense, informal, collective life.[30]

A remarkable growth of voluntary associations accompanied the emergence of immigrant family life. Czech newcomers to Chicago, for instance, formed forty-nine mutual benefit societies between 1870 and 1880, thirty-six of which began as branches of societies in homeland villages. Each society drew families and neighborhoods into wider circles

of mutual assistance and built a process of association which eventually
pulled most families into a round of organized life. Choirs and theater
groups performed almost daily in the new halls and saloons; self-improvement societies offered workers literacy in Czech and English; bakers' and
butchers' and framemakers' societies bound together men of a trade.[31]
Italians in Cleveland organized thirty-five mutual benefit societies between
1903 and 1910, twenty-five of which were branches of societies in Southern Italian villages.[32] In the Slovak community of Cleveland the formation of some twenty-five societies between 1885 and 1900 served to
create a stable community.[33] Rumanian immigrants to Cleveland began
to establish societies in 1902; four years later a complex network of associations linked probably two-thirds of the newcomers in an organized
round of life.[34] Wherever one looks in these new communities, whether
among Slovaks in Cleveland or Croatians in South Chicago, an extraordinary density of associational life was the case. In these new urban
settlements, voluntary associations became the characteristic social unit
that created "a matrix within which the group organized its policing
devices, family life, marriage, churches, educational system, and associations for cultural and social ends."[35]

The task of forming new communities fell on a generation already
familiar with the uses of associations in the creation of solidarities. Southern and Eastern European peasant communities were, on the eve of emigration, bound together with the strands of enormous varieties of associations. The work of creating the institutions of mutual benefit society,
parish, school, and labor union was carried out by men and women who
had learned to reach out, across lines of household and neighborhood, to
create agencies for the pursuit of collective goals. If one surveys the
emergence of ethnic leadership in American cities, one is confronted with
a bewildering picture of diverse institutional responses to what, for all
its variations in outward form, is esentially a common problem: the construction of collective means of coming to terms with the realities of
urban life.
    The new communities were, rather like apprentice pioneers, seeking
their own distinctive means of solving the problems of urban newcomers.
Transient, poorly recorded, ill-defined, uncertain, the solutions that ethnic
leaders adopted to common problems are difficult to classify and order.
Czech, Rumanian, Italian and other ethnic leaders shared a predicament,
but a predicament which provoked them to explore a variety of strategies
in order to supply immigrants with stable leadership. Not all of this
leadership was successful, by any means; for every successful experiment
several failures could be counted. But the urgency of adapting to a new
environment kept alive organizational innovation.

An attempt to examine the strategies of ethnic leaders and shifts in kinds of ethnic leadership must begin with a simple review of a number of communities, a setting out in brief of past experience. It should be possible, from such a review, to learn at least the kinds of strategies and leadership involved and to gain some notion of the social contexts within which aspirations took shape and found articulation. What follows, then, is not an attempt to isolate any constancies of ethnic leadership, but rather an effort to mark out limits within which variations took place. Here, a sense of the limits within which the hopes of various ethnic groups changed and the dimensions within which ethnic leaders both initiated and responded to changes can best be conveyed by a rapid review of continuities and changes in several selected ethnic groups. Czechs, Slovaks, Rumanians, Croats and Slovenes, and Italians share a peasant background, yet present a large enough variety of responses to furnish good subjects for this rapid survey.

CZECHS

By the late 1870s Czech immigrants had settled in a number of Midwestern cities and had begun the task of organizing mutual benefit societies, parishes, and schools. Many among the early leaders had no more claim to prominence than their position as heads of families. A gathering of the heads of young families on West 25th Street in Cleveland in 1880, for instance, marked the emergence of organized parish life in a neighborhood; a meeting of seventeen young men in Milwaukee in 1881 led to the founding of a Catholic mutual aid society; an assembly of young mothers in Chiago in 1886 produced a sodality.[36] Men who were natives of the same village or families who belonged to a widening circle of relatives bound themselves together in these new associations. Each association provided the needed relationships for which a periodic gathering of families was a metaphor; each gathering shaped expectations of community life.[37]

The essential feature of voluntary associations in Czech communities was their multiplicity, in which was expressed the fragmented character of leadership. The astonishing proliferation of saints' societies, each a mutual benefit organization as well, filled the calendars of urban parishes. The leaders of these societies—some of whose membership numbered ten or twelve families—characteristically came from Czech villages in which mutual aid societies were active. Among the forty-nine Chicago societies whose leadership I have been able to trace from 1870 to 1920, for instance, 60 percent of the presidents had belonged to a mutual aid society in their native village. Nine out of ten were of peasant house-

holds, and eighty percent worked at blue collar jobs in Chicago.[38] A
Similar kind of leadership developed in Cleveland and St. Louis, two
other cities of substantial Czech settlement. With these leaders Czech
immigrants carried on that characteristic ethnic activity of community
building.[39] Beginning with St. John Nepomuk in St. Louis in 1854 and
ending in the 1920s and 1930s in Cicero and Parma, Czech Catholics
participated in the formation of an urban Catholic establishment. A lively
growth of voluntary associations continued to furnish the leadership
which nourished the growth of the Czech communities.[40]

A second group of leaders was active as well, these in the task of bind-
ing together a wide variety of local associations. Their efforts were effective; in Chicago, for example, by 1900 the five hundred or so local mutual
benefit societies belonged to one or another of twelve national unions.
Ordinarily formed under the leadership of the officers of the oldest
mutual aid society in a city, these national federations grew slowly in
the 1870s and 1880s but began a period of rapid expansion in the 1890s.
In a transient community a national union furnished a means of trans-
ferring membership from one city to another. But most important, these
great federations provided an articulate leadership drawn from a burgeoning class of professionals in the Czech community. With membership
in some federations approaching 100,000 and with broadly circulated
newspapers sponsored by the unions, a powerful group of national
leaders had emerged by 1900.[41]

What this brief sketch suggests, then, is that the emergence of Czech
leadership can be understood only over the long run. Czech emigrants
left a changing homeland in which peasant families had created new styles
of community life. In coming to terms with the unsettling transformation of
village life, a group of leaders had acquired a communal sense, a capacity
to respond to collective needs. As Czech newcomers entered American
cities, they were prepared to seek ways of pursuing their collective needs.
Hence the Czech leaders of the first and second generation built institutions which were particularly responsive to the changeful reality of the
city. In the first thirty years of the twentieth century, however, it was
just these communities which were most exposed to the corrosive force
of mobility. In Chicago, for instance, the rapid dispersion of the original
Czech settlements and the development of satellite communities in more
than twenty suburbs created a new need for leadership and organized
life. As early as 1908 a Czech priest in an urban parish complained that
of one hundred and sixty families in his parish, one hundred and forty
lived more than five miles from the church. And so the exodus went, until
by 1910 the creative center of the Czech community lay among the
double-deckers surrounding the Western Electric plants in Chicago's
western suburbs.[42]

One of the responses of Czech leaders in the reconstruction of ethnic communities was to form new organizations in order to reach alliances with other ethnic communities. The National Alliance of Czech Catholics, for instance, grew out of a World War I patriotic association into a major representation of emergent middle-class immigrants. Its leaders, most of whom were drawn from professional ranks, had a large role in introducing to second- and third-generation Czechs the varieties of Catholic professional and action groups in the 1920s, and the Alliance served as an avenue through which a maturing ethnic community participated in a broadening religious life.[43] A variety of such groups developed during the 1920s, many of them religious organizations but several with secular, largely cultural, aims. As Czech leaders strove to keep pace with their changing clientele, then, they took their cues from the contemporary world. And so began that periodic assimilation and rebuilding which characterizes the activities of ethnic leaders.

SLOVAKS

Slovak immigrants began arriving in large numbers during the 1880s, and in a few years a number of Slovak communities had developed a complex system of organization. Many of the early leaders were saloon keepers and small merchants, pioneers who began, and often sponsored, migration streams from their homeland neighborhoods.[44] As newcomers settled into the tiny houses near Cleveland's or Pittsburgh's steel mills, these men established mutual benefit societies among immigrants from Drinova, Hermanovce, Čel'ovoc. These early leaders cultivated distinctive memories of place, perhaps in hopes that traditional bonds would provide some measure of stability to a society's membership.[45] But they did more than guard tradition, for their work brought them into contact with other immigrant groups and with the larger urban world. So they stood between immigrant newcomers and the city, transitional figures in the early stages of ethnic community life.

A shift in leadership, however, had become apparent by 1900. The local societies had come under the direction of working-class leaders. Of the sixty-four leaders of Cleveland mutual aid societies in 1900 whom I was able to trace, for example, 80 percent were semiskilled or skilled workers, and some impressionistic evidence suggests that the proportion may have been higher in 1910. Not until the 1950s would business men and professionals begin to move back into leadership positions on the local level.[46] It was on the regional and national level that Slovak businessmen and professionals continued to exercise leadership after 1900. The emergence and consolidation of two great national benevolent unions, the National Slovak Society (1888) and the First Slovak Catholic Union (1889) were the work of two powerful leaders, Peter Rovnianek and Stefan Furdek. The first—a ticket agent, real estate broker, banker, newspaper editor—consolidated his hold on the National Slovak Society and remained a dominant secular voice until the 1920s. Furdek, a Catholic priest, organized societies and parties indefatigably throughout the 1890s and became a major voice in the Slovak community through the Union's newspaper, *Jednota*.[47] The powerful federations created by these two leaders remained down to the 1960s the two channels in which flowed the organized life of the community. Yet their activities and initiative were severely limited, for the effectiveness of the national leadership depended always upon the health of the local organizations.

Some sense of the relationship between local organizations and national leadership can be gained in a brief review of some efforts to renew Slovak ethnic life. The frenetic nationalistic activities beginning in 1907, for instance, depended at every step upon the organizing abilities of local leaders. The great nationalist crowd at Cleveland's Gray's Armory in 1907, drawn from every local organization in the city, came because of the effectiveness of local leaders in staging neighborhood meetings through the months of April and May. The periodic revivals of Slovak days through the 1920s and 1930s, massive demonstrations of sometimes 20,000 people in Pittsburgh, Chicago, and Cleveland, were organized through neighborhood committees. Even the founding of the American section of the *Matica slovenska*, a nationalist cultural union, came through the active intervention of the leaders of local cultural organizations.[48] Hence, even though Slovak leaders early formed several powerful national federations, much of the leadership in the community has continued to work at the local level. Perhaps the leadership of the National Slovak Society realized this when, in 1974, they decided to cease publication of *Národné noviny [National News]* and to devote their resources to production of the *Ethnic American News*, a paper largely of neighborhood news.

RUMANIANS

The early Rumanian community was formed by characteristically mobile men; they had already moved about Rumania and Hungary in search of opportunity. Like Ilie Martin—laborer, storekeeper, self-taught writer—they were ambitious young men for whom migration to the United States was of a piece with their seeking of new situations in the homeland. So self-made men played a major role in the early organization of the community. "The time had come," remembered an early leader, "to shake off our lethargy and, by forming associations, to act as examples for the rest of the Rumanians in this country." These men and women shared a strong sense of participating in, as one of them said, the "founding era" of a community.[49]

The community they formed was markedly secular. Lay leadership predominated in organizational expansion; the clergy played everywhere a secondary role. In Cleveland, for instance, the leadership of the first mutual benefit society, Carpațina, helped form a second organization, the Rumanian Club, in 1904. The leaders of both these organizations, in turn, founded new benevolent and cultural associations. A growing density of organizational life was apparent after 1910. Choirs and theater groups, for instance, segregated the young by age and sex while providing formal training in the Rumanian language. Family associations emerged in the early 1920s, a means of assuring continuity in family life. Self-improvement societies taught laborers to read and write. Between 1910 and 1920, then a network of local clubs came to affiliate Rumanian immigrants with a formally organized community.[50]

The early leadership, as I mentioned earlier, was drawn from mobile men. As a priest remarked of these men in 1906, the migration and creation of new community "made them more conscious of their dignity; they doffed their shepherd's caps, sloughed off their old habits, and adopted a more business-like manner." But even then, during the first flush of their discovery of a new range of action, they became concerned about the welfare of the community. Ioan Babor, a well-known businessman, declared in 1906 that the leadership of the urban communities "belonged to the hard-working middle class of the community—men who will work with great zeal and sacrifice to create a national culture in America."[51]

The second generation of leaders, who began to appear about 1910, continued this emphasis on culture and mobility. The immigrant community, wrote a young leader in 1909, "had gained, by means of hard work, a small fortune. . . . Now we need to leave the life of the factory . . . and look for a more satisfying way." This new life should begin, he went on, with a renewed emphasis on ethnic culture—on books, newspapers, and libraries. And above all, the stress should fall on education, for it would prepare young men and women to lead the second generation. And so began a second round of organizing, of evening and weekend schools, of scholarship funds to sponsor the sons and daughters of Rumanian immigrants in universities and professional schools. It was from this group of men and women that the leadership of the second generation would come.[52]

The first generation of Rumanian leaders fashioned on the national level federations of local societies, unions which by 1912 were well established. The Union of Rumanian Societies (1906) and the Rumanian American Association (1912) succeeded in affiliating all but a handful of societies by 1915.[53] The leadership of these young federations came largely from local societies, in a pattern of advancement from city to national offices which continually recruited new talent. One of the striking aspects of this circulation of leadership in the Rumanian community is the constant movement from local to national offices, and the reverse. The leadership of both levels continued to be young, even during the 1920s and 1930s, when in similar federations of other ethnic groups a rapid aging of leadership had taken place. In 1930, as in 1910, the mean age of national leadership was thirty. The circulation of officers was rapid, few serving more than two terms in any national office. Through a vigorous educational program, and through active recruitment of leaders on both local and national levels, Rumanian benevolent federations have managed for two generations to develop an expanding and increasingly qualified group of leaders.[54]

A pattern of leadership, established and institutionalized early in the life of the community, assured a remarkable continuity in organized Rumanian ethnic life. Despite the transience of the community, despite the very rapid social mobility of many first- and second-generation Rumanians, a strikingly cohesive leadership has maintained an active associational life.[55]

SLOVENES

The great majority of Slovene immigrants to American cities came from peasant backgrounds. At first regarding themselves as temporary visitors, they had by the end of the 1890s begun to form Slovene economic, cultural, and religious organizations. And as this organizational process intensified in the first two decades of the twentieth century, not only the pioneers of the 1880s and 1890s, but also those who arrived after 1900 lived and worked in Slovene communities. By 1900, a growing proportion of Slovene families lived in their own houses, several Slovene Catholic parishes had been established in major American cities, and mutual benefit societies had proliferated so widely that most immigrants belonged to at least one. A burgeoning business community, most of whose members operated saloons and grocery stores, took the lead in sponsoring mutual insurance companies and other community agencies.[56] Their leadership, moreover, was rooted in a shared background, for 70 percent of these leaders—editors, businessmen, professionals—came of peasant stock. Peasant origins characterized as well another major group of Slovene leaders, Roman Catholic priests, 60 percent of whom were born to peasant parents.[57] This shared social background, together with a shared religious faith, made for a remarkably cohesive ethnic culture. This leadership founded an astonishing variety of benevolent and cultural associations. In Cleveland, for instance, the first Slovene mutual aid society emerged in 1895; by 1914, a newspaper listed over fifty lodges of mutual insurance companies. Twenty independent societies and cultural organizations flourished also. Once begun, an organizational momentum carried thousands of Slovenes into hundreds of associations, until every empty room in the Slovene communities of Chicago and Cleveland housed some insurance or cultural organization. These organizations reached a plateau of maturity in the 1920s, as their leaders then began some effort to adapt to a new generation's needs.[58] These were remarkably active organizations, of very broad appeal, whose leadership furnished direction to the Slovene community.

The consolidation of the Slovene community was achieved in the early twentieth century through the creation of seven powerful national federations. Beginning in 1894 with the Slovenian Catholic Union, these federations had completed the task of national affiliation by 1910.[59] A base now established, a vigorous national leadership pursued the now-familiar path of ethnic careers. A large number of newspapers, typically sponsored by national federations, reached into ordinary houses; a wide variety of cultural institutions were organized by each union; and a broad basis for the support of education, through both parochial schools and scholarships, assured the continuity of leadership across generations. Having developed both a dense associational life in communities and federated national organizations, Slovene leaders of the first and second generation could expect their work to last.[60]

CROATIANS

The growth of an urban Croatian community roughly paralleled that of the Slovene. As the immigration reached its flood after 1900, an organized community had already taken shape. In Chicago, for instance, there were more than seventy-five mutual aid societies in 1906, and the number reached one hundred in 1914. Most of the immigrants, as was the case of the Slovenes, were Catholic, although there was a significant Socialist movement in the Croatian community. But in the development of local leadership between 1900 and 1914, the division of Catholic and Socialist seemed to make no real difference. Of a sample of seventy-six local leaders active after 1900, men of peasant background make up the greater part—about 80 percent—of both Catholic and Socialist leaders. Moreover, their American careers are not significantly different, both groups being overwhelmingly blue-collar. Catholic and Socialist leaders both developed, in major urban settlements, the characteristic mix of ethnic institutions—mutual insurance societies, cultural groups, national halls. These organizational expressions of the Croatian community, in turn, served as recruiting agencies for second-generation leadership.[61]

When carried to the national level, this associational activity produced a number of strong unions of local societies. The National Croatian Society (1904), the Croatian Catholic Union (1921), and the Croatian Fraternal Union (1926) had all grown to 100,000 members by the late 1950s. By the mid-1920s, then, Croatian leaders had created enduring ethnic institutions which ensured a continual recruitment of new generations of leaders.

ITALIAN

The particularistic loyalties of Italian leadership furnishes a staple theme of most discussions of the Italian community.[62] One important element in this cultural localism was the pattern of Italian migration and settlement. The predominance of major chains of migration from a few villages formed a core population in urban settlements. In Cleveland, for instance, immigrants from ten villages in the Abruzzi and Sicily early organized the community around their own parochial loyalties. A similar dominance of immigrants from ten or twenty villages characterized the Pittsburgh and San Francisco communities, as well as the enormous Chicago settlement. It was during the massive influx of village streams of migration that the Italian community took shape. In this period of rapid growth, the development of associations around traditional loyalties and memories of place furnished an element of stability.[63]

This remarkable burst of organizational activity deserves a closer analysis, for it provides one means of observing the emergence of an ethnic leadership. In Chicago, for instance, mutual benefit societies numbered almost 400 by 1914, three-fourths of which began as branches of organizations in the homeland. I have been able to trace the careers of eighty-five of the four hundred founding presidents, and the data tell an interesting story. About 70 percent of these men came from peasant backgrounds in Southern Italy, and about the same proportion had held some leadership post in their native villages. They were a restless group, almost half of them having made at least one previous journey overseas in search of work, and all having migrated within Italy. All of them were members of major migration streams and often were among the pioneer imigrants from their villages. Their Chicago lives were equally interesting: eighty percent started their working lives as unskilled laborers, of whom two of every ten were able to move into skilled jobs within twenty years. As they acquired leadership positions, they developed skills highly prized by the community. Among these eighty-five leaders, more than half served as presidents of cultural and religious organizations as well, and eighty percent were officers in at least one other organization. Here was a communal leadership, recruited with a background of experience, whose presence shaped the emergence of a distinctive Italian ethnic community.[64]

By the 1910s a more cosmopolitan leadership had begun to develop as well, both in the cities and on the national level. The Italo-American National Union, for instance, a federation of local societies in Chicago, began its fitful career in the 1920s and reached a stable maturity in the 1940s. And there were other experiments in federation as well, in Pittsburgh and Boston after 1917, in San Francisco in the 1920s, and, most importantly on the national level, the Sons of Italy. The leadership of these federations, however, had different roots from those of the local societies. Collectively, the officers of the Italo-American National Union came largely from a rural petite bourgeoisie which had, even in the village, sloughed off most traces of peasant identity. Their loyalties were to the abstract community of Italians, rather than to the present gathering of villagers. Rarely did leaders of local societies move into larger roles in urban and national unions. Only in the rather small Socialist federations did any circulation of leadership occur. It is in this parallel development of institutions, this disjuncture between local and national leaders, that one finds the roots of the striking lack of an effective national leadership in the Italian community.[65]

This essay began with the notion that ethnic communities are partly a reconstruction of a past community, partly a choosing of an American future. I have looked for materials, then, which would bear on the experiences of leaders who worked to preserve an ancestral community as well as those men and women who fixed on the task of choosing communities appropriate to their conception of an urban future. Does anything emerge from this all-too-rapid review of diverse ethnic groups to suggest that any common development of leadership was at work?

First-generation ethnic communities were shaped by men and women familiar with the uses of voluntary associations in the creation of solidarities. Southern and Eastern European peasant communities were held together by the strands of voluntary associations. The real work of creating the communal institutions of the new immigrant communities was carried out by leaders whose village life had prepared them to reach out, across household and neighborhood lines, to create institutions for the pursuit of collective aims. As we have seen in the case of the ethnic communities reviewed here, the greater part of the leadership possessed the experience of building collective organizations in their homelands; hence they began their American work with some sense of continuity. The whole founding group of the Daia şasească society of Rumanian immigrants, founded in Chicago in 1905, was made up of the officers of the mutual aid society in the homeland village of the same name. Socialist locals among Croatians and Slovenes in South Chicago and Gary were typically organized by men experienced in peasant movements in the old country—and usually their recruits were fellow villagers. Hence there emerged in the early years of the twentieth century a large pool of skilled leaders in all of these ethnic groups, men and women especially adept at shaping peoples of quite particularistic loyalties into functioning voluntary associations. These early ethnic communities were largely very loose federations of particularistic organizations. Yet ethnic leaders had worked a remarkable achievement, within the span of ten years, in the context of astonishing transiency. They had created a network of associations which fulfilled in partial and particular ways a wide range of needs of new urban peoples. And this was an enduring achievement.

Another kind of ethnic leader emerged along with the communal leader. Beginning in the 1890s, but coming to maturity in the 1910s and 1920s, a new group moved into the leadership of Southern and Eastern European ethnic communities. Their intent was to create a more solidary community, to mark more clearly the boundaries of these various groups. Their strategy was federation, the formation of formal unions of cultural associations and mutual benefit societies, federations which both created a tangible organizational reality and served to maximize material and social gains in the larger society.[66] In this dual task of reconciling internal divisions and pursuing larger interests, a style of broker leadership was needed. The leaders who captured these organizations in the Slovak and Italian communities were often marginal in their identity with the ethnic community. Several of the important Slovak leaders in the powerful federations of the 1920s and 1930s, for instance, were men who came from families without close identification with either the Catholic or anti-clerical factions. Many important Italian leaders seemed to have no deep ideological commitments; their organizational strategies, as they tried to nourish a union of local societies, were couched in the language of power and the promise of mobility, rather than in the phrases of ancestral loyalties. Without strong ties to any one element in the ethnic community and characteristically self-employed professionals, these men were able to move easily across boundaries in order to perform the dual task of providing organizational reality to these boundaries and of creating access to resources and opportunities of the larger society.

Yet the experience of the Czech, Slovene, Croatian, and Rumanian communities illustrates a very different experience in the emergence of federated ethnic communities. In all of these groups there was a consistent continuity between local and national leadership, a circulation of leaders from one level to another which served to recruit fresh and able leaders in the second and even third generations. The aggregation of local communities in larger, more generalized ethnic blocs accomplished a reconstruction of primordial ethnic affiliations. How this happened, and how leaders in these communities were able to advance it, is something about which we know almost nothing. An intensive study of ethnic leadership, however, at least begins to point up that an ethnic community can accommodate itself to a changing society, and still maintain a strong sense of loyalties.

NOTES

1. Josef J. Barton, *Peasants and Strangers: Italians, Rumanians, and Slovaks in an American City, 1890–1950* (Cambridge, Mass., 1975), pp. 27–47.
2. Ibid.
3. Ibid.
4. Family reconstitutions, San Pietro in Guarano, Calabria, 1808–1914.
5. Family reconstitutions, Sibiel, Rumania, 1850–1920.
6. Jaroslava Hoffmannová, *Vystěhovalectví z Polné do Severni Ameriky ve druhé polovině XIX. století* (Havlickuv Brod, 1969), passim; Ludmila Karnikova *Vyvoj obyvatelstva v českých zemích, 1754–1914* (Prague, 1965), pp. 265–79; Giuseppe Galasso, *Mezzogiorno medievale e moderno* (Turin, 1965), pp. 350–79; Jozo Tomasevich, *Peasants, Politics, and Economic Change in Yugoslavia* (Stanford, 1955), pp. 119, 123, 129, 132, 177, 197.
7. The work of nineteenth-century ethnographers is a good approach to the character of village ceremonial; I have depended heavily on the work of Giuseppe Pitré and Giovanni Di Giacomo on Sicily and Calabria, and the studies of Kamil Krofta on Bohemia. My field notes from Sibiel, July–September, 1968, and from Alcara Li Fusi and San Pietro in Guarano, June and September, 1968, and June–September, 1971, are also useful.
8. Rosario Villari, *Mezzogiorno e contadini nell'età moderna* (Bari, 1961), pp. 63–64, 68; Domenico Demarco, *La Calabria: Economia e società* (Naples, 1966), pp. 78–79; Jaroslav Purš, *Dělnické hnutí v českých zemích, 1849–1867* (Prague, 1961), pp. 42–47; Imre Kovacs, "Despre nivelul dezvoltării agriculturii din Transilvania," *Anuarul Institutului de Istorie din Cluj* 9 (1966): 143–65.
9. On Southern Italy, see especially Sidney Sonnino, *I contadini di Sicilia* (Florence, 1877), pp. 82–83, 192–93; *Atti della Giunta per l'Inchiesta agraria e sulle condizioni della classe operaia*, 13 vols. (Rome, 1881–86), 9, fasc. 2, pp. 420–27; field notes, San Pietro. On Bohemia, see Ladislav Kmoniček, "Namezdní práce na zlonickém velkostatku před a po roce 1848," *Sborník archivních prací* 7 (1957):64–78; and G. Hoffman, "Blatenský velkostatek v polovině 19. století," *Sborník archivních prací* 8(1958): 124–27.
10. Family reconstitutions, San Pietro and Sibiel. Cf. Franca Assante, *Proprietà fondiaria e classi rurali in un comune della Calabria (1740–1886)* (Naples, 1969), pp. 79–85; Guido Vincelli, *Una comunità meridionale (Montorio nei Frentani)* (Turin, 1958), p. 210.
11. Field notes, Huslenký, September, 1972, Chicago and St. Louis, July–August, 1974; cf. Hoffmannová, *Vystěhovalectví z Polné*, pp. 10–20.

172   JOSEF J. BARTON

12. "Situazia," ca. 1929, fol. 2, p. 3, Sibiel, Parish Archives; ms. minutes of unnamed society, ca. 1900–1914, Tilişca, Parish Archives.

13. Field notes, Alcara Li Fusi; minutes, Società Agricola di Mutuo Soccorso, in the society's office, Alcara Li Fusi, January 15, 1893, March 8, 1914; "Elenco dei sodalizi . . . 27 aprile 1917," Messina, Archivio di Stato, Prefettura, fasc. 193.

14. Cf. Michael Anderson, "The Study of Family Structure," in *Nineteenth-Century Society: Essays in the Use of Quantitative Methods for the Study of Social Data*, ed. E. A. Wrigley (Cambridge, 1972), pp. 49–52.

15. Minutes, Società Agricola, Alcara Li Fusi, April 26, May 17, 1891; field notes, Alcara Li Fusi and San Pietro. Cf. the extensive materials in Palermo, Archivio di Stato, Prefettura, busta 120, and in Potenza, Archivio di Stato, Prefettura, busta 283.

16. "Situazia," fol. 2, pp. 3–5, Sibiel; field notes, Sibiel; and the enormous collection of materials in Sibiu, Arhivele Statului, f. Comitat, (Vicecomitele), esp. fascs. 34, 306.

17. Cf. Antonín Robek, *Příspěvky k historicko-etnografické monografii panství Zvoleněves v první polovině devatenáctého století* (Prague, 1966), pp. 75–81, 102–3. Two village chronicles, the first of a Slovene village, the second of a Croatian, tell a similar story: Šmihel chronicle, University of Minnesota, Immigration History Research Center, and Niko Nikolić, ed., *Kronika župe Bistre i agrarnoekonomska struktura Bistranske Poljanice* (Zagreb, 1962).

18. Augustin Deac, "Mişcarea muncitorească din Transilvania în ultimul deceniu al secolului al XIX-lea," in Institutul de Istorie a Partidului de pe lîngă C.C. al P.M.R., *Mişcarea muncitorească din România, 1893–1900* (Bucharest, 1965), pp. 328–36, 341–48; Imre Kovacs, "Mişcarile țărăneşti in Transilvania," in Vasile Liveanu et al., *Relaţii agrare şi mişcari țărăneşti in România, 1908–1921* (Bucharest, 1967), pp. 175–83; Augustin Deac and Ludovic Vajda, "Influenţia raşcoalei țărăneşti din 1907 in Transilvania şi Bucovina," in *Marea raşcoala a țărănilor din 1907*, ed. Andrei Oţetea and Ion Popescu-Puturi (Bucharest, 1967), pp. 563–69.

19. Minutes, Società Agricola, Alcara Li Fusi, 1891–1900; field notes, Alcara Li Fusi and San Pietro; notes and minutes of Cooperativa Cattolica di Credito, San Pietro in Guarano, in possession of Francesco Nocito, Rocigliano.

20. Cf. Frank Thistlethwaite, "Migration from Europe Overseas in the Nineteenth and Twentieth Centuries," XIe Congrès International des Sciences Historiques, *Rapports 5* (Uppsala, 1960):50–54.

21. Barton, *Peasants and Strangers*, pp. 48–63.

22. Ibid., pp. 64–90.

23. Sam Bass Warner, Jr., *Streetcar Suburbs* (Cambridge, Mass., 1962), *The Private City* (Philadelphia, 1968), and *The Urban Wilderness* (New York, 1972).

24. Cf. Herbert G. Gutman, *Work, Culture, and Society in Industrializing America* (New York, 1976), pp. 14–15, 24–25, 31–32, 40–41, 65–66; Marc A. Fried, *The World of the Urban Working Class* (Cambridge, Mass., 1973), pp. 166–69.

25. Quoted in Magyar Országos Levéltár, K-26/1909/XXII/1937 (microfilm, Immigration History Research Center).

26. Michael Gold, *Jews without Money* (London, 1930), p. 19.

27. Stephan Thernstrom, *The Other Bostonians: Poverty and Progress in the American Metropolis* (Cambridge, Mass., 1973); Barton, *Peasants and Strangers*, pp. 91–146.

28. Field notes, Cleveland, 1968–71, Detroit, 1974, and Chicago, 1974–75.

29. *Čechoslovan* (Chicago), November 20, 1886.

30. Field notes, Cleveland, Detroit, Chicago.

31. *Svornost* (Chicago), January 3, 6, 1888, January 14, 18, 31, 1897; *České Chicago* . . . (Chicago, 1900), pp. 13–33; Rudolf Bubeniček, *Dějiny Čechu v Chicagu* (Chicago, 1939), pp. 79–85, 210–17, 293–313, 457–83, 515–18. Cf. *Pokrok* (Cleveland), February 9, 1875; Jaroslav E. S. Vojan, *Velký New York* (New York, 1908), pp. 40–41, 48.

32. Ohio, Office of the Secretary of State, Acts of Incorporation; *La voce del popolo italiano* (Cleveland), 1909–22; field notes, Alcara Li Fusi and Ripalimosano, June 1971.

33. Konštantín Čulen, *Dejiny slovákov v Amerike*, 2 vols. (Bratislava, 1942), 1: 197, 206; *Národný kalendár* (Pittsburgh), 1926, p. 70; Acts of Incorporation, Ohio, vol. 37, pp. 173, 505; *Jednota kalendár . . . 1940* (Middleton, Pa.), p. 122; membership

records, 1907–10, First Slovak Catholic Union, Immigration History Research Center.

34. *Istoria Uniunei și Legei Societaților Române de Ajutor și Cultura . . . 1906–1931* (Cleveland, 1931), pp. 29, 31–32; *Românul* (Cleveland), February 18, 1906, March 9, 1907, May 2, 1908, January 23, 1910, February 19, 1911, August 8, 30, 1912, October 13, 1912; *America* (Cleveland), June 14, 1907; Magyar Országos Levéltár, K-26/1910/XIV/715/4856; Union and League of Rumanian Societies in America, *Proces verbal . . . 9-11 novembrie 1918* (Cleveland, 1918), p. 6; *Solia* (Detroit), October 25, 1936; Aureliu Hatiegan to John P. Farelly, June 25, 1916, Diocese of Cleveland Archives, Parish Files, f. "Most Holy Trinity."

35. Oscar Handlin, "The Social System," in *The Future Metropolis,* ed. Lloyd Rodwin (New York, 1961), p. 24.

36. *Hlas* (St. Louis), January 7, 1880, April 28, 1880, August 11, 1880; *Čechoslovan* (Chicago), June 12, 1886; *Věstník* (Chicago), January 1, 1903.

37. Cf. *Národ* (Chicago), February 17, 1895; *Památník osady sv. Jana Nep . . . 1863–1913* (Milwaukee, 1913), pp. 5, 7, 65, 69; *Památník na zlaté jubileum chrámu Paně Panny Marie Ustavičné Pomoci v New Yorku, 1887–1937* (New York, 1937), pp. 8–30, 47–53; *Hlas* (St. Louis), December 31, 1879, March 3, 1880, April 7, 1884.

38. Based on a survey of Czech newspapers, principally *Hlas* (St. Louis), 1872–1920, *Národ* (Chicago), 1894–1920, *Denní hlasatel* (Chicago), 1891–1920, and *Čechoslovan* (Chicago), 1883–1900, and on acts of incorporation, Illinois Secretary of State, Springfield.

39. *Pokrok* (Cleveland), December 26, 1874; *Národ* (Chicago), February 7, 14, 1895; *Památník zlatého jubilea osady sv. Václava . . . 1863–1913* (Chicago, 1913), pp. 37, 43, 47; *Hlas* (St. Louis), July 28, 1880, September 1, 1880, October 15, 1890; *Volnost* (Cleveland), June 3, 1882; *Katolík kalendář . . . 1905* (Chicago), pp. 170–171; *Hlas kalendář . . . 1916* (St. Louis), p. 183.

40. *Centennial of St. John Nepomuk Church . . . 1954* (St. Louis, 1954), pp. 40–43, 65–66; *Hlas* (St. Louis), March 30, 1898; *Národ* (Chicago), February 7, 1904; *Památník oslavy 25-letého trvání osady Blahoslavené Anežky Česke v Chicagu, Ill.* (Chicago, 1929), pp. 62–66, 72–114; "Celoroční zpráva osady sv. Víta, 1932," Archives of St. Procopius Abbey, Lisle Ill., f. "Chicago, St. Vitus."

41. Based on the Czech newspapers listed in n. 38 above and, in addition, *Pokrok* (Cleveland), 1874–1900, *Svornost* (Chicago), 1875–1900, *Hlas kalendář* (St. Louis) and *Kalendář Amerikan* (Chicago). Two reference works have been indispensable: Tomaš Čapek, *Padesát lét českého tiska v Americe* (New York, 1911), and Čapek, *Naše Amerika* (Prague, 1926).

42. *Zlatá jubileum osady Panny Marie Dobré Rady* (Chicago, 1939), pp. 6–8; *Zájmy lidu* (Chicago), March 28, 1924; Rudolf J. Pšanka, ed., *Zlatá kniha československého Chicagu . . .* (Chicago, 1926), pp. 190–91, 211.

43. *Bohemian Review* (New York) 1 (March, 1917): 15; *Hlídka* (Chicago), August 20, 1920, September 20, 1920, January 1, 1921; *Denní hlasatel* (Chicago), October 12, 1921.

44. Čulen, *Dejiny slovákov*, I, 98; *Jednota katolícky kalendár . . . 1902* (Cleveland), p. 78; *Hlas* (Cleveland), April 15, 1925, March 11, 1937.

45. Based on a study of the membership of eighteen mutual benefit societies in Cleveland, information drawn from First Slovak Catholic Union Papers. See also Jan Pankuch, *Dejiny clevelandských a lakewoodských slovákov* (Cleveland, 1930), pp. 21–22; *Amerikánsko slovenské noviny* (Pittsburgh), January 14, 1897; *Jednota kalendár . . . 1902*, p. 207; ibid., *1903*, p. 208.

46. Based on a sample of sixty-four men who served as presidents of Cleveland societies, 1900; cf. *Jednota* (Cleveland), September 20, 1905, April 11, 1906, 1910; field notes, Cleveland, April 1968 and September 1971.

47. Marian Mark Stolarik, "Immigration and Urbanization: The Slovak Experience, 1870–1918" (Ph.D. diss., University of Minnesota, 1974), pp. 69–100; Peter V. Rovnianek, *Zapisky za živa pochovaného* (Pittsburgh, 1924); Josef Paučo, *75 rokov Prvej Katolíckej Slovenskej Jednoty* (Cleveland, 1965).

48. Čulen, *Dejiny slovákov*, 2: 113–24; *Jednota* (Cleveland), April–May, 1907;

174 JOSEF J. BARTON

J. C. Hronský, *Cesta slovenskou Amerikou*, 2 vols. (Turčiansky Sv. Martin, 1940), 1: 338–44, 352–56, and 2: 171, 345–47, 474–75; Konštantín Čulen, *Slovenské časopisy v Amerike* (Cleveland, 1970), pp. 19–20, 27–29, 39, 44–49, 51–54, 75–83, 94–95.

49. *Românul* (Cleveland), May 20, 1906; minutes of Reuniunea de Cântări Traiană, June 25, September 15, 1909, Immigration History Research Center.

50. *Istoria Uniunei și Legei*, pp. 31–32; *Românul* (Cleveland), February 18, 1906.

51. *Românul* (Cleveland), March 25, 1906; *America* (Cleveland), December 28, 1906.

52. *America* (Cleveland), November 12, 1909; *Steaua noastră* (New York), August 20, 1913; *Românul* (Cleveland), October 1, 1912; *Solia* (Detroit), July 19, 1936; *Calendarul America . . . 1916* (Cleveland), pp. 137–43. Minutes of Union of Rumanian Societies in America, July 5, 1912, March 16, 1913; minutes of Asociația Liga și Ajutorul, July 4, 1916; Vasile Zdrobă to George Marhăo, April 29, 1923, f. marked "Aradană, 1923." (All in Union and League of Rumanian Societies Collection, Immigrant History Research Center.)

53. *Calendarul America . . . 1912* (Cleveland), pp. 103–53; *Românul* (Cleveland), January 18, 1908; *America* (Cleveland), December 15, 1907, January 21, 1909.

54. Based on a survey of officeholders in *Românul* (Cleveland), 1906–50, *America* (Cleveland), 1906–50, and *Calendarul America* (Cleveland), 1912–60.

55. See Barton, *Peasants and Strangers*, pp. 142–46.

56. Rudolph M. Susel, "Some Aspects of Ethnic Community Development: The First Generation Slovenes of Cleveland, Ohio" (unpublished ms., 1970), pp. 8–33; Jože Zavertnik, *Ameriški slovenci* (Chicago, 1925), pp. 229–313, 410–30.

57. Based on a sample of 104 biographies of Slovene leaders, drawn over the period 1890–1920, from the following newspapers: *Amerikanski slovenec* (Joliet), *Prosveta* (Chicago), *Ameriška domovina* (Cleveland), and *Glas naroda* (New York).

58. *Clevelandska Amerika* (Cleveland), May 5, 1914; *Ave Maria koledar . . . 1915* (Brooklyn), pp. 142, 150–51, and ibid., *1918*, pp. 140–42; *Ave Maria koledar . . . 1928* (Lemont), pp. 173–75, and ibid., *1930*, pp. 111–12, 124–25; John A. Arnez, *Slovenci v New Yorku* (New York, 1966), pp. 38–49, 85–92, 129–38. The long-term cohesiveness of local organizations is suggested in the following items: *Amerikanski slovenec* (Joliet), September 18, 1925, November 27, 1928; *Proletarec* (Chicago), May 1, 1927; *Glas naroda* (New York), July 26, 1948, December 20, 1948, September 26, 1952; *Prosveta* (Chicago), January 18, 1950, February 15, 1950; *Ave Maria koledar . . . 1968* (Lemont), pp. 30–32/g.

59. J. M. Trunk, *Amerika in amerikanci* (Celovec, 1912), pp. 450–51; Zavertnik, *Ameriški slovenci*, pp. 553–623; *Glas naroda* (New York), July 19, 1948; Ivan Mladinec, ed., *Narodni adresar* (New York, 1932), pp. 5–32.

60. On newspapers, Jože Bajec, "Petinsedemdeset let slovenskega časnikarstva v ZDA," *Slovenski izseljenski koledar* (Ljubljana), 14 (1967), 273–307; on continuity of leadership, *Glas naroda* (New York), February 17, 1948, May 31, 1957, February 1, 1963, September 26, 1963; *Prosveta* (Chicago), January 1, 1950, January 21, 1950.

61. Based on a survey of the following newspapers: *Američki hrvatski glasnik* (Chicago), *Radnik* (Chicago), *Hrvatski svijet* (New York), *Zajedničar* (Pittsburgh), and *Naša nada* (Gary). A useful compendium is George J. Prpić, *The Croatian Immigrants in America* (New York, 1971).

62. Rudolph J. Vecoli, "Contadini in Chicago: A Critique of *The Uprooted*," *Journal of America History*, 51(1964), 404–17, is a vigorous statement of this view. John W. Briggs, "Italians in Italy and America: A Study of Change within Continuity for Immigrants to Three American Cities, 1890–1930" (forthcoming, Yale University Press), chap. 4, is an equally sustained challenge to this argument.

63. Barton, *Peasants and Strangers*, pp. 60–63.

64. Based on a thorough reading of the following Chicago newspapers: *L'Italia*, 1886–1967; *La tribuna italiana trans-atlantica*, 1904–1908, 1914–31; *Avanti*, 1918–21; *Il lavoratore*, 1924–31; and *La parola del popolo*, 1921–23. The sample was chosen systematically from a list of officers compiled from newspapers and records of the

Illinois Secretary of State. The biographies were gathered from obituaries, anniversary publications, and interviews conducted in 1974–75.

65. The documentation is too extensive to cite in detail, so I shall simply list the newspapers I have found most useful: *Il progresso italoamericano* (New York); *La gazzetta del Massachusetts* (Boston); *Il corriere del popolo* (San Francisco); *La Trinacria* (Pittsburgh); *La voce del popolo italiano* (Cleveland); and *La luce* (Utica). The study of Chicago leadership is based on interviews and the *Bollettino* of the Italo American National Union.

66. Cf. the suggestive essay of Dominique Schnapper, "Centralisme et federalisme culturels: les émigrés italiens en France et aux Etats-Unis," *Annales: Economies, Sociétés Civilisations* 29 (1974): 1141–59.

The Irish

Robert D. Cross

WHETHER OR NOT Irish sailors reached St. Brendan's Isle, and so established an irrefutable claim to being the first Europeans to reach the New World and the real founding fathers of what was to be the United States, there were undoubtedly Irish Catholics in the British colonies from a very early time.[1] By comparison with immigrants speaking German and with the large numbers of Irish Protestants who would later insist on being called Scotch Irish, the numbers of Irish Catholics were not substantial. The prevailing anti-Catholic temper of the colonies would have in any case prevented any important Irish ethnic life, even if their numbers had been larger. Even those Catholics like the Carrolls of Maryland, whose faith was not covert, were not Irish and do not seem to have been any more notable in their interest in the well-being of the Irish than were the Catholic gentry of eighteenth century England. Too few to be singled out for opprobrium, the Irish Catholics experienced the mixed blessings of insignificance.

During the years when the new nation was being established, the Irish continued to be largely inconspicuous. If they were notably combative—a trait regularly attributed to them subsequently, and a source of reproach and obloquy in the next generation—the militance of a Commodore John Barry was, in Revolutionary years, highly welcome. George Washington's prohibition of traditional expressions of anti-Catholic feeling and festivity in the Continental army may have been calculated to prevent the alienation from patriot ranks of Irish Catholics as well as of Catholics of other stock. Certainly there was no disposition among the rebels to inhibit the deep-rooted hostility Irish felt toward British power. Similarly, the tentative efforts of patriot statesmen to develop a working alliance with those in Ireland resentful of the tyrannies of George III could not have failed to soften attitudes toward the Irish in America; probably, however, the connection between the righteousness of the Irish cause in Ireland and the well-being of the Irish in America was seldom made.

In the years after the Peace of Paris, and especially in the 1790s, however, the position of the Irish in America was more problematic. The Federalists, like the leaders of most new nations, were paranoid about any expressions of dissent or even any appearances of difference. Whether or not the Irish in America were disproportionately "Jeffersonian" in thought or affiliation and whether or not there was much connection between the Irish rising in 1798 and the hydra head of the French Revolution, Federalist guardians of America were terrified by the sight of hordes of "wild Irishmen" in America.[2] The Naturalization Act of 1795 and the Alien and Sedition Acts of 1798 certainly had the Irish in view— as well as dangerous Frenchmen, Englishmen, and treacherous natives. This flurry of legislative animus, though malevolent in intention and frightening in prospect, proved to be largely impotent. In any event, the Irish had neither the numbers nor the status to mount an effective protest. Native-born Jeffersonians, on coming to power, quickly obviated the need for Irish concern or action.

Irish Catholics continued to migrate to America in the early years of the nineteenth century, but still not in numbers sufficient to cause much alarm or to enable them to foster a vigorous ethnic life. With the progressive deterioration of American party organizations, political affiliation seemed less portentous. Anti-Catholic feeling was at a low ebb, and the creation of Catholic parishes in many cities did not provoke alarm. Irishmen were now more conspicuous, and Matthew Carey may be taken as a typical Irish-American leader.[3] Born in Dublin in 1760 and migrating to Philadelphia in 1784, he readily won, by his energy and manifest intellectual abilities, a prominent role as a publisher of classical and English writings, as an original economist, and as a spokesman for such causes of general interest as Greek independence. But he did not cease to be an "Irishman." As early as 1790, he helped organize the Hibernian Society in Philadelphia to aid emigrants from the old country. In his *Ireland Vindicated*, published in 1819, he was arguing not just for the rights of Ireland, as all Irish, then and later, were bound to do; he was also, however consciously, providing a rationale for the self-respect that the Irish, like every other ethnic group in America, would require and seek. This caused little controversy, if one came from an established homecountry. Unless there was a prospect of war with the United States, English immigrants could vaunt the achievement of Britain and French immigrants celebrate *la gloire* of France. But in a nationalist epoch like the nineteenth and twentieth centuries, emigrants from a weak or nonexistent state understandably felt inferior. Many Irish felt they would be denigrated as "slavish" just as long as Ireland was "enslaved." (Generations later, Poles, Czechs, and Serbs would have similar feelings.) German Americans supported Bismarck; Italian Americans would be proud of Mussolini.[4] Certainly, for Carey, and probably for most Irish nationalists in subsequent years, there was no felt conflict between a strenuous Irish nationalism and a whole-hearted Americanism. Unhappily, many native Americans would never be able to conceive of a benign double loyalty.

As the numbers of Irish imigrating to America rose from a trickle to a flood in the 1830s and remained at high tide until late in the century, the "leadership" of a Matthew Carey was no longer sufficient. Not one, but many, emigrant aid societies were desperately needed. Concern for bleeding Ireland, though in no way slackening, yielded preeminence and importunacy to concern for the well-being of the Irish in America. Appeals to the fair-minded in the western world were supplanted by demands for power in this country. The increasing totals of Irish immigrants, though frightening to native Americans and a source of despair to aid societies, gave these demands for power and respectful attention more than mere poignancy.

More than numbers buttressed the Irish claim. Unlike most immigrants, almost all the Irish spoke English, even if with a mockable accent. They could not, therefore, be quite so easily ignored, quite so readily exploited, quite so simply shunted aside from jobs or positions of status; enough Irish immigrants could read English, so that it was necessary (as it was not for Italians and Slavs later) for the prejudiced to write up signs "No Irish Need Apply."

Furthermore, they brought with them familiarity with techniques of representative government. For most, no doubt, this amounted to little more than a sorrowful experience of the ways in which a "democratic" political system could be manipulated to injure them. But however little the Irish had gained in Ireland by the 1830s and however few of them had actually worked with, or even seen, Daniel O'Connell, few probably were unaware of the tactics available to the resourceful: the formulation and publication of grievances; the organization of rallies; the inspiriting oratory; the dissemination of newspapers and pamphlets. Many immigrant laymen and most immigrant priests had learned what "O'Connellism" could do, even if Catholic Emancipation had brought little practical benefit to them. Equally important, many of the immigrants had learned the political importance of violence. The "Establishment" in Ireland had never mobilized such overwhelming counterterror as to make "Whiteboyism" seem counterproductive. Politically minded at the same time that they were as a group open minded about the kind of methods to be employed, the mass of Irish immigrants arrived in the United States at a propitious time. Restrictions on adult white male suffrage were disappearing fast; the founding fathers' aversion to party organization seemed increasingly anachronistic; and William Marcy could believe he was only being candid in declaring that to the victors belong the spoils. Such a scene was congenial to the Irish, who had a clear notion of the spoils of office and of how they had been deprived of them; ironically, the scene made more sense to an Irish immigrant than it did to nostalgic native Americans, typified by a Philip Hone or a George Templeton Strong.[5]

At first, the Irish were content to follow the many who volunteered to lead them. But even at an early date they demonstrated a certain ornery fractiousness. In 1817 a group departed from Dooley's Long Room in New York City to express their severe displeasure at the unwillingness of Tammany to nominate the Irish Protestant, Thomas Addis Emmett, for Congress.[6] Though it took several years and several subsequent riots to be persuasive, by the 1840s, Tammany, like Democratic organizations in most cities, had learned to defer, if not surrender, to Irish Americans. Mike Walsh was probably the first immigrant to make the full hegira, reaching Congress in the 1850s after years as leader of New York's "Spartan Band."[7] His upward progress in American politics was paralleled by John O'Sullivan's editorship of *The Democratic Review* and mimicked by the Whigs' feeble attempt to create in 1852 *The Irishman*, edited by Patrick O'Dea.

Irish immigrants soon gave their special tone to American politics. Whether as leaders or followers, they placed extraordinary emphasis upon the virtues of loyalty. This trait, hardly surprising in those who had suffered so much from those who had purported to "represent" them in Ireland, at once enhanced the strength of the leader in his often difficult negotiations with non-Irish America and infuriated those native citizens to whom "independence" politically—not loyalty—was the supreme virtue. "Gratitude is the finest word I know," Richard Croker, boss of Tammany Hall at the close of the century, declared. "I would much prefer a man to steal from me than to display ingratitude. All there is in life is loyalty to one's family and friends."[8] Of course, Irish Americans were capable of deserting a leader; the history of Tammany Hall makes an account of fifteenth century Florence read like a Boy Scout narrative. But when a Curley deserted a Honey Fitz, he did so not to manifest his independence but to support a Martin Lomasney.

Irish Americans did not want their leaders to amend the Constitution or to reform in other ways the body politic. Indeed, "reform" was a suspicious notion, connoting all too often the subversion of traditional institutions like the state, the church, and the family. The Irish hoped their governors would neither succumb to such an ideology as led that generous man, Lord John Russell, to acquiesce, in the name of laissez-faire, to the shipment of food out of Ireland during the Great Hunger, nor wipe out saloons in the name of temperance, nor destroy the state in the interests of the emancipation of Negroes.[9] The Irish *did* expect of their political leaders uncalculated acts of kindness and sympathy—the visit to the wake, the basket of food at Christmas, the off-the-record word to the district attorney in extenuation of a son's petty violation of the law. To the reformer, such services were not trivial; they were disgusting and patronizing payoffs for a license to loot the treasury and to betray the public interest. When the Tammany district leader, George Washington Plunkitt, distinguished "honest graft"—the willingness of a political insider to benefit from advance knowledge of contracts to bid on or land to be confiscated—from the blatant shakedown of helpless prostitutes, criminals, and innocent businessmen—reformers grumbled that no higher ethic could be expected of the Irish. In fact, Plunkitt and his spokesman, William Riordan, did less than justice to Irish-American political attitudes.[10] It was true enough that few Irish immigrants or their children shared the fantasies of the popular Social Gospeler, W. T. Stead, about the wonderful things that would happen "if Christ came to Chicago."[11] They did not suppose that political leaders would be Godlike. They were neither surprised nor dismayed if the men they elected saw their opportunities for self-enrichment—and took them. They may even have indulged in private satisfaction that fellow Irishmen could lead expansively prosperous lives in a culture where they themselves were obliged to endure grinding hardship. What they could *not* endure, or tolerate, was the political leader who lost "touch" with them—who by word or deed denied a common humanity with them. They supported a politics and a set of politicians who did not make them feel alien or excluded. With no high opinion of mankind, they gloried in outrageous expressions of hate for their "enemies." They did not boggle at the chicanery of Tammany leaders like "Honest John Kelly"; the buffoonery of James Michael Curley; or the aloofness of Richard Croker. They admired these worthies, and for nothing more than for their ability to get and to use power. They were not much concerned about the ways in which this power was exercised or the goals toward which it was applied, for they were viscerally sure that the result would be good for the Irish. Still, it would misrepresent their convictions to impute to them a belief that politicians, any more than priests or businessmen, would win either for themselves or their followers lasting success. To the Irish American, life in this world was a losing proposition. But the ends for which one fought, and even more the style with which one comported oneself, were the criteria of grandness, the prerequisities for loyalty.

In the nineteenth century political prowess was of great importance not just in bestowing psychological satisfaction and in warding off the forays of an unsympathetic political system but also in enabling the immigrant to make his way economically. Aside from the relatively few who could be awarded a job in the street-cleaning department, or on the "force," or in municipal construction, or in the political machine itself, there remained a large mass of immigrants who needed help in finding a way to earn a living. Arriving in America as "unconditioned labor," the Irish inadvertently demonstrated all too dramatically the illusionary character of the myth of the self-made man. In both factory and construction work, the decision as to whom to employ rested with a foreman or boss. Where that foreman or boss was an Irishman—especially an Irishman from one's own neighborhood in Ireland—the prospect of employment was fair. Failing that, if the employer could be subjected to the importunities of an economic or political leader benignly disposed toward the Irish, the immigrant had a chance. By and large, however, it was only late in the century that an Irish immigrant could hope for intercession in his behalf from an Irish American magnate—a Grace or a Cuddahy— or, more reliably, from a labor union dominated by Irishmen. Until then, he usually needed assistance from the "personal friend" of a friend.

With increasing frequency, that friendly figure would be a priest. Irish-American experience has been so intertwined with Catholic-American experience that almost until the post–World War II period it has been possible to regard the two as virtually indistinguishable. Certainly that was the way in which most Irish immigrants thought—and with justice. For centuries in Ireland, Catholicism was the sign and seal of being Irish.[12] The Roman Catholic Church, beleaguered as it was, organized the life of the Irish peasant and gave meaning to it. Immigration to America changed little. To the Irishman, birth, marriage, and death were meaningless apart from the theology and the ceremonies of Catholicism. The hardship of daily life, the apparent prosperity of non-Catholics, and —perhaps most egregious of all—the opprobrium bestowed on them by enemies of the Faith—all such incongruities were explained by the Catholic plan of salvation, which reiterated that whatever the appearances of this world, there was salvation for no one outside the Church; colloquially, Irishmen were assured that God in His inscrutability had ordained that non-Catholics were allowed to fatten in this world so that they would fry the hotter in the next. Sunday mass, Easter duty, confession and penance, and the last rites made it possible for an Irishman to endure in a non-Irish world.

All such consolations depended on the presence of a Catholic clergy, preferably an Irish Catholic clergy. And, in contrast to the predicament of many Catholic immigrants, there was never any real shortage of Irish clerics in America. Many had come to America early; a surprisingly large number accompanied the famine migrants; the Church in Ireland took special steps to ensure a steady flow of priests to America; and American bishops found a gratifying response to their regular pleas for more priests and nuns for the missions in America.[13] Furthermore, Irish-American families gave strong support to their offspring who undertook lives dedicated to the Church. Whether born in Ireland or, like James Gibbons, born in America but receiving his education in Ireland, the Irish clergy presented Irish immigrants in America with a special kind of leadership. It was largely uncomplicated. Priestly deference to bishops was pretty much unquestioned; few immigrants—until late in the century —ever had to choose between loyalty to parish priest or loyalty to bishop, or to Pope, or to a remembered Church back home. In Ireland, where the parish priest was frequently the only authority to summon up against a Protestant landlord, a "political representative," or, for that matter, an unsympathetic neighbor or father, the priest could assume virtual infallibility. In an era when Catholics in other lands were troubled over questions of papal infallibility, it was a commonplace that no problem existed for the Irish; no good Catholic questioned that the priest, and so the Pope, and so the Church, was infallible. There was no need to indulge in theological or historical quibbles.

In America Irish priests in the nineteenth century were, even more effectively and spectacularly than in Ireland, the real leaders of the Irish. Given their backgrounds and the needs of their people, it is scarcely surprising that they were conservative. Few of them were innovators in theological speculation; even fewer gave much attention to the growing debate elsewhere in the Catholic world over liturgical "reform"; probably still fewer devoted much attention to the problematic relations of the Irish to those non-Irish non-Catholics of seeming good will.[14] The Irish American priest, like the Irish American politician, concentrated on being *available* to the immigrants, in bad times as well as good. A friendly critic could complain that the layman regarded the priest not just as "teacher, father, and friend, but boss-teacher, boss-father, boss-friend, perhaps boss-politician."[15] For most immigrants in the nineteenth century, such worries were nonexistent. Enough that the Irish priest was willing to help in every way conceivable.

When, for example, the Presbyterian John Breckenridge of Philadelphia began to publish a series of insulting attacks on Catholics and Catholicism, the Irish Catholic priest John Hughes was willing to answer charge with charge, billingsgate with billingsgate.[16] When states threatened to intensify discriminations against Catholic schools, or against the religious life of Catholics in public schools or caring institutions, priests like Hughes were more than ready to take up the cudgels. Later in the century, when employers exercised undue force against all workers, or against Catholic workers particularly, "labor-priests" like Peter Yorke were quick and sturdy in their intervention.[17] Even in the twentieth century, Father William Dorney of Chicago was popularly and affectionately known as "king of the Yards" because of his ability to help his parishioners to get jobs, to keep them, and to improve their wage rates.[18]

Given both the ability of and the deference granted to the Irish priesthood and given also the steady if slow evolution of an American Irish lay leadership in politics, in business, and in society, it is understandable that eventually the Irish in America at times suffered not from a lack of leadership but from a surfeit. A dramatic example early in the nineteenth century was the series of sporadic contests over control of the property of Catholic parishes: should control be exercised by bishops, by priests, by the laymen who had contributed most of the money, or by some combination of these? Occasionally the "trusteeship" controversy extended even to the prerogative of selecting an appropriate priest for the parish. American civil law tended to assign control of property to those persons, usually laymen, who had provided it. It did not seem implausible, furthermore, that laymen with demonstrated skills and accomplishments in the world of business should have the decisive voice in deciding business options confronting a parish. But it seldom proved the case that matters of worldly moment could be neatly separated from matters of felt spiritual significance. Anyway, priests and bishops were not disposed to defer to, or even to cooperate as equals with, lay "leaders." A large number of the conflicts which ensued involved Irish priests and non-Irish congregations, but quite enough conflicts pitted Irish clergy against Irish laity to make the very word "trusteeism" a bugaboo. In the upshot, partly because of the abilities, determination, and persistence of the clergy and partly because most American states eventually made it legally possible to vest control of all church property in the bishop as a "corporation sole," by the end of the century "trusteeism" was for the Irish little more than an unpleasant memory of a time when they were sorting out which leaders to follow. Henceforth, among Irish Catholics the clergy would be the unquestioned leaders in all matters remotely involving the Church.[19] When the Catholic University of America was established with a board of trustees that included wealthy Catholic laymen along with a preponderance of bishops, it was tacitly understood that the laymen would withdraw whenever "sensitive" measures were under discussion.[20] It was the duty of the faithful to be faithful—just as it was the duty of the precinct worker to follow the direction of the district leader.

By the time of the Civil War, therefore, with at least two million Irish-born or children of Irish parents in America, patterns of leadership highly suitable to the Irish past and present had developed. In a deeply politicized society, Irishmen had established their usefulness as leaders of street gangs, as "shoulder-hitters," as district leaders and ward bosses

who could turn out the vote—through friendship, through rational persuasion, through "hurrah," through not very seriously disguised techniques of coercion and violence. Only a few had yet achieved the prestige
of being aldermen; most Irish political leaders were still outside the civics
textbook table of formal political organization. The Irish, therefore, could
satisfy only imperfectly the natural desire of an immigrant group for
"recognition." They were reasonably suspicious of appeals made to them,
they felt, out of necessity rather than shared sympathies, such as that of
General Winfield Scott in 1852: "I think I hear again that rich brogue that
betokens a son of old Ireland. I love to hear it! I heard it on the Niagara
in '14, and again in the Valley of Mexico. . . ." To which, not unfairly, the
Irish American replied, "Gineral, Gineral, you are a big delulherer!"[21]

The predicament of the Irish, possessed of very considerable but not
decisive political power (except in local elections), was painfully demonstrated by the unmistakably anti-Irish elements in the Know-Nothing
surge in the 1850s. Though nativists of that type were unable to carry
through any permanent legislative proscription of ethnic political or social
activity, they were able to exclude for a time Irish Americans from most
political offices in states like Massachusetts. At least as galling, they
were able to harass the Church by authorizing "sniffing" investigations of
churches and convents, as well as making life miserable for prominent
Catholic clergymen, especially Gaetano Cardinal Bedini, sent by the Pope
to assess the progress of Catholicism in America.[22] From the perspective
of later generations, Know-Nothingism was really "the last hurrah" of
overt, nationwide, anti-Irish politics.[23] Even in the 1850s it helped
strengthen the hand of defenders of the faith like Archbishop Hughes,
whose militant leadership seemed entirely appropriate. Nearly a century
later, an Irish politician like James Michael Curley found it useful in
consolidating Irish American support to invoke the memory of the preposterous and often obscene antics of the Know-Nothings.[24]

By about 1860, too, the Irish had also succeeded in gaining effective
control of the Roman Catholic Church in America. Not only had trusteeism been squelched; even more, though non-Catholics continued to
proselytize, the clergy was in a position to take vigorous and confident
steps to prevent "leakage." Men like Hughes devoted only a small part
of their time to exchanging apostolic blows and knocks with Protestant
seducers; they devoted even less effort to putting down such articulate
non-Irish Catholics as Orestes Brownson, who dared to question Irish
hegemony within the Church; most of the energy of the clergy could be
devoted to building the churches, schools, and charitable institutions
which, staffed by Irish priests and nuns, would serve and safeguard the
Irish immigrant and his family.[25] To describe Catholicism as the church
of the immigrants was to speak of the present and the future with confidence, not with apprehension.

In firm control of the Church and with a good grasp on the lower rungs of the political system, Irish Americans in the latter half of the nineteenth century were confronted with new problems requiring new types and new techniques of leadership, not so much to supplant as to supplement the old. An enormously absorbing issue was the possibility that the Irish who had fled to America might be the key figures in securing the redemption of the old country from British misrule. From the ignominious failure of Young Ireland in 1848 to the establishment of an independent Ireland in 1921, Irish in America were intimately involved in virtually every effort to expel British soldiery, to secure a juster representation in Westminster, or to reform the system of land tenures.[26] One of the earliest, most straightforward, and most completely unsuccessful enterprises was the series of Fenian adventures. Sinn Fein, and its parallel organization, the Irish Revolutionary Brotherhood, were founded before the American Civil War; American membership burgeoned during the War, when Irish Americans, north and south, imagined that their hard-earned military skills would serve them well against Britain. Sinn Fein, rent with factionalism from the beginning, did manage to establish a headquarters in Union Square in New York, from which the Fenian flag was conspicuously hung and from which the organization issued letters of marque and reprisal and in other ways conducted itself as a sovereign nation—until President Grant finally balked. No doubt his decision stemmed partly from the smashing of the Irish rising in 1867, in which a few "Americans" took part, and even more from the pathetically inept invasions of Canada from St. Albans, Vermont, in 1866 and 1870. At its height, the Brotherhood may have counted 45,000 members; yet over 100,000 persons attended a picnic in Yorkville in 1866. Years later, Finley Peter Dunne was to wisecrack that if Ireland "cud be freed by a picnic, it'd not only be free today, but an empire."[27] But such turnouts of Irish Americans were important. Their presence affirmed the solidarity they felt in America; the oratory they heard demonstrated that even if Canada or Westminster or Dublin was beyond their reach, they were no hapless, feckless, insignificant peasant immigrants, but independent Americans to be reckoned with; they were affirming their right to a full measure of self-respect. The point was not lost on either Irish American or native American leaders.

Still, throughout the long, shifting struggle—replete with New Departures, preoccupation with Home Rule, or Land Leagues, or the reform of the land system—and despite the huge popularity in America of such striking figures as O'Donovan Rossa, John Devoy, Alexander Sullivan, and Michael Davitt—leadership in Irish America remained pretty firmly in the hands of those unmistakably committed to life in America. The increasingly prosperous businessmen tended to grumble that Irish nationalist endeavors were "a waste of time"; the clergy were obliged to condemn all calls for violence and to reproach as "socialism" some of the proposals for land distribution or nonpayment of rents; those New York Irish, now in control of Tammany, while yielding to no one in the bitterness of their vituperation of the English, were unwilling to ask their supporters to follow Henry George when he campaigned for the mayoralty of New York on a platform of justice to Irish and American farmers; Tammany had nominated Abram Hewitt who was safely Democratic and (it was hoped) more unqualifiedly committed to American interests.

Incarnating the proper balance of Irish and American interests was Patrick Ford. Born in Ireland in 1837 and brought to America at the age of seven, he served an apprenticeship with Garrison on *The Liberator*. Probably more important, as editor for many years of *The Irish World*, he rallied Irish Americans to a wide variety of causes and indignations, but he always stopped short of demanding that they choose, irrevocably, between support of change in Ireland and their dearly won gains in economic, religious, and political status in America. Better than most Irish American nationalists, he recognized the precariousness of the Irish achievements; they lacked, for example, the wealth of the German Jews, and they needed, unlike British immigrants, to prove that Gaelic interests were as "legitimate" as Anglo-Saxon ones. Under Ford's leadership, *The Irish World* managed to tread the narrow line between "despair and enthusiasm, jealousy and cynicism."[28] If Ford was obliged to forego the gratification of leading a gloriously noble lost cause, he never forfeited the respect of American priests, politicians, and businessmen, nor the affection of the Irish American masses.

By the late nineteenth century, an increasing number of Irish Americans had scrambled their way up to middle-class amenity. Looking through the lace curtains they could afford at the newcomers from Ireland and at the "shanty Irish" who still considered themselves fortunate to have a hod to carry or a wheelbarrow to shove, these "successful" Irish Americans were all too painfully aware that their curtains were necessary to shield *them* from the not generally friendly gaze of non-Catholics. All too easily lampooned by Harrigan and Hart in plays like "O'Reilly and the Four Hundred" and too frequently reproached by such social arbiters as Lelia Hardin Bugg, who deplored the "low manners" of the "people of our parish," the lace-curtain Irish required a different kind of spokesman.[29] One such was John Boyle O'Reilly. His "Irish" credentials were unchallengeable. Born in the old country to a middle-class family, he had early laid to rest any suspicion of being a member of the establishment, by being sentenced to death and exiled to Australia on his conviction of treason against the British Army which he had, with conscious duplicity, joined.[30] Escaping to America, he helped edit *The Boston Pilot*, from 1870 to 1890, at the same time publishing a large amount of poetry and prose. He publicly sympathized with the plight of the black freedmen, hoping that many would some day become Catholics and intermarry with whites. He certainly incurred no shame, and yet avoided suicide, in boxing with John L. Sullivan. He wanted good done, but he effectively ridiculed "do-gooders." He was not terrified by the epithet of "socialism" which he saw flung at those working, admirably he thought, to improve the conditions of the working class. Yet his own political science was "Jeffersonian" enough to reassure the Catholic and non-Catholic bourgeoisie.

He was the premier figure among an increasing number of writers, many of them women, who in poetry, prose, and drama helped the Irish to see themselves as they wanted to be seen. His esthetic was conventionally Victorian, though he no doubt pleased his compatriots with his contention that Anglo-Saxons were preoccupied with facts while Irish poets reached toward Truth. Most of his writing is eminently forgettable, but he wrote one sharp-edged couplet about

> the organized charity, scrimped and iced
> In the name of a cautious, statistical Christ.

It was characteristic of him that he wanted "pride without bitterness," and he succeeded remarkably, and not only with the Irish; he became, also, in the patronizing phrase of the Brahmins, Boston's favorite Irishman. He was asked to deliver poetic tributes on the death of Wendell Phillips and at the dedication of the monument to Crispus Attucks. Strikingly, he was asked to write the poem for the dedication of Plymouth Rock in 1887. O'Reilly's life in America was a continuously troubled one. Irish nationalists and socialists, lace-curtain and shanty Irish, condescending Brahmins and close friends like William Dean Howells, rabid anti-Catholics and the Catholic hierarchy to whom he sedulously deferred, rebellious priests—all these and others looked constantly over his shoulder. He deeply felt his marginality, suffered desperately from insomnia, and died at the age of forty-six, probably from an overdose of sleeping pills. He felt more of the pains than the exhilarations of leadership.

By the late nineteenth century, a substantial number of Catholic workers had acquired the skills and the time-in-rank to regard themselves, and to be regarded as, more than casual labor. On the industrial and mining frontier, this was not always the case; in the coal fields of Pennsylvania, the "Molly Maguires" responded to what they regarded as soulless oppression by American and British employers and supervisors with a movement that combined inarticulate rage, the rhetoric and primitive organization of the Ancient Order of the Hibernians, an embryonic trade-unionism, and a ready recourse to violence. Overwhelmed by economic and political power and driven to secrecy by the brutal tactics, legal or tacitly sanctioned, of the standing order, the Molly Maguires produced no important leaders; their legacy was the need for more careful organization, more prudent tactics, and concentration in areas where Irish workers had achieved a more commanding position. All these conditions were met in the American Federation of Labor. Except in the needle trades, most of the workers in the federation were Irish; they were completely in sympathy with the aspirations of Gompers for "more and more" and with his predilection for working "within the system."[31]

The Knights of Labor from its beginnings in 1869 had less clearly defined notions about membership or goals. Terence V. Powderly, born in Pennsylvania in 1849, became Master in 1879. He was well aware that the order's rituals seemed quasi-Masonic (and so intolerable) to many Catholic clergy and that its commitment to secrecy—even if, as he arranged, it could be breached in the confessional—appeared to jeopardize the clergy's exclusive responsibility for the care of souls.[32] "Between the men who love God and the men who don't believe in God," he lamented, "I have a hard time of it."[33] Threatened with condemnation by papal authorities, the Knights were cautiously but effectively supported by James Cardinal Gibbons and other "Americanist" prelates; after years of maneuvering, Rome declared in 1886 that the order "can be tolerated." Whatever relief this brought Powderly was vitiated by a series of defeats the Knights suffered in the next few years in the economic arena. In the 1890s Powderly abandoned the labor movement when he was appointed Commissioner of Immigration by President McKinley; later he left the Church. His own travails and those of his clerical supporters were not without meaning, however, for the Irish in America. They benefited from the prominence of an Irish labor leader, even one more gifted in flamboyant rhetoric than in ability or willingness to foster labor militancy. The existence of the Knights—and Gibbons' deft defense of them in Rome—made it possible for Irish workers to seek to improve their lot without confining themselves to the all-Irish or all-Catholic unions which conservative Catholics in America and Rome considered the only appropriate modality. If Powderly was condemned to be a marginal man because of the times in which he lived, William Green and George Meany were confronted with no such predicament.

Meanwhile, Irish power increased steadily, especially in the cities. Tweed was the last non–Irish Catholic to be the leader of Tammany until the 1950s, and though it was necessary at first—in the 1880s—in order to win mayoralty elections in New York or Boston to nominate lace-curtain Irish like Hugh O'Brien and William Grace, by the turn of the century the Irish-dominated machines could be defeated only by a precarious "fusion" of Republicans, "renegade" Irishmen, independents, and other ethnic groups.[34] Control of city politics meant not only that Irish in need could receive aid more regularly, and on a larger scale, than had been the case when it was necessary to depend on a sympathetic Irish alderman. It also ensured that such key instrumentalities of civil power as the police were now firmly in Irish hands. It was strikingly different from the 1850s, when, after considerable effort, Barney McGinniskillen, twenty-two years in the United States, could win appointment to the Boston force only to be dismissed shortly afterward as an unworthy cop, too "fresh from the bogs of Ireland."[35] Whatever the intentions of Americans in developing a "professional" police force in the major cities, the result was that by the end of the century Irish Americans had acquired a near monopoly of the police power. This power was large by statute and enormous in fact because of the great discretion entrusted to officials whose theoretical obligations to preserve law and order were limited only by the occasional, usually ineffectual, protest against excesses or willful obliviousnesses. As a result, the Irish cop became a more effective and ubiquitous leader than either the local political leader or the parish priest.[36]

Many Irish Americans had, by the end of the century, also won positions of prominence on the managing boards of public asylums, prisons, and schools. The Third Plenary Council of the Church, meeting in Baltimore in 1884, had adjured priests to establish parochial schools, and, where these were created, they rested—like the Catholic high schools which also began to be built—firmly in the hands of clerical, usually Irish, leaders.[37] But at no point were more than one-half of the Catholic children attending school able or willing to attend church schools, so the ability of Irish laymen to ensure that most public schools would not be blatantly anti-Catholic was an important gain. In addition, many young Irish American women became teachers in the public schools. If they were regarded as less omniscient than the nuns in parochial schools, they did enjoy prestige; and their presence rendered it unlikely that Catholic children would have to choose between the injunctions of Catholic priests, Catholic parents, and Protestant public school teachers.

Precisely because the Irish leaders of city machines no longer faced effective challenges from native Americans, they were able, and often willing, to abandon a narrow tribalism. They could solicit support from newer ethnic groups. For example, the large number of Jews in New York were induced not to elect a Jewish Socialist to Congress because Tammany under Charley Murphy had secured the election of Henry Goldfogle.[38] Murphy also recognized that second- and third-generation Irish, like Al Smith, favored a kind of state action which earlier Irish leaders would have rejected out-of-hand. Jane Addams, in Chicago, received crucial, if unexpected, support from Boss Tim Sullivan.

An increasing number of Irish Americans came to realize that the traditional near-automatic identification of Irishmen with the Democratic

party was deleterious to Irish interests; many simply found the somewhat more bourgeois commitments of the Republican party more congenial to their ideals than were the compromises of the Democratic party.
The most striking illustration of this trend was Archbishop John Ireland
of St. Paul.[39] Born in Ireland and migrating at an early age with his
family to the midwest, Ireland rose rapidly in the Church and in the
estimation of non-Catholic America. A much-revered chaplain with the
northern armies in the Civil War, a lionized figure in Minnesota political
and economic circles, he came to believe deeply that the well-being of
the Irish and of the Church was inextricably tied to the well-being and
progress of the United States. He could not conceive that any real conflict of interest could exist. A vigorous supporter of parochial schools, he
was quite willing to affirm to the National Education Association his support of the public school system; "withered be the hand," he declared
melodramatically in 1890, "raised in sign of its destruction!" Though his
attempts to work out compromises by which schools with Catholic students and Catholic teachers could be absorbed, financially, within the
Minnesota public school system were frustrated by the protests of militant
Catholics and non-Catholics, he was not dismayed. He also supported
"total abstinence"—to the consternation of visiting French Catholic
friends—and was an advocate of anti-saloon legislation and, at least in
rural areas, of state prohibition legislation. He disliked Irish nationalist
agitation, fearing that such enterprises would persuade Americans that
Catholics were unpatriotic. He persuaded his friend, Cushman Davis,
Republican Senator from Minnesota, to attack in Congress the efforts of
German Catholics and others to persuade Rome to appoint prelates of
German, Polish, and Italian origin. He refused to heed the not very
subtle requests from Rome that he declare himself an unqualified supporter of the rights of the Pope to be a temporal ruler of part of Italy.
He was an outspoken Republican; his pamphlet attacking Bryan's notions
on free silver was circulated throughout the United States. He was probably the key man in persuading McKinley to appoint Joseph McKenna
as Attorney General and later to elevate him to the Supreme Court. His
offices were decisive in securing an effective Catholic voice in the commission which negotiated the disposition of the Friars' Lands in the
Philippines after the American occupation. If to many Irish Catholics he
was too much the sycophant to non-Catholic power, he was undeniably
effective in modifying the total identification of Catholics and Irish Americans and Democrats with the dangers attendant on such an identification.
No man was more influential than Ireland in precluding any real successes by the American Protective Association (APA), that ominously
anti-Catholic organization of the 1890s. If he could not persuade McKinley to denounce the APA explicitly, he was effective behind the scenes.

Many Irish Catholics in New York wanted a show-down with the APA at that state's constitutional convention; Ireland's allies effectively maneuvered to block APA initiatives, with the result that though state aid to parochial schools was outlawed, a constitutional provision safeguarded the right of Catholic clergy to visit Catholics in state asylums and penitentiaries. No doubt the APA was an anachronism, given the growth of Catholic power in America. But men like Ireland played a crucial role in denying it more attention than it deserved and in hastening its passage into oblivion.[40]

Ireland's willingness to work with non-Catholics and his conspicuous lack of charity toward German Catholics and the more militant Irish Catholics—Bishop Bernard McQuaid of Rochester for example, and Archbishop Michael Corrigan of New York—prevented Ireland from ever being the leader he wanted to be in the Church. Even James Cardinal Gibbons of Baltimore, the most dulcet of men, did not escape the accusations of McQuaid and Corrigan of truckling to non-Catholic America. As Irish Americans achieved diverse positions, they needed and sought out diverse leaders and supported diverse strategies. It was inevitable, therefore, that conflict among Irish leaders would occasionally break out.

Perhaps the most poignant example of such conflict was the career of Edward McGlynn, pastor of St. Stephen's in New York City, a man characterized by an admiring biographer as "rebel, priest, and prophet."[41] His vigorous support of social reform, and especially of the ideals and campaigns of Henry George, won him a wide following among his large, lower middle-class parish and also among many other Catholics and non-Catholics. It did not endear him to Tammany, nor to diocesan leaders. A Democratic politician inquired of Thomas Preston, Archbishop Corrigan's vicar-general, whether McGlynn spoke for the Church. In an open letter, Preston replied that "the great majority of the Catholic Church in this city are opposed to the candidacy of Mr. George," believing his principles unsafe and "contrary to the teachings of the Church." Solemnly disavowing any attempt to intervene in a civil election, Preston continued that the Church "would not wish to be misunderstood at a time when the best interests of society may be in danger."[42] After George's defeat, Archibishop Corrigan issued a pastoral letter condemning George's theories, and McGlynn countered with such a vigorous defense both of George and of his own rights to speak out, that he was suspended from the priesthood. When he refused to go to Rome, he was excommunicated for his contumacy. Somewhat later, Ireland and his allies, worried about the public reaction to this treatment of a popular priest, paved the way for the restoration of McGlynn; "this will break Corrigan's heart," Ireland uncharitably added.[43]

Though only handfuls of Irish immigrated to America in the twentieth century, the Irish Americans have not disappeared from sight, nor have distinctively Irish-American leaders. Andrew Greeley, growing up in Chicago in the 1930s, would recollect forty years later that the Irishness of his family was real if "unself-conscious."[44] In his parish and in the resort in Wisconsin to which his family was able to migrate in summertimes, he encountered few non-Catholics. In Chicago he was more aware of his neighborhood than of his parish. His father was a stalwart member of the Knights of Columbus. Moderately prosperous, his family was on easy, but not especially deferential, terms with priests and with politicians, Irish and non-Irish alike.

In a less heterogeneous metropolis like Boston, the lines between the Irish and "the others" were both more real and more self-conscious. There, a professional Irishman like James Michael Curley could carry on a generally successful political career on the old bases of Christmas baskets for the Irish poor and of mellifluous attacks on both blatant anti-Catholics like the second Ku Klux Klan and the sense of superiority shown the Irish by the Lodges, Cabots, and Saltonstalls.[45] Elsewhere in the country, Irish city leaders retained for a time their control over political machines by their sensitivity to the wants of newer arrivals and by their skill in forging electoral coalitions. Ultimately, such leaders were rendered largely superfluous by the activities of the welfare state and the welfare nation. But a highly skillful and able commander like Mayor Daley of Chicago not only weathered this competition, and the obloquy of liberal critics, but with exquisite timing delivered the crucial delegates to the presidential candidacy of Jimmy Carter in June, 1976.

Nationally, a steadily increasing number of Irish Americans won positions of prominence. It was the "bad luck of the Irish" that one of the ablest of them, Governor Al Smith of New York, should seek to be elected president in 1928. In that year, no Democrat, certainly no one so proudly representative of urban America, certainly no one so openly contemptuous of the noble experiment of prohibition, could have defeated Herbert Hoover, the symbol of peace and middle-class prosperity. Smith's Catholicism and his proud Irishness undoubtedly hurt him, and his overwhelming defeat at the polls corroborated Irish Americans' sense of the ineluctable hostility of non-Catholic America. If Smith could not be elected (it was easy to conclude), America was as alien as ever to legitimate Irish demands for "recognition."[46]

The bitter memory of Smith's defeat made all the more glorious the election of John F. Kennedy in 1960. No more than in any election could one scientifically conclude that one attribute was decisive. But, beyond dispute, it was a "great day for the Irish." Ironically enough, the close circle of O'Briens and O'Donnells whom Kennedy brought with him to the White House came to be called the "Irish Mafia." Equally ironically, that epitome of Yankee America, Robert Frost, adjured Kennedy to be more "Irish than Harvard." But such ironies could be ignored. It was enough that the long proscription—the long heritage of "No Irish Need Apply"—was ended in the most dramatic way America could demonstrate.

Irish Americans also achieved in the twentieth century almost complete emancipation from the responsibility of promoting Irish nationhood. President Woodrow Wilson, though speaking feelingly of the right of national self-determination for peoples, maintained, like many Americans, some reservations about separatist movements from Great Britain. And his relations with outspoken Irish-American nationalists like Daniel Cohalan were openly hostile. But if Wilson did little in America, or at the Versailles Peace Conference, to advance the cause of an independent Ireland, other American politicians were more sympathetic.[47] They welcomed in 1921 the formation of the Irish Free State. During World War II, Irish-American leaders were not harassed for the balky neutrality of Eire. Even when, beginning in the late 1960s, some Irishmen proved willing to kill or be killed in order to incorporate Ulster into Eire, only a handful of Irish Americans attempted to act out a dual loyalty, confident that American patriotism *required* a militant support of total Irish independence of Britain. Irreconcilables like Paul O'Dwyer, a prominent Democratic leader in New York, helped raise money to aid the suffering Catholics in Northern Ireland and to provide munitions for tiny groups like the "Provisional" faction of the IRA seeking to advance the cause of unification by blowing up passersby in Ireland and England. But the great majority of Irish Americans, as well as the Irish government in Dublin, openly condemned violence. *Ireland irridenta* was not a fighting faith in America any longer.

The progress of the Irish in America toward psychological autonomy— away from the helplessness and near-destitution that had for generations made necessary special political, religious, and social leadership—was steady but slow, especially when measured, as many Irish Americans did measure it, by the rise of American Jews. The onset of the Great Depression in the 1930s belied the promise of American life. Andrew Greeley's father, for example, lost almost everything he had earned, and he subsided, his son records, into a kind of "somber, serious" mood.[48] It was no doubt similar reversals, occurring just when the achievement of middle-class status seemed certain, that made attractive the demagoguery of Curley in Boston and, nationwide, the spectacular popularity of Father Charles Coughlin, "the radio priest," who preached in reassuring brogue his demands for economic and political reform—demands which he laced with assaults on international Jewish bankers and on the gradualism of New Deal experiments.[49] After Catholic Church leaders had cracked down, and after the boom produced by World War II rendered

Coughlin's extremism implausible, fears of Russian power abroad and communist subversion in America gave to Senator Joseph McCarthy of Wisconsin a brief moral authority. Both Coughlin and McCarthy sought, and found, a constituency by no means identical with Irish America. Indeed, the influence of each was limited by the outspoken opposition of other Irish Americans; Monsignor John Ryan was Coughlin's most implacable and most effective antagonist, and McCarthy might temporarily silence but he never eliminated the aversion of Irish Americans who, no less opposed to Communism, saw no need to adopt his "rule or ruin" tactics.[50] Each man distracted Irish America; neither was able to command its whole-hearted loyalty. In the long run, the economic power of Joseph Kennedy was more important; the "eldest Kennedy" could obtain the ambassadorship to England for himself, high-status education for his children, senatorships for three of his sons, and the presidency for one of them.

Finally, Irish Americans, remaining loyal to the Roman Catholic Church, no longer needed to look to priests and bishops for the same kind of leadership as in previous years. A rapidly increasing number of men and women brought to Catholic life the higher education and the professional skills which relieved the clergy from providing leadership in every area of life, social and intellectual. Even in specifically religious spheres, Irish Americans increasingly looked to the clergy for enlightenment and persuasion rather than uncomplicated *ipse dixits*.[51] Especially after Vatican II, with its emphasis on "the people of God," the clergy found themselves assigned a far more defined, though no less exigent, leadership. And they could not rely on a united clerical front. With a capable theologian like the Reverend Charles Curran of the faculty of The Catholic University making public his dissent from the encyclical of Paul VI, *Humanae Vitae;* with Jesuits like the Berrigan brothers taking issue with both civil and religious authorities in calling for militant opposition to the Vietnam War; with a persuasive publicist like the Reverend Andrew Greeley regularly censuring not only Curran and the Berrigans but all his ecclesiastical superiors; and with the proliferation of lay journals like the *National Catholic Reporter* joining the hitherto lonely *Commonweal* and *Catholic Worker* in espousing norms for Catholic thought and action; the priest or diocesan still might win a role of leadership, but he had to win it; it was not bestowed upon him by his ordination.

Furthermore, the Church, though still drawing a disproportionate number of its leaders from among Irish Americans, now responded more generously to the very large numbers of Germans, Italians, Poles, and other European ethnic groups in its constituency, as well as to swelling numbers of emigrants of Catholic denomination from Latin America.[52] By the middle of the twentieth century, the Church in America was moving toward ecumenicism, not just in regard to Catholic immigrants but also to non-Catholics, white and black. The leadership of Robert Lucey, Archbishop of San Antonio, was as important to Irish Americans as that of John Hughes of New York a century earlier, but it was of a very different character. Similar changes affected Catholic educational institutions; parochial schools enrolled many non-Catholics, especially blacks in the inner cities. And Irish Americans saw no anomaly in supporting "the fighting Irish of Notre Dame," coached by Ara Parseghian, an Armenian Protestant, and starring players who were Protestant and Catholic, black and white.

An ethnic group, if it is to survive, finds, or is given, or develops the leaders it needs. Over the long history of the Irish in America, there has been no dearth of Irish needs, and the variety of leaders—charismatic or programmatic, eloquent in voice or effective in achievement, rogues or saints, those anathema to the non-Irish, or favorite Irishmen among the most reluctant Boston Brahmins—is evidence of the variety of Irish Americans and of their resources and resiliency. Hoping for everything in American life, they secretly expected little. The combination of exuberant optimism and mordant pessimism conduced to a proliferation of leaders whose enterprises ensured that Irish Americans would never be ignored. It was characteristic of Irish America that its most prepotent hero, John F. Kennedy, demurred when he was told that his election had finally laid to rest the awful bugaboo of anti-Catholicism (and anti-Irishness). That would depend, he rejoined, on the course of subsequent events.[53]

NOTES

1. I have drawn freely upon a wide variety of excellent general histories of the Irish in America. Among the most useful are: Carl Wittke, *The Irish in America* (Baton Rouge, 1956); William V. Shannon, *The American Irish* (New York, 1963), John B. Duff, *The Irish in the United States* (Belmont, Calif., 1971), Andrew M. Greeley, *That Most Distressful Nation* (Chicago, 1972); Thomas N. Brown, *Irish-American Nationalism, 1870–1890* (Philadelphia, 1966); Nathan Glazer and Daniel P. Moynihan, *Beyond the Melting Pot* (Cambridge, Mass., 1963); and Oscar Handlin, *Boston's Immigrants, 1790–1880* (Cambridge, Mass., 1959). Lawrence McCaffrey's excellent *The Irish Diaspora in America* (Bloomington, Ind., 1976) was published after I had finished this paper.
2. Harrison Gray Otis of Massachusetts, cited in Maldwyn Jones, *American Immigration* (Chicago, 1960), p. 85.
3. Biographical details are drawn from Brown, *Irish-American Nationalism*, p. 25.
4. John A. Hawgood, *The Tragedy of German-America* (New York, 1940); John P. Diggins, *Mussolini and Fascism: The View from America* (Princeton, 1972).
5. Moynihan, "The Irish," in Glazer and Moynihan, *Beyond the Melting Pot.*
6. Shannon, *The American Irish*, p. 52.
7. Ibid., pp. 52–54.
8. Ibid., p. 78.

9. Cecil B. Woodham-Smith, *The Great Hunger: Ireland, 1845–1849* (New York, 1962).

10. William L. Riordan, *Plunkitt of Tammany Hall* (New York, paperback ed., 1963).

11. W. T. Stead, *If Christ Came to Chicago* (Chicago, 1894), is a fair example of the Christian perfectionism of many Protestant exponents of the Social Gospel.

12. Emmet Larkin, *The Roman Catholic Church and the Creation of the Modern Irish State, 1878–1886* (Philadelphia, 1975).

13. In 1852 at least one-third of the 1,500 Roman Catholic priests in the United States were Irish-born or of Irish stock. See T. T. McAvoy, "The Irish Clergymen," in *The United States*, vol. 6, in *A History of Irish Catholicism*, Patrick J. Corish, ed. (Dublin, 1970), p. 19.

14. The Paulist fathers, whose special mission was to non-Catholic America, were sometimes slightingly referred to as "Protestant priests." Quoted in Robert D. Cross, *The Emergence of Liberal Catholicism in America* (Cambridge, Mass., 1958), p. 51.

15. Quoted in ibid., p. 168.

16. Ray A. Billington, *The Protestant Crusade, 1800–1860: A Study of The Origins of American Nativism* (New York, 1938).

17. B. C. Cronin, *Father Yorke and the Labor Movement in San Francisco, 1900–1910* (Washington, 1943); A. I. Abell, "The Reception of Leo XIII's Labor Encyclical," *Review of Politics* 7 (October, 1945):486.

18. Gregory Baum, ed., *Journeys: The Impact of Personal Experience on Religious Thought* (New York, 1975), p. 170.

19. R. F. McNamara, "Trusteeism in the Atlantic States, 1785–1863," *Catholic Historical Review* 30 (July, 1944): passim.

20. Quoted in Maurice F. Egan, *Recollections of a Happy Life* (New York, 1924).

21. Quoted in Shannon, *The American Irish*, p. 51.

22. Billington, *The Protestant Crusade*, passim.

23. John Higham, *Strangers in the Land* (New Brunswick, N.J., 1955).

24. Stanley Coben, "The Assault on Victorianism," *American Quarterly* 27 (December, 1975):621–23.

25. J. P. Dolan, *The Immigrant Church: New York's Irish and German Catholics, 1815–1865* (Baltimore, 1975) shows, however, that despite the strenuous efforts of priests and laymen to provide "bricks and mortar," immigration continued at such a rate that at no time in the nineteenth century were there more than half the churches and schools needed. Shortages continued in the twentieth century when other Catholic immigrant groups surpassed in numbers those from Ireland.

26. In the section that follows, I have relied especially heavily on Brown, *Irish-American Nationalism*, for both interpretation and specific details.

27. Quoted in ibid., p. xv.

28. Ibid., p. xvii.

29. On Harrigan and Hart, see Shannon, *The American Irish*, p. 143; Lelia Hardin Bugg, *The People of Our Parish* (Boston, 1900).

30. On O'Reilly, see Arthur Mann, *Yankee Reformers in the Urban Age: Social Reform in Boston, 1880–1900* (Cambridge, Mass., 1954), pp. 24–51.

31. Shannon, *The American Irish*, p. 140; Philip Taft, *The AFofL in the Time of Gompers* (New York, 1957), and Taft, *The AFofL from the Death of the Gompers to the Merger* (New York, 1959).

32. Terence V. Powderly, *The Path I Trod* (New York, 1940); Henry J. Browne, *The Catholic Church and the Knights of Labor* (Washington, 1949).

33. Shannon, *The American Irish*, p. 127.

34. See, for example, Edwin R. Lewinson, *John Purroy Mitchel: The Boy Mayor of New York* (New York, 1965).

35. Roger Lane, *Policing the City: Boston, 1822–1885* (Cambridge, Mass., 1967), p. 93. In New York considerable numbers of Irish were on the force in the 1850s; see James F. Richardson, *The New York Police: Colonial Times to 1901* (New York, 1970).

36. Leadership in American localities has always been handicapped by the enor-

mous geographic mobility of the population. A stream of local studies has demonstrated that "persistence rates"—whether in Trempeleau County or Newburyport—have been very low. In such a milieu, longstanding *personal* leadership was seldom possible. Instead, one was more likely to be recognized as a leader because one occupied a recognized position in a recognized institution: the church, the political machine, the police force. Because the Irish early came to dominate such institutions, they were leaders in a way not readily available to outstanding men in other ethnic groups.

37. Robert D. Cross, "Origins of the Catholic Parochial Schools in America," *American Benedictine Review* 16 (June, 1965):194–209.

38. Arthur Gorenstein, "A Portrait of Ethnic Politics: The Socialists and the 1908 and 1910 Congressional Elections on the East Side," *Publication of the American Jewish Historical Society* 50 (March, 1961):202–38. See also Nancy J. Weiss, *Charles Francis Murphy, 1858–1924: Respectability and Responsibility in Tammany Politics* (Northampton, Mass., 1968).

39. Biographical details are to be found in James H. Moynihan, *The Life of Archbishop John Ireland* (New York, 1953). See also Cross, *Emergence of Liberal Catholicism*, passim.

40. Donald Kinzer, *An Episode in Anti-Catholicism* (Seattle, 1963).

41. Stephen Bell, *Rebel, Priest, and Prophet: A Biography of Edward McGlynn* (New York, 1937).

42. Quoted in Cross, *Emergence of Liberal Catholicism*, p. 121.

43. Ibid., p. 123.

44. Quoted in Baum, ed., *Journeys*, p. 171.

45. Shannon, *The American Irish*, pp. 201–32.

46. Ibid., 151–81.

47. Carl Wittke, *The Irish in America* (Baton Rouge, 1956), p. 282; John B. Duff, "The Politics of Revenge: The Ethnic Policies of Woodrow Wilson" (Ann Arbor Microfilms, 1965).

48. Baum, ed., *Journeys*, p. 171; Greeley, *Distressful Nation*, p. 185.

49. Sheldon Marcus, *Father Coughlin: The Tumultuous Life of the Priest of the Little Flower* (Boston, 1973).

50. On Ryan, see Francis L. Broderick, *Right Reverend New Dealer: John A. Ryan* (New York, 1963); on Irish Catholic reaction to McCarthyism, see Shannon, *The American Irish*, pp. 367–91.

51. Daniel Callahan, *The Mind of the Catholic Layman* (New York, 1963).

52. For example, see Victor Greene, *For God and Country: The Rise of Polish and Lithuanian Ethnic Consciousness in America* (Madison, Wisc., 1975).

53. Shannon, *The American Irish*, p. 413.

Ethnicity and Leadership: An Afterword

Sidney W. Mintz

THE KIND OF ETHNICITY these authors intend to help us to
understand is, I believe, political ethnicity, ethnicity in the service of
politics, or—as political scientists sometimes prefer to call it—ethnic
mobilization. For some scholars, there might not seem to be any other
important way to reveal what ethnicity is—as if difference takes on its
significance only when expressed in the form of *claims*. Thus Abner
Cohen draws the distinction between "ethnic category" and "ethnic
group"; and John Bennett, introducing a recent collection of papers on
ethnicity, refers to ". . . the proclivity of people to seize on traditional
cultural symbols as a definition of their own identity—either to assert the
Self over and above the impersonal State, or to obtain the resources one
needs to survive and consume."[1]

Surely claims are what ethnic leadership is so commonly about; and
while that assertion is broad enough to hold for the Kurds, the Quaeshqai,
and the Catalonians, I mean it here to refer particularly to groups within
these United States.

In a society that has vaunted, at once, a credo of equal opportunity and
of inherent equality *(among the equal)* for much of its corporate and
sovereign existence, figuring out how privileges are accorded and what,
indeed, the citizenry thinks about the rules of distribution has become,
more and more, an absolutely necessary undertaking. We may agree that
women, homosexuals, and the handicapped are none of them what usually
are called ethnic groups; yet we ignore at our peril the need to understand those processes by which being shortchanged socially, economically, or politically can become any group's motto or battle standard.

198

Ethnicity was for very long an uncomfortable and unacknowledged fact of North American cultural and social life; it has long been a political fact, too, but now it is fully acknowledged as such. "One need not be a Marxist," Cohen tells us, "in order to recognize the fact that the earning of a livelihood, the struggle for a larger share of income from the economic system, including the struggle for housing, for higher education, and for other benefits, and similar issues constitute an important variable significantly related to ethnicity."[2]

Surely this is the case for a society such as the United States, and the availability of pressure-producing devices (such as the secret ballot, opinion and communication media, and public education itself) leaves open the continuous possibility that "new" ethnic groups will emerge, while "old" ethnic groups may take on a different, politically more instrumental shape. "Any 'ethnic' group," writes Emmanuel Wallerstein

exists only to the extent that it is asserted to exist at any given point in time by the group itself and by the larger social network of which it is a part. Such groups are constantly created and re-created; they also constantly "cease to exist"; they are thus constantly redefined and change their forms at amazingly fast rates. Yet through the physical maelstrom, some "names" maintain a long historical continuity because at frequent intervals it has been in the interests of the conscious elements bearing this "name" to reassert, revalorize the mythical links, and socialize members into the historical memory.[3]

The insistence that we view ethnicity situationally, circumstantially, as an aspect of the historic moment and of the economic and sociopolitical context in which it expresses itself, strikes me as useful. Yet it is also necessary to remember that ". . . the heritage . . . the mythical links . . . and the historical memory" are symbolic constructions, only variably confirmable by the record of the past. Ethnicity is not a phantasm, the result of an act of sheer imagination; but its peculiar and particular expression in the form of claims—ethnicity *for* something—is the precipitate of wider forces, acting in conjunction upon the awareness of people for whom *some* aspects of their preexisting likeness have become sociologically relevant.

The stress on ethnic leadership, however, which is both illuminating and called for, may tend to distract us slightly from the question of what ethnicity is, and how it comes to be—how it crystallizes, hardens, dissolves, changes shape. It is almost as if, in order to concentrate on the nature of group leadership, we must treat ethnic identity, and the groups that express it, as givens. Yet I suspect that, had the question been raised, most if not all of the contributors would have agreed that ethnicity is not so much given, as a situational description. You cannot, I think, have *an* ethnic group; you can only have ethnic *groups*. "The term ethnicity will be of little use," writes Cohen,

if it is extended to denote cultural differences between isolated societies, autonomous regions, or independent stocks of populations such as nations within
their own national boundaries. The differences between the Chinese and the
Indians, considered within their own respective countries, are national not
ethnic differences. But when groups of Chinese and Indian immigrants interact
in a foreign land as Chinese and Indians they can then be referred to as ethnic
groups. Ethnicity is essentially a form of interaction between culture groups
operating within *common* social contexts.[4]

Joan Vincent, making the same point somewhat differently, stresses the
idea that it is "the other" who endows ethnicity with a structural meaning
that transcends cultural content. Borrowing E. P. Thompson's comment
that love requires its lovers and deference its squires and laborers, she
adds that "what ethnicity requires in its barest essence is 'we' and
'they.' "[5] "We" and "they" signify that there are boundaries, however
much such boundaries may be crossed, or even changed; we know well
that the boundaries themselves may endure at times, in spite of the movement of objects, ideas and even personnel across them, as Fredrik Barth
has so eloquently argued.[6] We know, moreover, that their capacity to
endure by no means signifies that they are rigid, fixed, unchanging:

I would urge that we take a more "neutral" stance in the analysis of intergroup
boundaries. Such boundaries are complex phenomena; they are also potentially
very fluid. They may or may not involve significant cultural or institutional differences . . . over time, they may come into existence, be maintained, break
down, or disappear . . . they may become more flexible or more rigid . . . they
may be impermeable for the members of the groups involved (as in situations
of apartheid), or may permit an intergroup flow of personnel . . . institutional
differentiation may occur without the development of ethnic differentiation . . .
boundary maintenance and modification may be going on simultaneously in different sectors within the same ethnic/institutional arena . . . and so on.[7]

We see people migrating from one place to another, carrying with
them what they can of their material goods and of the processes by which
they maintain and replace those goods; of the ideas, rituals, beliefs, etc.,
which give meaning and continuity to their social lives; and of the stat-
uses and officialdoms that incarnate the social structure of their group.
Such transmissions are never complete or perfect; expectably, some parts
of these heritages—material, technical, social—are lost or radically modified. At any rate, whatever the continuities with the past, there will be
changes, losses, and additions, too. The new, revised forms presumably take
on their differing character in the context of *other* groups, of differing cultures; the people of whom we speak become an ethnic group (or, at least,
they become an ethnic group of a different sort) in the new setting. And
thus I believe it has been for all of the groups the contributors here have
dealt with, whose problems of ethnic leadership they have analyzed. It is

understandable that, in analytic treatments of this sort, "culture," in the older conventional anthropological usage of the term, should not figure importantly. We find here no Ukrainian embroidered tablecloths, no descriptions of how to dance the *krakowiak*—not even a passing reference to the pleasures of eating ham hocks, sashimi or blood pudding. Indeed, ethnicity as a question of content of culture, while a worthwhile subject and an interesting one, only surfaces adventitiously in this collection.

I have suggested that the reasons for this are good, given the concentration on leadership of groups the bounded and coherent character of which seems hardly arguable, for most purposes. But shifting our emphasis in the study of ethnicity from what Fredrik Barth has called "the cultural stuff" to the boundaries that enclose groups does not allow us to assume, however, that the particular traits, markers or diacritica employed in defining "we" and "they" are all necessarily of the same phenomenological order. Even if the structural character of the social field within which ethnic groups operate takes precedence over the traits by which group membership is tagged, the traits themselves merit careful reflection. To begin with, some hierarchical social systems, by enabling individuals to change their dress, their religion, and even their language, also may permit thereby movement of individuals from one group to another. But those systems which employ inherited physical diacritica (such as skin color, hair form, and the like) in establishing or maintaining boundaries settle the issue for those who carry the features used in demarking and maintaining such social hierarchies. In short, some societies let one change one's religion; others may change the social meaning of skin color, or of a particular skin color; none, obviously, changes skin color itself. Physical (genetically acquired) markers and cultural (socially acquired) markers are, I believe, qualitatively different, even though both sorts of marker are significant only as they are informed with symbolic meaning by those who employ them.

By these statements I mean to oppose some tendency in recent parlance to assimilate the idea of "minority" to the idea of "ethnic group," and to support my own feeling that this is at best euphemistic, and in any case misleading. There are no "half-Negroes" in contemporary North American life, unless one of one's parents is foreign. All "half-Negroes," both of whose parents are North American, are not half-Negroes but all black— unless, of course, they are phenotypically white, in which case (if their genealogy is not known) they are not black at all. What I am underlining here is obvious, yet I believe that it cannot be omitted from our consideration. Some minorities, in these terms, may also be ethnic groups; but not all ethnic groups are minorities. I do not find it useful, myself, to treat diacritica of difference based on perceptually dramatized features that are inherited, and those based on socially acquired features (such as

SIDNEY W. MINTZ

posture, gesture, language habits, and the like) as if they formed a single class, or were arranged along some sort of continuum, or could be handled in exactly the same way—and I suspect that it is usually confusing, perhaps at times even disingenuous, to treat them thus. Historically, structurally and otherwise, populations which fall within the categories once called "racial minorities" in North America differ qualitatively, I believe, from other social groups, such as the Jews, the Irish, and the Poles. I do *not* mean by this to say that group disadvantages maintained in part by the employment of nonheritable diacritica have never been acute, in the United States as elsewhere. But some diacritica are genetically determined, while others are not, and this difference cannot be treated as merely one of degree. Following Abner Cohen, I consider ethnicity as alluding to the quality of relationships among individuals who share some cultural behavior. To the extent that this view applies to groups for whom the major diacritica are, however, physical and not cultural, in the eyes of the majority, I would consider them "racial minorities" that might also be ethnic groups. In my opinion, such a concession does not make the terminology synonymous, however.

Having avoided so far much reference to the question of ethnic leadership, concentrating instead on some of the difficulties anthropologists face in confronting the term "ethnicity" itself and what it might stand for, I would like to turn briefly to the major concern of the contributors. To what extent can we speak of ethnic leadership as a general sociological or political problem in North American life, available to disciplined analysis? I submit that future inquiry might fruitfully take a slightly different tack. Instead of asking what kind of leadership typified particular ethnic groups in North American life, we might consider what kinds of ethnic group produced the sorts of leadership these papers have described. I shall raise tentatively only one dimension of that perspective.

To invoke an almost mystical term like "values" may seem inappropriate; but as the author of a concluding comment, perhaps I can be excused for doing so. If we wish to look at ethnic leadership in part as an expression of the character of particular groups, and not only of the structural constraints and situational features operative in each case, it may be useful to touch briefly on the idea of values. Values seem to be quite unmanageable anthropologically; and in spite of several serious attempts to operationalize their study, not much progress has been made. My resort to their discussion here, however, is more in accord with asking an anthropological question about ethnic leadership, than because of any optimism about our ability to provide answers. I would suggest that we might, in thinking about any particular ethnic group, ask ourselves about two aspects of in-group values. One aspect I would call—for lack of a better term—a performance-positive value. A performance-positive value will be functional in a specific socioeconomic and political context in North American life because its expression is consonant with that wider context. An example, perhaps not trivial, might be the valuative stress on verbal articulateness among East European Jews. It is a value that happened to—and happens to—fit with things in North American life: with salesmanship as an American theme, with aggressiveness in selling as a moral good (for males only), with the idea of "selling oneself," with the growth of the legal profession, with teaching, with mass media, with advising the government on policy, and with much else. The retention of this value managed to be consistent both with prior ethnic experience and with at least some of the new situational contexts, such as graduate school, law school, and municipal administration, within which group leadership might both develop *and* find its front-rank constituencies.

The other sort of value I propose has an equally inadequate label—I call it a performance-negative value. By this I mean only a value the perpetuation of which is dysfunctional for conventional socioeconomic mobility and the discarding of which might be advantageous. In contrast to my first example, I would counterpose the quiet, rather laconic verbal style that seems to be learned by Oriental children. My impression is that Oriental and Jewish children make disproportionately good showings on most of the conventional written measures of excellence in primary and secondary school. I suspect they would make rather different showings in measures of verbal performance alone, however. What is more, I think this contrast simultaneously reflects the values of the groups under consideration and those of the majority society, as well as highlighting the measures of performance used to determine fitness for certain tasks by the society. Performance-positive values and performance-negative values, to the extent that they can be identified at all, raise serious questions, it seems to me, for any pluralistic social scheme. Thus, when we talk about equal opportunity in the future (or about making opportunities equal beginning now, which is unfortunately proving not to be the same thing at all),* we owe it to ourselves to keep in mind what the *requirements* are for validating such opportunity, and how such validation does, or does not, confirm prior value commitments.

My example is again purely impressionistic. I suspect that the children of first-generation East European Jews are more fully socialized into the school situation than are the children of first-generation Italians, and that this is an expression of differing values. I would expect Jewish children to be more strongly reinforced for striving for good grades, and that their

---

*It is my impression that university faculties, like most other people, are wildly enthusiastic about future equality, and notably reluctant to think very hard about how eventually to achieve it, beginning now.

school performance in general would receive more attention, be regarded more seriously by their parents, than would be the case with Italian children. Finally, I would expect such differences to express themselves in the degree to which children who have internalized parents' expectations for themselves would conclude that their parents' values were positively functional for them. Put differently, the extent to which parents are committed to imposing secular, professional goals upon their children may differ ethnically (culturally); whether such goals can be achieved will depend, *among many other things*, on the fit between the values of the ethnic group and the values of the majority society; the success of members of different groups will reflect back upon the groups themselves; such successes (and failures), consistent with the original values of each such group, will affect the emergence and quality of group leadership. Or, to state it otherwise once more, what gets left out so often in our ethnic group perspective is the character of cultural endowment, of relevant valuative and behavioral features, that facilitate or hamper performance as judged by imposed, external standards in the wider setting. Yet without some reflective consideration of such endowment, and of its fit or lack of fit with the values of the society at large, talk about equality that goes beyond mere opportunity (among other things) may continue to remain empty.

It need hardly be added that the North American conception of shedding one's foreign cultural attributes in order to "become American" carried with it the general expectation that such virtues as industry, discipline, honesty, and so on would be all that might pardonably survive from the alien past; language, cuisine, costume, custom, coiffure, etc., were all to change. Such a view could hardly leave room for the specification of performance-positive and performance-negative values; yet plainly, the culturally different were always being judged in precisely these ways, and negative traits were commonly seen as genetic, even when they were socially acquired. How terribly important, then, the fact that socially acquired features of behavior are *not* inherited and can be changed, while physically inherited features of appearance *are* inherited and cannot be. If I seem to overstress the differences between inherited and socially acquired traits, let me say that I do so because I believe the recent trend has been in the opposite direction.

My wider insistence would be that some attempt to relate structural constraints (and I include here those originating in the use of physical diacritica in imputing membership) to some aspects of the value systems of ethnic groups may throw some light upon the ways in which ethnic leadership takes on its characteristic shape in each case. Having said as much, I want to make clear that I am not contending that the *fate* of

ethnic groups is a function of the group's values but rather that leadership may in some way be a precipitate of the relationship of those values
to wider values in North American society. At present, it seems to me,
relatively little attention is being paid to the connections between older
group values and future success in North American life. We talk a good
deal—too much, perhaps—about differences in performance, including
what are supposed to be group differences. But we talk rather less about
the relationship of such performances to ethnic group values, on the one
hand, and about the relationship of such performance to the *real* (often
subtly concealed) criteria of acceptability—for higher educational training, for instance—on the other.

I have tended to avoid here the issue of leadership itself, also resisting
an obvious temptation to fall back on the repository of anthropological
curiosa, even though such recourse might be intellectually defensible. I
think that the North American case is, if not unique, at least fairly special. Surely one aspect of its special character is our adherence to the
occasionally conflicting themes of equal opportunity and individual
achievement, and our apparent continuing inability to align those themes
in any satisfactory way with the day-to-day facts of North American
social life. Ethnic leadership is not only a matter of who gets how much
of what, and by which means, but also of understanding certain, sometimes only grudgingly acknowledged, prejudices that seem to me to mark
us off as a society too often egalitarian in pronouncement and racist in
fact.

NOTES

1. Abner Cohen, *Custom and Politics in Urban Africa* (Berkeley, 1969); John Bennett, ed., *The New Ethnicity*, 1973 Proceedings of the American Ethnological Society
(St. Paul, 1975), p. 3.
2. Abner Cohen, ed., *Urban Ethnicity*, Association of Social Anthropologists Monograph, no. 12 (London, 1974), p. xv.
3. Emmanuel Wallerstein, "The two modes of ethnic consciousness: Soviet Central
Asia in transition?" in *The Nationality Question in Soviet Central Asia* (New York,
1973), pp. 168–69.
4. Cohen, *Urban Ethnicity*, p. xl. Italics added.
5. Joan Vincent, "The Structuring of Ethnicity," *Human Organization* 33, no. 4
(Winter, 1974):376.
6. Fredrik Barth, ed., *Ethnic Groups and Boundaries* (London, 1969), pp. 13–17.
7. James R. Gregory, "The Modification of an Interethnic Boundary in Belize,"
American Anthropologist 3, no. 4 (November, 1976):703.

Notes on Contributors

Josef J. Barton is associate professor of history at Northwestern University. His comparative study, *Peasants and Strangers: Italians, Rumanians, and Slovaks in an American City, 1890–1950* (1975), is based on extensive research in European villages and archives as well as in Cleveland, Ohio.

Robert F. Berkhofer, Jr., is professor of history at the University of Michigan. He is well known as a theorist and generalist of the "new social history," particularly for his book, *A Behavioral Approach to Historical Analysis* (1969). He is also a historian of the American frontier, who has written *Salvation and the Savage: An Analysis of Protestant Missions and American Indian Response, 1787–1862* (1965) and *The White Man's Indian* (1978). In both capacities his work draws substantially on anthropology.

Robert D. Cross, professor of history at the University of Virginia, has special interests in American church history, the social history of the twentieth century, and the history of immigration. He has written *The Emergence of Liberal Catholicism in America* (1958) and edited *The Churches and the City* (1966).

Roger Daniels is a professor in and head of the department of history at the University of Cincinnati. A specialist in the history of American immigration, he has written *The Politics of Prejudice: The Anti-Japanese Movement in California and the Struggle for Japanese Exclusion* (1962), *Concentration Camps, USA: Japanese Americans and World War II* (1971), and *The Decision to Relocate the Japanese Americans* (1975).

Nathan Glazer is professor of education and social structure at Harvard University. Among sociologists, he is probably the most widely known authority on the subject of ethnicity. Principal author of *Beyond the Melting Pot: The Negroes, Jews, Italians, and Irish of New York City* (rev. ed., 1967), Glazer has also co-edited *Ethnicity: Theory and Experience* (1975) and has written *Affirmative Discrimination: Ethnic Inequality and Public Policy* (1976).

John Higham is John Martin Vincent Professor of History at The Johns Hopkins University. In addition to works on historiography and American intellectual history, he has published *Strangers in the Land: Patterns of American Nativism*

(1955) and *Send These to Me: Jews and Other Immigrants in Urban America* (1975).

Nathan Irvin Huggins is professor of history at Columbia University. His books, which span the history of black Americans, include *Harlem Renaissance* (1971) and *Black Odyssey: The Afro-American Ordeal in Slavery* (1977). He is also co-editor of *Key Issues in the Afro-American Experience* (1971).

Frederick Luebke is professor of history at the University of Nebraska and author of two books: *Immigrants and Politics: The Germans of Nebraska, 1880–1900* (1969) and *Bonds of Loyalty: German Americans and World War I* (1974). Much of the research for his chapter in this volume was done as a Fulbright research fellow at the Institute für Auslandsbeziehungen in Stuttgart.

Sidney W. Mintz is professor of anthropology at The Johns Hopkins University. His publications include *The People of Puerto Rico*, with Julian H. Steward *et al.* (1956), *Worker in the Cane* (1960), *Caribbean Transformations* (1974) and, with Richard Price, *An Anthropological Approach to the Afro-American Past* (1976).

Index

Abiko, W. K., 44
Aboriginal Lands of Hawaiian Ancestry
ALOHA, 14–16
"Accommodationist" leaders, 3–8, 20,
30–31, 52, 57
Addams, Jane, 189
African Methodist Episcopal Church, 104
Afro-American Council, 102
Afro-American League, 102
Afro-Americans: and "Black Power," 112;
and caste patterns, 96; and
intermarriage, 95; leadership of, 2–3
Akaka, Daniel, 16
Alcara Li Fusi, 154, 158
Alcatraz, 119
Alexian Brothers Novitiate, 137
Ali, Mohammed, 93
Alien Land Acts, (1913, 1920), 41, 44
Aliens, Issei, 46
American Association of Foreign
Language Newspapers, 3
American Civil Liberties Union (ACLU),
59
American Dilemma, An (Myrdal), 3, 92
American Federation of Labor (AFL),
106
American-German Review, 81
American Gymnastic Union, 69
American Indian Chicago Conference,
139
American Indian Movement, 119, 140
American Jewish Assembly, 28
American Jewish Committee, 23, 26, 28,
30, 31
American Jewish Conference, 28
American Jewish Congress, 26–27, 30
American Jewish Defense League, 31
American Monthly, 66, 74, 79
American Protective Association, 190
American Turners, 69, 86
Amerikanische Turnzeitung, 69
Anti-Defamation League, 27
Armstrong, General Samuel Chapman,
100
Asian American, The, 37
Atlanta Exposition, 99

Balfour Declaration, 30
Baltzer, John, 69
Barth, Fredrik, 200
Bartholdt, Richard, 79
Bedini, Gaetano Cardinal, 184
Bendetsen, Karl R., 54
Bennett, John, 198
Berrigan brothers, 194
Bingham, Police Commissioner, 22
Blackfeet, 135
Blue Lake, 119
B'nai B'rith, 27
Bohemia, 150
Boston Brahmins, 195
Boston English, 113
Boston Pilot, 186
Brandeis, Louis, 11, 25
Brando, Marlon, 119, 139
Breckenridge, John, 182
Brotherhood of Sleeping Car Porters, 106
Brown, Dee, 119
Brownson, Orestes, 184
Brown v. Board of Education, 111
Buddhist temples, 47
Buffalo Express, 73
Bugg, Lelia Hardin, 186
Bulgaria, 153
Bureau of Indian Affairs (BIA), 11, 120,
124–25, 132–34, 136, 143
Burns, John A., 13
Bury My Heart at Wounded Knee
(Brown), 119

Cabot family, 192
Carey, Matthew, 177
Carl Schurz Memorial Foundation, 80
Caste patterns, and blacks, 95–96
Castro, Fidel, 116
Catholic Central-Verein, 86
Catholic University, 183, 194
Catholic Worker, 194
Cayuga, 134
Chavez, Cesar, 2

212   INDEX

Kishinev pogrom, 22
Kitchen Workers' Union, 55
Knights of Columbus, 192
Knights of Labor, 188
Know-Nothing Party, 184
Korz, Charles, 79
Kristallnacht pogrom, 85
Kuhio Kalanianaole, Prince Jonah, 12–13, 16
Kuhn, Fritz, 83
Ku Klux Klan, 93
Kurihara, Joe, 55

Labor leaders: Hawaiian, 13; Irish, 187–88; Jewish, 25, 26
LaFollette, Robert M., 75–76, 77
Land Leagues, Irish, 185
Language schools, Japanese, 48
Laws, immigration, 36, 138
Leacock, Eleanor, 129
Leupp, Ariz., isolation camp, 56
Lewin, Kurt, 2–3
Liberator, 186
Lieber, Francis, 79
Light, Ivan, 48
Liliuokalani, Queen, 14
Lincoln University, 103
Lodge family, 192
Logan, Rayford, 92, 107
Lomasney, Martin, 179
London, Meyer, 23
Los Angeles Times, 52
Louis, Joe, 93
Lower East Side Committee, 23
Loyalty Leagues, 93
Lucey, Robert, 195

McAdoo, William, 78
McCarran-Walter Act of 1952, 36
McCarthy, Senator Joseph, 104
McClatchy, V. J., 42
McCloy, John J., 56
McGinniskillen, Barney, 189
McGlynn, Edward, 191
Mack, Judge Julian, 26
McKenna, Joseph, 190
McQuaid, Bishop Bernard, 191
Macy's, 24
Magyar immigrants, 3
Malcolm X, 11, 114
Manzanar riot, 53, 54
Marshall, Louis, 11, 22–23, 24, 27, 30
Martin, Ilie, 164
Matica slovenska, 164
Mencken, H. L., 64, 69, 79, 85
Menominee, 137
Meriam Report of 1928, 119
Metcalf, Richard, 126
Metcalf, Victor H., 41
Minorities, definition of, 201–2
Minorities Treaties, 30
Missouri synod, 69
Moab, Ut., isolation camp, 56

Modell, John, 47
Modernization, 11–12, 14–16
Mohave desert, 56
Molly Maguires, 187, 188
Momaday, N. Scott, 11
Moravia, 152
Moton, Robert Russa, 104
Mueller, Paul, 74
Murphy, Charley, 189
Myrdal, Gunnar, 3, 20, 48, 92

Nagel, Charles, 66, 77
Naples, 152
Narodne noviny, 164
Narragansett, 129
National Academy of Sciences, 19
National Alliance of Czech Catholics, 163
National Association for the Advancement of Colored People (NAACP), 12, 94, 105, 110
National Catholic Reporter, 194
National Congress of Americans of German Descent, 80
National Congress of American Indians, 7, 119, 138
National Croatian Society, 168
National Education Association, 190
National German-American Alliance, 70, 80
National Indian Youth Council, 139
National Negro Business League, 102
National Slovak Society, 164
National Tribal Chairmen's Association, 140
National Urban League, 12
Native-American leaders, 6–7, 11
Navajo, 130
Nazism, 28, 30; in America, 5, 83–86
New Yorker Staats-Zeitung, 73, 79
New York Times, 72
Niagra Movement, 102
Nichibei Shimbun, 44
Niebuhr, Reinhold, 69
Niemöller, Pastor Martin, 85
Nisei, 40, 47–52
Norwegians, 8

Oberlin College, 85
O'Brien, Hugh, 188
O'Connell, Daniel, 178
"O'Connellism," 178
O'Dea, Patrick, 179
O'Dwyer, Paul, 193
Office of Economic Opportunity (OEO), 135, 143
Oglala Sioux, 141
Ohio Synod, 69
Ojibwa, 131
Omaha Tribüne, 77
Order of Kamehameha, 13
O'Reilly, John Boyle, 186
"O'Reilly and the Four Hundreds," 186
Orthodoxy, Jewish, 27

Library of Congress Cataloging in Publication Data
Main entry under title:
Ethnic leadership in America.
(The Johns Hopkins symposia in comparative history; no. 9)
Papers from a symposium held at Johns Hopkins University Feb. 5–6, 1976.
1. Leadership—Congresses. 2. Ethnicity—Congresses. 3. Minorities—United States—Congresses.
I. Higham, John. II. Series.
HM141.E86   301.15'53   77–17257
ISBN 0–8018–2036–7